THE QUEST FOR
EQUALITY IN FREEDOM

THE QUEST FOR
EQUALITY IN FREEDOM

Francis M. Wilhoit

Transaction Books
New Brunswick, New Jersey

Library of Congress Catalog Number: 78-55940
ISBN: 0-87855-240-5 (cloth)
Printed in the United States of America

Library of Congress Cataloging in Publication Data

Wilhoit, Francis M.
    The quest for equality in freedom.

    Bibliography: p.
    Includes index.
    1. Equality. 2. Liberty. I. Title.
JC578.W48   323.4   78-55940
ISBN 0-8755-240-5

To the memory of

Ellen Wilhoit Thompson

"We hold these truths to be self-evident, that all men are created equal."

Thomas Jefferson,
Declaration of Independence (1776)

"Four score and seven years ago, our fathers brought forth on this continent a new nation, conceived in liberty, and dedicated to the proposition that all men are created equal."

Abraham Lincoln,
Gettysburg Address (1863)

". . . nor shall any State deprive any person of life, liberty, or property, without due process of law; nor deny to any person within its jurisdiction the equal protection of the laws."

Amendment XIV,
U.S. Constitution (1868)

CONTENTS

PREFACE

This book describes and analyzes the gravest crisis now facing constitutional democracy: the fundamental conflict between liberal and egalitarian values. Particularly stressed in this analysis are such aspects of the crisis as its origins, ideological tensions, and public policy ramifications.

Equality and freedom are not only among the oldest dreams of human beings, they are also the most basic themes of modern democratic government. Yet the potential threat they pose to the United States and other political systems, when both are pursued with uncompromising vigor, is scarcely better understood today than it was two centuries ago. This is true despite the existence of a vast body of scholarly literature purporting to explain the institutions and policy conflicts of constitutional government.

Any study of equality must invariably be a study of fulfillment and incompleteness, a study of how myths are born and perpetuate themselves, and a study of how each generation helps to liberate the succeeding one. The march of equality, in other words, is cumulative; that is a central point of this work. Substantively, this book is intended as a contribution to two fields: the discussion of equality in political philosophy, and the analysis of political controversies that involve the issues of freedom and equality. Throughout the book, an effort is made to interpret and clarify basic democratic concepts while emphasizing the inevitable contradictions in logic and values inherent in the democratic ideology.

In addition, this work, which is intended for non-specialists as well as scholars, seeks to link the great battles over freedom and equality with the specific circumstances, historical and sociopolitical, in which they arose.

To understand any of these battles it is necessary to understand what specific *conceptions* of freedom and equality were stirring the minds of the leading proponents of these values. As thus told, the story of the ongoing quest for equality in freedom has much to reveal from the successive ages of U.S. and Western history and especially from the reformers who sought, with varying degrees of success, to lead and at the same time enlighten their zealous and sometimes fanatical followers. And much of what is revealed, we shall discover, is peculiarly relevant to our own age and its problems. For, after all, the basic aspirations of human beings do not greatly change from age to age.

A serious effort to survey so panoramic a subject must clearly entail large debts to numerous friends, colleagues, and scholarly experts. I should like, therefore, to acknowledge in the first instance my incalculable debt to the U.S. Congress which, at the height of World War II, enacted into law the G.I. Bill, thereby granting me the equality of educational opportunity I had long sought in order to realize my personal goals. Moreover, as a Harvardman-by-Act-of-Congress, I am deeply indebted to my Harvard professors who, though working in a quasi-aristocratic ambiance, taught me more about the true nature of equality than any other mentors I have ever had. Finally, I must acknowledge a substantial debt to my graduate and undergraduate students at Drake University who have been an unfailing source of inspiration and encouragement as I probed ever deeper into the freedom-equality dilemma.

For all errors of omission and commission in the text, I, of course, am solely responsible.

September 1977   *Francis M. Wilhoit*

THE QUEST FOR
EQUALITY IN FREEDOM

1

THE LOVE OF EQUALITY

If the love of money is the root of all evil, the love of equality is the root of much if not most of the restlessness that has agitated humankind since the dawn of history. Revolution and civil war, religion and social change, utopian strivings and pressure group confrontations: what aspect of society and government has not in some way been colored by the passionate love and pursuit of equality? Today, indeed, the love of equality is vastly stronger than any other motivant of political behavior, except perhaps the thirst for money and power, with which it is closely connected.

Few mythic ideals have impelled the human race to such extremes of action and reaction as the ideal of equality. The consequences of that extremism, revealed through great triumphs and equally great failures for the dreamers, are solidly documented: rags-to-riches sagas and crushed expectations, revolutionary glory and counterrevolutionary terror, dreams fulfilled and dreams turned to nightmares. In a thousand simple and complex ways, the love of equality has inspired and moved people in every conceivable circumstance—very much like the love of God. The compelling power of this ideal was recognized by Aristotle more than two thousand years ago when he wrote that "inequality is generally at the bottom of internal warfare in states, for it is in their striving for what is fair and equal that men become divided."[1]

If it was true in fourth-century Greece that the striving for equality lay at the heart of political reality, it is infinitely more true today. In fact, what in Aristotle's day was but an episodic, amorphous thing has become since the

1

Renaissance a fixed and ubiquitous fact of daily life. Furthermore, the contemporary striving for equality is part and parcel of a more fundamental phenomenon—the quest for democratic justice, which surely ranks as one of the protean forces of modern history.

For all we know, the love of universal equity may well go back to the birth of homo sapiens, and among the lower classes it may indeed be a basic human instinct. It is certain that the dialectic of mass equality, ever seeking to countervail the vested interests of the classes, has been a dominant leitmotif of Western civilization since record-keeping began. This is true even though, or because, inequality rather than equality has been the organizing principle for most social communities here on earth. Still, if the pages of history appear to be monopolized by the injustices of tyrants and despots, it must not be forgotten that there have always been closet Tom Paines, biding their time until the seed of equality, sown in the soil of endless revolts and insurrections, comes to fruition and temporarily quenches the hunger of the world's pariahs for true social justice. They may be unknown until violence erupts but they are always around.

The details of the social conflicts of ancient and medieval times are today of interest to few but scholars; yet it was precisely in those early upheavals that the Western world began its long march toward equality and simultaneously started autocracy's descent from a position atop the world to an embattled place in the midst of the masses and their tribunes. What Cyrus and Alexander found easy to achieve in their stratified societies, the later Bourbons, Stuarts, and Romanovs found ultimately impossible to maintain. Moreover, though the people of the United States—at least the whites—were "born free," they have still benefited enormously from the pioneering struggles of European egalitarians, some of whom, in fact, were models for our own Founding Fathers.

Figuratively speaking, one might say that the search for equal justice in freedom has permeated Western experience like a Bach fugue, with its ideological imperatives erupting suddenly in the voices of a given people and then being contrapuntally developed in neighboring and distant lands through a broad range of voices, modes, and instruments. Ineluctably linked to the class struggle, so central to Marxian thought, this equality fugue has become in a profound way the theme around which all modern history revolves. Sometimes cacophonous but always exciting, it is something that will almost certainly continue to disturb our days and haunt our nights as its fascinating counterpoint evolves into ever more complex, insistent patterns. One may ask at this point if there has ever been a country untouched by the equality theme. The best answer is probably not. For though the theme, along with the love it reflects, may be disguised in this or that way, it is so old, so multi-faceted, and so basic a component of civilization that it may well turn out to be coterminous with history itself.

As the preceding discussion has suggested, it is both the love for and the striving after equality that will be the focus of this interpretive analysis. In that regard, it must be conceded at the outset that the subject is one that invites all sorts of pertinent and difficult questions. What, for instance, are the origins of the worldwide quest for equality, and in what crucial ways has this quest influenced history? What did the great thinkers of the past say about the nature and justifications of equality? How in the West did the pursuit of equality come to be linked, in theory and practice, with the pursuit of freedom and constitutional democracy? What is the possibility of ultimately resolving the policy dilemma posed by conflicting democratic goals? And what is the future likely to hold for egalitarians and libertarians and for the programs they espouse?

As the argument of the book progresses, it will be necessary to stress not merely the positive achievements of the equality movement but also the tough problems that inevitably arise when public officials, with the best of intentions, seek to rectify the abuses of unjust, inegalitarian social systems with a maximum of pragmatic tinkering and a minimum of philosophic thought. These intractable problems underscore one of the most difficult processes of democratic governments—that of balancing, through wise public policy, the values of a congeries of competing interest groups, all of which may be perfectly legitimate and entitled to an equal hearing. This line-drawing crisis of values will be especially central to the latter chapters of the book.

It needs to be emphasized here that freedom and equality need not be, and have not always been, antipodal ideals or myths. And yet, throughout much of Western history, politicians and informed citizens alike have perceived them as antithetical. This is shown by the fact that whereas liberals, radicals, and revolutionaries have beaten the drums for equal rights for all, conservatives and reactionaries have just as insistently shown a preference for the drums of freedom, though of a limited kind of freedom. Reflecting the belief that freedom and equality are indeed mutually exclusive, John Randolph of Roanoke once exclaimed, "I love liberty, and I hate equality."[2] On the other hand, the anarchist Mikhail A. Bakunin took an opposite view when he insisted that "equality is an absolutely necessary condition of freedom."[3] So it has gone throughout the course of recorded history—leftists lauding the love of equality, rightists denouncing it as an opium of the dispossessed.

Prophets, writers, and artists, no less than social and political reformers, have been deeply addicted to the love of equality—so much so, in fact, that some among these groups have been in the vanguard of the struggle against privilege. In a line stretching from the Hebrew prophets through the Stoics to the proletarian artists of the 1930s and the civil rights activists of the 1960s, tens of thousands of committed people from the private sector have fought the good fight of equality, thereby serving as spurs to remedial action. After their protests have been made with sufficient vehemence and tenacity, the reluctant policy makers in the public sector fall into line by implementing, incrementally, the dreams of the "visionary" equality lovers. Public officials rarely act without being prodded.

Of course not all prophets and artists have loved equality with the same intensity or for the same reasons. Still, over the centuries, most have agreed on one point: equality is central to the Western concept of justice, and blatant inequality has no warranty, moral or otherwise.

The most implacable opponents of this premise, not surprisingly, have been in all times and places the vested interests, the power elites, the privileged few. Such as, for example, the ancient kings, the tyrants of the Mediterranean world, the nobles of the Middle Ages, the absolute monarchs of the Renaissance, and such modern capitalists as the Fuggers, Krupps, Carnegies, and Vanderbilts. The anger of dedicated egalitarians against such men of privilege is aptly dramatized by a famous statement of the French revolutionary François (Gracchus) Babeuf: "From time immemorial it has been repeated, with hypocrisy, that *men are equal;* and from time immemorial the most degrading and the most monstrous inequality ceaselessly weighs on the human race. . . . The moment has arrived for founding the Republic of Equals."[4]

Examples of such fulminations from the Left could be multiplied a thousandfold, for they saturate the pages of Western history, but Babeuf's words are quite adequate to suggest the passionate impatience of those moved by the overwhelming love of equality. Today's world, by general agreement, is a far cry from a Republic of Equals, though nearly two hundred years have elapsed since Babeuf uttered his *cri de coeur.* Nevertheless, progress toward the goal he emotionally articulated has been substantial, if not everywhere continuous, and millions still dream daily of its ultimate realization.

Scholars who study such things have long known that the world's equality lovers have always been moved by a mixture of motives—some nobler than others—as they sally forth under the banner of justice to battle the vested interests. But motives notwithstanding, the cry of "Equality now!" has today become a tornadic force in nearly all countries of the world. The reality of this is in no way altered by the knowledge that numberless crimes and atrocities, as well as worthy deeds, have been, and are still being committed under its mythic banner. For, as Victor Hugo reminded us, nothing can stop an idea—especially a mythic one—whose time has come.

Of all the tragic aspects of the equality dream, of which there have been many, one of the most disheartening is the well-documented fact that egalitarian reforms hardly ever equally benefit the disadvantaged. Indeed, more often than not they primarily benefit a handful of opportunistic demagogues. Little wonder, therefore, that conservatives and other right-wing critics of the dream adamantly refuse to put egalitarian values above libertarian ones in their ideologies. It must, however, be stressed that in modern democratic countries such as the United States, equality, like freedom, has long been an established moral, legal, and cultural norm; hence, good citizenship requires at least a nominal commitment to egalitarian values. This means that dissenters from the democratic norm are invariably on the defensive, if not outright counterrevolutionaries. This is but another way of saying that in the contemporary world equality is being increasingly viewed as an epochal heroic myth embodying the march of destiny.

Clearly, any serious in-depth study of the equality passion involves far more than the mere quantification of certain material factors, useful though that may be in providing a handy index to progress. It involves likewise an evaluation of legal, constitutional, moral, and psychological factors; an analysis of both the theory and the practice of equality, in the past and at the present time; and, no less important, a careful scrutiny of the gap between theory and practice. Only if all of these aspects are considered will there be a demystification of equality and a clarification of its practical ramifications.

Throughout this descriptive and theoretical analysis of equality, its complex relations to the concepts of justice, democracy, and freedom must and will be constantly emphasized. This emphasis will chiefly be on the United States and the contemporary world though the early history of equality will be examined in order to provide a clearer perspective on the current dimensions of the struggle. To ignore entirely what the ancient Greeks, Romans, Hebrews, and early Christians thought and did about equality would be to deal with the subject in a vacuum. Granted the theory and practice of equality are today quite different from what they were in both the ancient and medieval worlds; nonetheless a hard core of the equality ideal has remained fairly constant through the centuries, as has the common man's attachment to the ideal. Furthermore, though the definitions and rationales of equality have become more intricate and sophisticated over time, the mythic, chiliastic nature of the ideal—which is what really moves most people—has changed only in the scope of its influence.

At the present time it would appear that only a few hardened rightists openly and explicitly condemn the common man's drive for greater equality. Yet, before the Great Depression, such condemnations—even by high public officials—were a common occurrence in the most advanced democracies. But it must be quickly noted that the silence of most conservatives on the issue today does not mean that they have undergone a transformation of values: it simply means they have prudently changed their tactics in this egalitarian age. In this regard, it should also be stressed that while most Westerners pay lip service to the equality ideal, the majority are no doubt thinking mainly of equal opportunity for themselves. For it is extremely difficult for middle-class people, whether liberal or conservative, to extend the concept to the truly disadvantaged minorities, many of whom make unseemly noises about their rights and a few of whom are downright uncivil in their defiance of authority. Empathy with the lower classes is now and always has been a hard task for ruling elites.

Perhaps in no other field of democratic policy making do we find so many interests and countervailing values that must be considered before the policy lines are authoritatively drawn to favor this or that group and its core values. Further complicating the matter, as noted earlier, is the fact that most if not all of the interests involved in the freedom-equality struggle are equally legitimate from the democratic standpoint, and often equally influential. It is, therefore, scarcely surprising that conscientious politicians have recurring nightmares over this issue, as medieval statesmen and philosophers agonized over the church-state problem.

So long as the courts, in this and other countries, insisted on a sharp distinction between the public and the private sectors, the active promotion of equality was a legal and constitutional imperative of certain agencies of the state but not of voluntary organizations. Of course, the latter have perhaps always had a moral obligation to advance equality within their jurisdictions, but that is another matter. Now, however, because of a number of key judicial and legal changes explained in subsequent chapters, the private sector is as involved in implementing equality aspirations as the state. This means that today's churches, private schools, labor unions, and business organizations can no more escape the consequences of the expanding quest for equality than can public officials—unless they are totally divorced from the public sector, a situation that is increasingly rare these days.

In a very deep sense, the quest for equality in the last century or so has become all but indistinguishable from the quest for that cluster of humane values embedded in the theory of democratic pluralism. What is more, democracy and equality, in the present age, have become virtually synonymous terms—a linguistic transformation that is as pleasing to radical democrats as it is dismaying to conservatives and right-wingers.

As a result of this extraordinary development, it can perhaps be said that the main reason we ought to be concerned with the deepening love of equality is because a knowledge of this phenomenon should lead to a better appreciation of the problematic nature of the constitutional system under which most Westerners live. To be sure, a comprehension of the nature and scope of the equality drive will not tell us everything we ought to know about constitutional democracy. It is, however, a vital aspect of any theory that seeks to explain what democracy is, how it works in an advanced society, and what its practical limitations in the matter of conferring benefits are.

The crucial question of whether democracy ought to be viewed as merely egalitarian government or whether it is a lot more than that will be touched on at various points in this book. Also to be touched on is the important question: In what ways, and to what extent, is equality today linked to majority-rule government and popular sovereignty, and is equality always advanced by the latter? Such questions, of course, are essentially questions about the scope of *political* democracy, a subject to be dealt with in some detail in Chapter 3. By way of anticipation, it might be noted here that the political aspects of the equality problem are among the oldest issues confronting democratic governments. Fortunately, they are no longer quite so intractable as they once were.

When one examines the long story of the quest for human equality, one cannot but be struck by the way in which the continuing struggle born of that quest has always posed both a challenge and an opportunity for public officials. It is a challenge to the extent that it calls into question all the values and traditions of the status quo while provoking successive confrontations between the "in" classes and the "out" masses. On the other hand, it is an opportunity in the sense that it offers officials endowed with the requisite skills and imagination a dramatic chance to use, rather than be used by, the myth of equality, particularly in the direction of restructuring outdated institutions that have lost their legitimacy or usefulness, or both. The record of how, over time, various political systems have dealt with this challenge-opportunity dichotomy is one of the more fascinating aspects of the equality saga and one that deserves far more attention than it has hitherto received.

By no stretch of the imagination can it be said the Western world, let alone the other worlds, has marched steadily forward from inequality to equality; far from it. Nonetheless, it does seem to be true that in most Western countries, in modern times, the general direction of change has been toward more rather than less equality. Sometimes the progress that stands out has been achieved by sudden, revolutionary leaps; more often it has been the result of slow, grudgingly-granted change. Though one cannot say with certainty whether the future progress toward equality will be primarily revolutionary or incremental, one can safely predict that the intensifying love of equality, being as pervasive as it now is, will inexorably accelerate the rate of social change and, in the process, afflict additional millions with the Tofflerian disease of Future Shock. Everything, it now seems, is accelerating and shocking.

Even in the most democratic countries there still remains a vast credibility gap between the imperatives of egalitarian theory and the practices of everyday life. Moreover, though the gap in many countries appears to be narrowing, it is still sufficiently wide to cause an endless succession of social, economic, and political problems that defy the best efforts of statesmen to solve them. It was precisely the growing public awareness of this age-old gap that mainly provoked the youth and other liberation movements of the 1960s, both in the United States and abroad. It is true that an even wider credibility gap exists in authoritarian countries between theory and practice, but there the governments can manage the dissent by outright repression or harassment of the complainers—at least up to a point.

If the preceding judgments are valid, equality is indeed a complex, many-faceted phenomenon, being at one and the same time myth, ideal, faith, doctrine, ideology, democratic end-value, and catalytic motivant of both individual and group behavior. The fatal symmetry of authoritarianism with its illusions, elaborate power-jealousies, obsession with rank, and attachment to inequality is proving less and less a match for this fiery passion when the Ins and Outs collide in one of those apocalyptic confrontations that have become commonplace in recent times. Those who call themselves egalitarians may frequently be unaware of the varied roles this core value plays in their lives and interpersonal relationships, and the scholars who study it find it empirically difficult to distinguish the roles. But, of course, disentangling the roles is less important in a practical sense than knowing that they exist and exert a powerful influence on all aspects of modern society.

Regarding the wellspring of the equality passion, it probably arises from the same source that Professor Heilbroner has pinpointed as the source of the "Acquisitive Itch": the general recognition that it is a "means to a more fully satisfying life."[5] Most people today realize that in large industrial societies, the good life requires that everybody enjoy at least a minimal degree of equal opportunity in such vital areas as education, health care, economics, politics, and criminal justice. They also realize that the drive for equality, like the drive for wealth, is linked in a fundamental way to "the drive for existence."[6] That is especially true in the modern world, where economics and politics play such a critical part in determing the quality of a person's life. Philosophers, to be sure, have more sophisticated justifications for equality than merely the promotion of material well-being. Yet behind the love of and the push for egalitarian goals there will doubtless always lurk the specter of self-interest, often veiled by ingenious rationalizations but never wholly absent.

This book, then, has as its purpose the clarification of a near-universal component of human behavior: the quest for equality in freedom. It disclaims any effort to show that maximizing equality, taken generally, is always justified, or is never justified. Justifications for equality, as for all other democratic values, are contextual and must be evaluated in the light of past traditions and present circumstances.

Finally, it needs to be said that equality, however perceived, is a difficult subject to explain, and one not susceptible to the facile treatment, rhetorical sleights of hand, or glib oversimplifications typical of the polemics of ideologues, whether of the Right or the Left. Whether the future of democracy is to be cataclysmic, as conservatives fear, or gloriously bright, as egalitarians hope, it behooves all devotees of social justice to approach the moral and other dilemmas of constitutional government not as life-and-death confrontations but as moments of truth that demand selfless statesmanship and cool reason. That is particularly true of the freedom-equality dilemma, which, unless it is eventually resolved, could well turn into a terrifying nightmare.

NOTES

1. Aristotle, *The Politics,* trans. T.A. Sinclair (Baltimore: Penguin, 1974), p. 191.
2. Quoted in Max Lerner, *America As A Civilization: Life and Thought in the United States Today* (New York: Simon and Schuster, 1957), p. 362.
3. Quoted in George Seldes, *The Great Quotations* (New York: Pocket Books, 1972), p. 320.
4. Ibid.
5. Robert l. Heilbroner, *The Quest for Wealth: A Study of Acquisitive Man* (New York: Simon and Schuster, 1956), p. 13.
6. Ibid.

2

A SURVEY OF THEORIES OF

EQUALITY

It is axiomatic today that "Few terms of political discourse have had as long a life and as important a role in the making of modern history as the idea of equality."[1] Indeed, the roots of the idea go all the way back to the pre-Christian era of Western civilization, to certain Judaic and Greek beliefs.

Although Biblical Hebrew had no specific word for "equality," the Jews were told, in a well-known passage of the Old Testament, "Ye shall have one law for the stranger and citizen alike; for I the Lord am your God."[2] Moreover, since the ancient Hebrews conceived of their God as wholly just, they naturally assumed that all persons, whatever their differences, were equal before the law. Equality, in other words, was the ideal norm and inequality a deviation that needed justification. This did not, of course, rule out the concept of hierarchy; it merely required that hierarchical distinctions be rational and clearly legitimated.

In addition to their insistence on equality before the law, the ancient Jews stressed these forms of equality: that stemming from the divine image God had planted in all people, and that derived from the human race's common descent from Adam. The former of these is clearly set forth in at least two places in the very first book of the Old Testament,[3] while the latter is also discussed in that book.[4] The gist of these passages is that since God created man "in his image," all human beings have equal rights in the sense that they *ought* to be similarly treated. It is perhaps no exaggeration to say that the creation of all persons in the image of God is the most fundamental basis for the idea of equality in the Hebrew Bible.

It should be noted here that historic Judaism, unlike Christianity later, had no doctrine of Original Sin, nor any dogma of *selective,* other-worldly salvation through grace.[5] Therefore, it is accurate to state that Judaism, in the soteriological sense, was less elitist and thus more egalitarian than orthodox Christianity. It has, in fact, been conjectured that if Christianity had not introduced the doctrines of Original Sin and of selective, personalized saving grace into the Western world, the progress toward human equality would probably have been more rapid than actually it was.

One aspect of equality that concerns theorists today more than formerly is the relationship between male and female. In ancient Judaism, as in Christian thought, there are certain doctrines that could be called sexually egalitarian and others that perhaps merit the anti-feminist label. The former would include the idea that women as well as men share the divine image, and the concomitant assumption that the lives, limbs, and property of females are to be shown the same respect as those of males. "Anti-feminist" conceptions would include the derivation of Eve from Adam's body, the acceptance of polygamy in the partriarchal age,[6] and the male-centered Hebraic divorce law. Though contemporary theorists assume sexual equality is an integral part of the democratic dogma (see Chapter 7), remnants of the early sex-discrimination doctrines persist in the writings of conservatives, especially those with strong religious orientations.

The toleration of slavery, like the acceptance of male supremacy, was a limitation on the Hebraic theory and practice of equality. Judaism not only countenanced slavery, it also legitimated the preferential treatment of Jewish slaves over those who were non-Jewish (Canaanite).[7] Here, quite obviously, the element of discrimination derived from religious values that were in basic conflict with secular egalitarian values. Generally speaking, though, Jewish jurisprudential theory afforded a more humanitarian status to slaves than did Greek, Roman, or other Middle Eastern legal systems.

In the field of naturalization, Jewish law, like its modern democratic counterparts, assured theoretical equality to all converts. True, Jewish law permitted a few minor restrictions, as does American constitutional law in denying naturalized citizens access to the presidency, yet the ideal was that converts had the same responsibilities and duties as natural-born Jews. This patently assumed that a common faith is more important than common blood.

Concerning the concept of hierarchy, Judaism definitely recognized the need for strong leaders in government, religion, warfare, and learning, but at the same time posited equal and open access to all, or to most leadership positions. In practice, this meant Jewish leaders were recruited from all ranks, including converts. It can, thus, be argued that ancient Judaism actually created the modern democratic doctrine of the "free circulation of intellectual and other elites." In theory at least, it seems that no bar was ever recognized to the emergence of new leadership from any source. Moreover, though the Bible did establish a hereditary priesthood, Judaism eventually evolved to the point where most of the theoretical as well as the practical distinctions between laity and clergy were obliterated.

Whatever the actual practice may have been at a given point in history, there is no doubt that Hebraic thought anticipated modern democracy by positing social and economic equality of opportunity as a basic ideal. When hierarchy or some form of elitism was sanctioned, the legitimating rationale was usually age, excellence, piety, or scholarship—never mere wealth. In respect to economic equality, the Levitical law of the Jubilee went so far as to authorize a major redistribution of the Promised Land every half century, at which time Hebrew slaves were also to be manumitted.[8] It is true that subsequent Jewish law revised and even rescinded some of the features of this Biblical legislation, but it remained in the Old Testament as a kind of beacon, inspiring people in all ages to raise the level of their aspirations.

Perhaps only in the concept of the Chosen People did Judaism manifest a rather advanced form of elitism. Yet even here Judaic thought was no more elitist than modern democracy, with its increasing stress on such xenophobic ideas as "sovereign nationalism." More to the point, the "chosenness" of the Jews never really constituted a foundation for a legal norm.[9] And, far from viewing "being chosen" as a question of racial privilege, most Jewish scholars today see it as entailing larger spiritual responsibilities and more demanding standards on the part of those whom God has chosen to preserve his revelations.[10]

Among Greek philosophers, the Stoics appear to have contributed most to the evolving doctrine of equality. Less God-centered than the Hebrews, the Stoics considered human beings to be equal in a common brotherhood "because the part of them that reasons, their 'souls,' is the same in all men."[11] This conception of spiritual equality, based as it was on a metaphysical faith, was closer to medieval Christianity than to modern democracy, since it postulated a kind of religious, trans-national universalism that is negated today by the aggressive secularism of the sovereign nation-state.

Like earlier Jewish conceptions, the Stoic view of equality not only accepted the legitimacy of legal and political rankings but also acquiesced in the institution of slavery. At the same time, however, it included belief in a limited type of equality between master and slave. As the great Roman Stoic Seneca wrote, "Kindly remember that he whom you call your slave sprang from the same stock, is smiled upon by the same skies, and on equal terms with yourself breathes, lives, and dies. It is just as possible for you to see in him a free-born man as for him to see in you a slave."[12] Seneca, like Augustine after him, insisted that servitude to one's passions is actually worse than being enslaved to another human being. As he aptly put it, "No servitude is more disgraceful than that which is self-imposed."[13]

Though the Stoic philosophy did not embrace the ideals of legal and political equality, it resembled modern democratic theory in its firm opposition to any sort of forced egalitarianism, which is tantamount to saying it espoused the principle of freedom of choice. Reflecting the Stoic penchant for apolitical social reserve and privacy, Seneca once wrote:

> We ought to enter cautiously into . . . social intercourse with . . . laymen, remembering that it is impossible for the man who brushes up against the person who is covered with soot to keep from getting some on himself. . . . You are wrong to trust the countenance of those you meet.[14]

The Roman Stoics, even more than their Greek progenitors, were strong proponents of the Golden Age myth and of man's egalitarian condition in the so-called state of nature. This did not, however, mean that they were precursors of modern communism. As they viewed the matter, the state of nature, though golden enough, was quite irrelevant to actual society, and it is generally agreed that their primitivism was more an aesthetic ideal than a political or social imperative. It is hard to dispute the view that the Stoics' "call for a return to the ways of nature is less an advocacy of the community of goods than an attack upon superfluous possessions. The man of wealth was to be pitied, not pillaged."[15] The Cynics, on the other hand, might have gone further.

Even before the appearance of the Greek Stoics in the Hellenistic Age, Plato and Aristotle had had a good deal to say on the subject of equality and inequality. Plato certainly did not share our view of essential equality as self-evident, and in the *Republic* as in other dialogues he clearly favored an organic functional-natural hierarchy as the basic organizing principle for society. In the *Laws* he observed that "Equal treatment of unequals causes inequality when not harmonized by proper proportion," and that "for the sake of equal opportunity, qualifications of property must be unequal." In the *Republic,* he noted, ironically, that "Democracy is a charming form of government, full of disorder, and dispensing a sort of equality to equals and unequals alike." Further showing his disdain for democracy, he wrote, also in the *Republic,* that an excess of liberty and equality "seems only to pass into the excess of slavery."[16] It is clear from such passages as these that Plato was proposing a conservative concept of equality—a concept still very much alive—and that he believed not in democracy as the most natural or best form of government but in some form of authoritarian elitism.

Plato's brilliant student Aristotle was quite familiar with his master's views on equality as well as with the practice of substantial equality among Athenian citizens in the fourth century B.C. In his own political theory, Aristotle was careful to distinguish two basic kinds of equality: simple numerical equality, according to which all people enjoy identical rights; and proportionate equality, according to which rights and rewards are distributed on the basis of merit. The latter, he believed, embodied true justice while the former did not. Although he himself was clear enough about the general principle of proportionate equality, he conceded that its actual realization in a given society would be difficult. For, as he once wrote, "Some take the line that if men are equal in one respect, they may consider themselves equal in all; others take the line that if they are superior in one respect, they may claim superiority all around."[17]

Ultimately, Aristotle's theory of proportionate equality—or "distributive justice," as it is better known—came down to a conviction that rights, privileges, and other prerogatives in a just society ought to be distributed, not in accordance with mere "arithmetic" but rather with "geometric" proportion. Or to put it more simply, he believed that distributive justice requires equality of opportunity for all, coupled with the recognition that distinctions based on personal merit and achievement are legitimate and, indeed, essential to the proper functioning of a good society, however hard it may be to define with precision the distinguishing criteria. Unlike certain later utilitarians, Aristotle did not suggest that the more equal the distribution of wealth in a society, the greater the total amount of happiness and justice in that society. He did, however, oppose extreme disparities in wealth.

Among Roman thinkers, Seneca and Cicero were the chief commentators on equality, and both were closer to the Stoic conception of the ideal than to that of Plato and Aristotle. Dismissing the Aristotelian view of the natural inequality of human nature, Cicero maintained that all people are basically equal and have similar rights because they have been endowed with the gift of reason. He wrote in this regard that:

> This fact will immediately be plain if you once get a clear conception of man's fellowship and union with his fellow-men. For no single thing is so like another, so exactly its counterpart, as all of us are to one another. . . . And so, however we may define man, a single definition will apply to all. . . . For those creatures who have received the gift of reason from Nature have also received right reason, and

therefore they have also received the gift of Law, which is right reason applied to command and prohibition.[18]

Along with Cicero and Seneca, a number of other Roman Stoics, such as Epictetus (once a slave) and Marcus Aurelius (an emperor), vigorously propounded the idea of the essential equality and unity of all human beings. Indeed, given the quantity and clarity of the Roman Stoics' writings, one wonders why their formulations did not have more effect on Roman government and society. The answer would seem to be that their conception of equality was abstract rather than issue-oriented and at the same time lacked the penetrative force of an evangelical religious carapace. Still, despite the abstract, derivative nature of the Roman Stoics' theory, they kept the flame of equality alive and thereby affected the course of subsequent history.

The Christian ideal of equality embraces a number of features borrowed from Hebraic, Greek, and Roman sources. Christianity has always accepted the principle of hierarchy in both church and society, while at the same time holding the doctrine of equality to be relevant "only in terms of eschatological promise."[19] It is true that the Apostle Paul once wrote that "There is neither Jew nor Greek, there is neither slave nor free, there is neither male nor female; for you are all one in Christ Jesus."[20] But far from being a call to revolution, the implicit message of this passage is that while all people have an equal personal dignity before Christ, full equality for all is an ultimate ideal which can be realized only through redemption. Given the existing conditions here on earth, inequality must remain the rule, save for certain elites such as monastics.

This equality-inequality dualism was central to Apostolic and Patristic Christianity, and was brilliantly encapsulated in Augustine's famous distinction between the City of God and the Earthly City. Earthly inequalities, he maintained, are the result of sin, which came into an otherwise perfect world with the fall of man.[21] This is but another way of saying that equality was the original condition of mankind, but is no longer applicable, at least until the completion of redemption. "In the meantime the ideal is suspended and the justification of inequality becomes the justification of all temporal authority."[22] Only in heaven will paradise be regained.

Today it is difficult for us to appreciate how wholly "natural" the concept of hierarchy seemed to both classical and medieval thinkers. To most people in this democratic age, the "great chain of being" idea that derived from the belief in a cosmic, ordered hierarchy must seem paternalistic, authoritarian, and certainly inegalitarian. To medieval Christians, on the other hand, the idea of hierarchy was not so much anti-equality as simply the most practicable way of reconciling ideal and reality and maintaining an equilibrium between the tensions of existence. As they viewed the matter, justice was necessarily hierarchical, and a certain degree of inequality was therefore not unjust. Though eventual equality was indeed a glowing eschatological promise, "That all men were not equal—and certainly not equal in all respects—was a platitude confirmed daily by the most casual observation."[23]

The Christian attitude toward equality has been well summarized in the following passage from an essay by Professor Paul Sigmund:

> Christianity adopted the Stoic belief in man's original equality, though on the basis of different premises. Christian equality was not related to a common rationality as in Stoicism but was based on a common faith in the fatherhood of God, common descent from the first parents and a sharing in their sin, and a common redemption by Christ. Yet the Christian ideas of religious equality were not applied to society or politics any more than the earlier classical theories had been.[24]

With the revival of legal studies in the twelfth century, equality ideas received increasing support from Roman law, which, as codified by Justinian's jurists, had assumed the original natural equality of all human beings. It needs also to be emphasized that Church canon law, which grew concomitantly with Roman law, was yet another source of the idea of natural equality coexisting with hierarchy. But this coexistence was always a tenuous one, and the hierarchical aspects of it were intermittently challenged—without success—by radical or heretical sectarian movements.

During the Middle Ages, Islam, strongest in Africa and the Middle East, was in many ways more egalitarian, both practically and philosophically, than Christian Europe. Islam, being an ecumenical and a missionary religion, was able to incorporate diverse elements of race and culture into a universal nation-state, embodied in the concept of the *ummah*—a close-knit community of freemen, under God, with similar values and beliefs. Since religion provided the foundation of the political community, as in ancient Israel, only believers were considered as fully equal members of the community. Unbelievers, however, were tolerated and given a special status. Moreover, though it is true that Christians and Jews were subject to certain discriminatory rules, it is important to recall Jews were treated far more harshly in Christian Europe than were Christians or Jews in Islamic lands.[25]

It needs also to be stressed that the greatest of medieval Islamic political theorists, Alfarabi (circa 870-950), was sympathetic to certain aspects of the ideal of equality. In such neglected political works as *The Virtuous*

City, The Virtuous Religion, and *The Political Regime,* which may be viewed as attempts to reconcile Islam with classical political thought, Alfarabi emphasized that the best political order is one which has the realization of human excellence or virtue as its guiding principle. Although he generally disparaged extreme democracy, such as that criticized by Plato and Aristotle, he thought it might at least be a starting point for the setting up of the virtuous regime; and he agreed that the two fundamental principles of democracy were freedom and equality. As he perceived democratic government, he understood it to mean two things above all: that "no man is superior to another in anything at all," and that "Authority is justified only on the basis of the preservation and promotion of freedom and equality."[26] Alfarabi, like Plato and Aristotle before him, never ceased decrying the "pure," egalitarian forms of democracy about which he had only read. Yet his writings, taken as a whole, are evidence enough that he embraced a more moderate form of equality that did not disparage hierarchy or functional discriminations among people.

During the Reformation, some—though by no means all—Protestant reformers, disturbed by the gap between Christian ideals and Christian practices, tried with more zeal than patience to make the ideal of equality operative as well as ultimate. Of course, few of the reformers outside the Anabaptists were thinking of anything more than religious equality, but even that kind of advocacy was an advance over traditional Christian practice.

On the subject of equality, Luther, like so many of his Reformation colleagues, was more than a little ambivalent. In his social, political, and economic views, he was as conservative as the medieval popes, most notably in his *Secular Authority: to what extent it should be obeyed.* Yet, by opposing the Roman Church's practice of hierarchical co-optation and by advocating a "priesthood of believers," he was laying the foundation for a quite liberal and modern conception of equality. Above all, he was insisting, like modern liberals, that human beings are capable of governing themselves and should be given the maximum equal opportunity to do just that. This was especially true in the church but also in society at large.

Calvin, like Luther, was vehemently opposed to the Catholic Church's rigid hierarchical structure, and in his *Institutes of the Christian Religion* he advocated something akin to an egalitarian republican polity. However, in sixteenth-century Geneva, which he controlled for many years, he instituted a government that was at least semi-theocratic. Also like Luther, he refused to extend his theological egalitarianism to the social, economic, and political realms; yet his psychological theory was, in some respects, even more radically egalitarian than Luther's. The core of that theory was the doctrine of equal and universal depravity, according to which all human beings, with the possible exception of a few saints, are totally depraved in their natures and capable of doing good only if infused with saving grace. Calvin's successors could, and did, reach two varying conclusions about the imperatives of equality stemming from this doctrine: one, that no individuals should be trusted with prolonged authority, and so in church governance the congregation should settle all matters of importance; or two, given the sinfulness of most men, the few saints who are God's elect should rule with unquestioned authority. Radical congregationalists preferred the former conclusion, while mainstream Presbyterians preferred the latter. It is obvious that both the theory and the practice of modern democracy are closer to the former than the latter.

The scholar Josef Bohatec has brilliantly summarized the innate tension between equality and inequality in Protestant, and general Christian, thought in the following passage:[27]

> The incontestible [*sic*] equality of all human beings before God, their equality of value as all being stamped in God's image, does not mean that all are alike in *kind*. Order presupposes difference and adjustment, hence the inequality of gifts and duties, of dignity and achievement within the social body. The antithesis between their natural equality and their inequality as members of one body loses its force when we consider that both, the equality and the inequality, are based on the creative will of God. Equality and inequality are obligations. The privileges and dignities implied in inequality simply mean greater rights for higher duties. . . . The unequal distribution of gifts implies unequal tasks and a mutual exchange of capacities.

In sum, then, the Reformation theory of equality stands essentially as a middle ideological position between two extremes, which may be defined as medieval Catholic authoritarianism on the Right and radical antinomian Protestantism on the Left. It is a position that is still predominant in the United States and in much of the rest of the Western world, and its influence on modern society has been enormous.

Following the Renaissance and Reformation, the quest for equality, for perhaps the first time in history, became a central issue in almost all Western countries, along with nationalism, church-state relations, constitutional government, and the broad question of political obligation and its relation to civil disobedience. Equality was not only a major issue in and of itself, it was also a significant aspect of the whole spectrum of controversial issues that convulsed the post-Renaissance world.

After the classical era and until the seventeenth century, most political theorists were also theologians; since the 1600s, most have not been. Among the secular theorists who succeeded Luther and Calvin as philosophers of equality, two were outstanding and both were Englishmen. Their names were Thomas Hobbes and John Locke.

In such political works as *De Cive* (1647) and the *Leviathan* (1651), Hobbes, who is generally looked upon as an apologist for authoritarianism, argued that in the pre-societal state of nature, each individual was the final authority as to what he could and could not do, since each was equal to everyone else in power. But then, following the establishment of society and government, all persons surrendered their right as individuals to judge the best means of extending their wills and egos. This surrender of a "natural right," Hobbes emphasized, represented an *equal* sacrifice by all, and did not preclude the right of individuals to defend themselves in the future if rulers sought to kill them. Hobbes was saying, in other words, that the transition from the state of nature to the state of organized society was essentially the result of an egalitarian convenant, the basic premise of which was that although the equality of nature had been freely exchanged for subordination to a ruler, the rights and duties of civil society would be equally distributed. Civil society, therefore, may be described as authoritarianism in governance coexisting with a substantial degree of equality among the citizenry.[28] Ironically, though Calvin would doubtless have found many of the ideas of Hobbes abhorrent, it was the Calvinist concept of the free covenant that, at least indirectly, inspired the Hobbesian view of an authoritarian polity established by equals.

In his always fascinating political philosophy, Hobbes was both a traditionalist and a modernist. He was clearly a traditionalist in his use of the contract idea, his postulation of a divinely ordered universe, his pessimistic psychology, his emphasis on obedience, and his frequent resort to theological rhetoric. He was, on the other hand, a modernist in his secular orientation, his preference for civil over ecclesiastical polity, his "scientific" methodology, his "natural" set of values, his frequent use of mechanistic imagery, and his substitution of earthly security and order for the Christian heaven. As has well been said, "The equality of the Hobbesian civil society is . . . an equality of domination, which is sustained, at least in part, by an identification of those dominated with the holder of authority. . . . Because the sovereign is the personification of the citizens, they all are considered to be equally the authors of any . . . distinction."[29]

Such a view of equality, representing as it does a kind of secularization of Calvinist thought, is congenial enough to conservatives but wholly unacceptable to liberals. That is so for it denies the basic premises of participatory democracy, and in so doing replaces political and socioeconomic equality with psychological equality in a national security framework. Even Calvin, liberals might argue, offered more, since he promised not only Hobbesian law and order but eternal life in heaven as well—at least for the elect.

At the end of the seventeenth century, John Locke argued, as had Hobbes before him, that there was undoubtedly human equality in the state of nature. But Locke went on to stress, especially in his *Second Treatise,* that this condition was basically an equality of status, not of innate endowments. He maintained, moreover, that this natural equality by no means precluded a tacit acquiescence in an unequal possession of the earth—even *before* the compact establishing political society.

Within the realm of politics, Locke believed in a high degree of legal and governmental equality along with the equal right of all people to individual freedom. But he was certainly no leveller; and in the area of economics, he espoused a doctrine generally known as competitive equality, which made possible great disparities of wealth and was based on the premises of a free market, abundant land, and a more or less equal ability among men in the pursuit of wealth. In compacting to form society and government, our ancestors, according to Locke, consented to money, and in so doing "assented to the consequences which flow from the use of money, including the possibility that through the market and exchange mechanisms some of them may be deprived of adequate property in material goods."[30] Which is but another way of saying that industry is, and ought to be, rewarded with extra benefits in the just society—a conclusion that Calvin came to long before Locke.

Since he was a moderate constitutionalist rather than a radical, Locke placed an enormous emphasis on the importance of private property and found no difficulty in justifying it ethically. As a result of this emphasis, he anticipated, though he did not resolve, the most difficult problem attending the quest for socioeconomic equality: how to reconcile that quest—morally and otherwise—with the individual's freedom to own and accumulate private property and rise above the masses in wealth and power. If Locke never really grappled with this problem in a frontal way, he at least spotlighted it. And while it is true that his theories of property were used to buttress the burgeoning institutions of modern capitalism, as well as to rationalize the later dichotomy between human rights and property rights, it must not be forgotten that Locke's sometimes ambiguous conception of property was *social,* not Social Darwinist or exploitative, and was so comprehensive in scope as to embrace a person's life, liberty, and estate. In addition, it needs to be stressed that Locke's philosophy always implied a preference for personally-developed over inherited property, something that is too often forgotten. Finally, as Locke viewed the matter, the only ways of getting rid of inequalities in wealth were to abolish money and homogenize all people till they were identical in industriousness. Neither of these, he believed, was desirable or possible.[31]

The most passionate lovers of equality in the post-Renaissance era were not philosophers like Hobbes and Locke but certain radical reformers whose commitment to equality often literally drove them to the barricades in defense of their ideal and, sometimes, to a violent death at the hands of society's defenders. Among the best known and interesting of these were the Anabaptists of the sixteenth century and the Levellers and Diggers of the next century.

The Anabaptists, whose name meant adult "rebaptizers," constituted the extreme left wing of the Protestant Reformation, in which role they were equally detested by Catholics and mainstream Protestants. Their somewhat amorphous ideology was an amalgam of antinomianism, religious fundamentalism, quasi-pacifism, populist politics, communitarian sociology, Biblical ethics, and radical economics.[32] In one sense, they were extreme elitists, for they believed that the Christian Church was an exclusive community of the redeemed, and as such should separate itself as fully as possible from the secular world. Yet, in most other respects, the Anabaptists were among the most advanced egalitarians of their age. Furthermore, in seeking equality, they were more interested in practical than theoretical results. Of course, they had differences among themselves, as all groups do.

Contrary to the belief of many people, the Anabaptists generally supported the principle of private property, though a substantial minority did indeed move in the direction of religious communism for their own group, and all of them strongly emphasized the moral obligation of mutual aid. As for government, they advocated an absolute minimum of external authority, coupled with a maximum of decentralization and local voluntarism. Easily the most radical of the Anabaptists was Thomas Müntzer, who sought to turn the Reformation into a genuine social revolution, and who later was executed after the collapse of the German Peasants' Revolt (1524-25) that he had led. According to Luther's colleague, Philip Melanchthon, Müntzer "taught that all goods should be common, as it is written in Acts 4:32 that the Apostles made goods common. With this he made the mob so mischievous that they no longer wanted to work . . . [and he] threatened all princes in the neighboring area."[33]

It is difficult for us today to "think ourselves" into the historical situation of the Anabaptists in order to discern precisely what their premises, motives, and ultimate hopes were. But it can be said without hesitation that they had a significant impact on the evolving theory of human equality, particularly in their call for the restoration of primitive equality. Their critics point out today that their view of communistic equality went little beyond that of Plato's guardians or of the medieval monastic orders, and that their fanatical demagoguery led straight to modern "totalitarian democracy." There is a good deal of truth in such criticisms—except when they are applied to Müntzer. He was quite clearly *sui generis,* and as such should perhaps be labeled only a quasi-Anabaptist. In any event, Müntzer was a bona fide egalitarian revolutionary, who took the mainstream Anabaptist eschatological doctrines and both secularized and universalized them, the way Hobbes secularized Calvin. Thus, it is understandable that contemporary socialists, following Engels, look upon Müntzer's social radicalism as a forerunner of modern socialism. The Marxists are especially prone to do this, knowing as they do that the Anabaptists were the Bolsheviks of the Reformation period.

In the seventeenth century, the Levellers and Diggers proved to be far more fanatical partisans of equality than the Anabaptists had been. As the latter had been the far Left of the sixteenth-century religious revolt, so the Levellers and Diggers were the radical democratic wing of those anti-monarchical, anti-Anglican forces that precipitated the great English Civil War of the 1640s. Originating around London in the mid-1640s, the Levellers put forward an egalitarian program of social and political reform that included, among other things, manhood suffrage, parliamentary reapportionment, a written constitution, religious toleration, prohibition of military conscription, anti-monarchicalism, free public schools, and the use of reason instead of Biblical authority to legitimate public policy decisions.[34] Their most famous leader, John Lilburne, was often accused of wanting to "level men's estates," though the truth is that both he and his followers were more democractic and republican than communistic.

Near the end of the 1640s an even more radical group emerged from the cauldron of the Civil War. They were promptly, and pejoratively, labeled Diggers because of the "dig-ins" they conducted in the common lands of certain areas. Their egalitarianism was so advanced that they might accurately be described as agrarian communists. They believed, for example, that the land of the great estate owners should be distributed among the poor for cultivation by them, that waste lands should be communally developed, that money should be abolished, that education should be made free and universal, and that government should be returned to the town or parish level. Whereas the Levellers had been legal and political egalitarians only, the Diggers proposed to extend the concept of equality to the social and economic realms. Of course, neither program was acceptable to the Cromwellians, who ran the English Commonwealth. And though many of the ideas of the Levellers and Diggers have been absorbed into the mainstream of modern social democracy, both groups were so harassed by the English authorities that by the early 1650s they had ceased to exist as organized political forces. Clearly, the Diggers' view of equality, which was best articulated by Gerrard Winstanley and William Everard, was an idea whose time had not yet come.[35] What is more, the Diggers were generally detested by the Levellers.

The eighteenth century, ironically, was both the era of Evangelical Methodism and the Age of Reason. Also interesting is the fact that the two defining phenomena of the period, Christian revivalism and the mid-century intellectual revolution, both gave a substantial practical and theorectical boost to the increasingly popular ideal of equality, though in different ways.

Methodism, founded by the Anglican revivalist clergyman John Wesley, started as a secessionist movement within the state church of England and soon became a major force behind the Great Religious Awakening that swept throught the American colonies before the Revolution. Aggressively evangelistic and related to Arminian Calvinism, Methodism emphasized "faith working by love," "sitting loose" on all theology, simplicity in worship, complete freedom of the will and contrary choice, a more humanistic conception of the Christian life, and a more ethical view of faith. In addition to the egalitarian leanings of their religious doctrines, Methodists promoted the ideal of equality in society at large by evincing a deep concern for the underprivileged and by demanding better social conditions for all people. They eventually succeeded in converting large segments of the British and American lower classes from Anglicanism and old-fashioned Calvinism and, in England at least, may well have helped to forestall a violent social revolution. Though the debt is not always acknowledged, both the English Labour Party and American liberalism have absorbed, directly or indirectly, most of the egalitarian emphases of the Methodists and of their evangelical descendants. So have hundreds of other progressive movements.

The Age of Reason was most dominant in France where the *philosophes,* or popular philosophers, created an intellectual revolution that came to be known as the Enlightenment. Building on the scientific doctrines of the sixteenth and seventeenth centuries, the often eccentric *philosophes* disagreed on many things while generally supporting such ideas as skepticism or Deism in religion, laissez-faire in economics, constitutional monarchy or republicanism, full freedom of speech and press for intellectuals, and some form of utilitarianism in ethics.

Many, perhaps most, of the Enlightenment theorists were both intellectual and social elitists, not egalitarians; yet a few of them made important additions to the literature of equality, thereby enhancing the legitimacy of the ideal. Foremost among these was the Swiss-French philosopher and political theorist, Jean-Jacques Rousseau, whose widely read writings were a major inspiration for both the French Revolution and the Romantic movement in the arts. To a significant degree, Rousseau secularized the Christian doctrines of paradise lost and paradise regained by positing a series of closely-interwoven propositions. Following Locke, he characterized the state of nature as idyllic and relatively innocent, where the only inequalities are the products of nature. Then, veering toward Hobbes and Calvin, he posited next the "fallen" state of man, in which innocence was succeeded by vicious passions and great vanity. This transformation led, in turn, to society and the state, which brought not only a measure of security into the world but also social and political inequality. Finally he postulated "paradise regained," which in his scheme of things was neither heaven nor violent revolution but a small republican community about the size of Corsica, where the public interest would take precedence over private interests, where the people would always be sovereign in a direct popular government, and where there would be almost complete political, governmental, legal, and social equality. Since Rousseau did not really expect such a utopian recovery of Eden to evolve from the status quo of his day, and since he was unwilling to advocate violence to bring it about, he ended up prescribing little more than conservative resignation. It must be stressed, however, that his utopian rhetoric was immensely appealing to millions of people and remains appealing to vast numbers down to the present day.[36] That is especially true of *The Social Contract,* which, after all, was not written as a work of scholarly history but as an imaginative blueprint for the realization of the good life in the best of all possible worlds. It is, thus, an "as if" work.

Sounding at times like a modern left-wing polemicist, Rousseau wrote far more about inequality than about equality, yet he was also the first theorist to study seriously the history of egalitarian thought. Easily his most famous work on this subject was his *Discourse on the Origin of Inequality* (1755), which he submitted to the Academy of Dijon as a contest entry in response to the question, "What is the origin of inequality among men, and is it authorized by natural law?" He did not win the contest, but he achieved something more important. He produced a masterpiece of egalitarian thought, which also turned out to be one of the most influential works of modern political philosophy.

Rousseau in the *Discourse* was careful to distinguish two kinds of inequality: *natural* and moral or *political* inequality.[37] The first is relatively unimportant and is simply the result of differing physical and mental endowments among human beings. The second is the heart of the problem of inequality in the world and is strictly a socially-determined matter. Nature should definitely not be blamed for its existence and proliferation.

In this study of inequality (an earlier *Discourse on the Moral Effects of the Arts and Sciences* won the Academy of Dijon's essay prize in 1750),

Rousseau anticipated socialist doctrine by about a century as he explained the origin of society (and inequality) in these oft-quoted words: "The first man who, having enclosed a piece of ground, bethought himself of saying 'This is mine,' and found people simple enough to believe him was the real founder of civil society."[38]

Using that sweeping generalization as his point of departure, Rousseau then proceeded to argue that "The new-born state of society . . . gave rise to a horrible state of war," as all men "ran headlong to their chains, in hopes of securing their liberty." As for the laws passed by society's established governments, they merely "bound new fetters on the poor, and gave new powers to the rich; which irretrievably destroyed natural liberty, eternally fixed the law of property and inequality, converted clever usurpation into unalterable right, and, for the advantage of a few ambitious individuals, subjected all mankind to perpetual labour, slavery, and wretchedness."[39]

Throughout his life Rousseau was obsessed by the differences between nature and society, and, indeed, roughly half of the *Second Discourse* dealt with the state of nature. On the very last page of that work he brilliantly summarized the gist of his theory about the origins of political inequality when he wrote:[40]

> It follows from this survey that, as there is hardly any inequality in the state of nature, all the inequality which now prevails owes its strength and growth to the development of our faculties and the advance of the human mind, and becomes at last permanent and legitimate by the establishment of property and laws. Secondly, it follows that moral inequality, authorized by positive right alone, clashes with natural right, whenever it is not proportionate to physical inequality . . . [present in all] countries; since it is plainly contrary to the law of nature . . . that children should command old men, fools wise men, and that the privileged few should gorge themselves with superfluities, while the starving multitude are in want of the bare necessities of life.

The passionate jeremiads of Rousseau in this *Discourse* were surely the apotheosis of egalitarian rhetoric up to that time. Above all, they capture a crucial moment for the egalitarian ethic, the moment when incantatory language transforms the hatred of inequality into an overwhelming visceral revulsion. The massive polemical juggernaut, as it were, finally exhausts its energy as the reader is left to wonder, why go this far and not all the way to the revolutionary barricades? After putting down the *Discourse*, one inevitably finds a deathly chill falling over the status quo and its conventional vision of reality, however reasonable both may formerly have seemed. But then, casting around for a solution, one scarcely finds it in Rousseau. One finds, alas, only the "Corsican solution" of a small society run by the General Will, and those desperate words at the start of *The Social Contract:* "Man is born free; and everywhere he is in chains."[41] Small comfort, indeed, for those downtrodden souls who have never been in doubt about their legal, governmental, and social chains, and who are seeking exits, not more rhetoric, however moving. Such exits did not, and could not, come from the Genevan Puritan, who was never at home in the Bohemian salons of pre-revolutionary France, and who never quite had the courage of his ideological convictions. Exits of a sort would shortly be proposed by a new breed of prophet-theorist, but they involved the kind of extremism in action that Rousseau was never able to bring himself to support. Nevertheless, he had demythologized the subject of inequality, and with such effectiveness that the burden of proof in future quarrels over justice would lie with those who seek to legitimate the status quo, and not with their opponents. In addition, private property would never in the future seem quite so blameless.

Less well known than Rousseau but considerably more advanced in their radicalism were four additional *philosophes* of the Age of Reason: Condorcet, Mably, Morelly, and Babeuf. Since each of these made significant contributions to egalitarian theory, their careers and writings will be briefly examined in order to round out this overview sketch of Enlightenment philosophies of equality.

Unlike Rousseau, the Marquis de Condorcet was not only a vigorous theoretical proponent of equality but also lived to be an active, if ultimately tragic, participant in the French Revolution. His most famous philosophical work was *Outlines of an Historical View of the Progress of the Human Mind.* Though the *Outlines* was written while he was in hiding from the Jacobin Terror, it was certainly one of the most optimistic works ever written by any theorist and as such differed markedly from the pessimistic writings of men like Voltaire and the early Rousseau. He did not, however, live to see it in print, since he was arrested after nine months of hiding and died his first night in prison.

As an intellectual godfather of the Revolution that devoured him, Condorcet was in many ways the perfect ideologue. Though he espoused many ideological principles, three were as basic to him as geometric axioms: the natural goodness and equality of all humans, the perniciousness of man-made institutions, and the inevitability of human progress through enlightened education.

In his confidence about the certainty of human progress, Condorcet in effect turned Calvin on his head. He did this by accepting much of Calvin's predestinationist "determinism," while at the same time postulating a steady unilinear progress toward human perfectibility as a substitute for Calvin's gloomy prediction of a general retrogression toward

Armageddon. Morever, just as he was sure that in the past inequality and ignorance had gone hand in hand, he had no doubt that equality and enlightenment would advance together in the future and usher in the dawn of a new and more glorious age. Indeed, he believed that the equality-focused French Revolution had produced just such an age, and he was serenely confident that the perfectibility of the human species would henceforth be accelerated in every aspect. As for the kind of equality envisaged by Condorcet as a result of the French Revolution, it was essentially individualistic. That meant in politics, popular participatory government; in economics, something like laissez-faire; and in society, self-reliance and voluntarism. Condorcet maintained that the three main barriers to equality in the past had been income differentials, differences in inherited wealth, and discriminatory education. The future, he predicted, would see the surmounting of all three barriers, and he did not hesitate to say that equality-minded governments would have a major role to play in the tearing down of all barriers of discrimination.

In the final analysis, it would appear that education played the kind of role in Condorcet's thought that Providence played in Calvin's, that the General Will played in Rousseau's, and that the dialectic of the class struggle would later play in Marx's. Education, in other words, was the ultimate motor of change, the *sine qua non* for achieving a truly just and therefore egalitarian society. Few thinkers before or since have been so ebulliently optimistic about the causal efficacy of education, and only the Marxists and utopians have dared paint such a glowing picture of the chances for perfecting humanity in a state of blissful equality. Though public education has never achieved all that Condorcet hoped it might, it remains one of the cornerstones of everybody's equality theory.[42]

Less famous than Condorcet and far more viscerally pessimistic about man's fate, Gabriel Bonnet de Mably was a French *philosophe* who wrote as provocatively on the subject of nature, equality, and property as almost any thinker of the eighteenth century. Mably agreed with Rousseau and the Diggers—and disagreed with Locke—that the introduction of private property had, indeed, ended mankind's golden age. This came out especially in his numerous arguments with the Physiocrats and other libertarians of the Enlightenment who argued that private property must be a fundamental institution in any just society. What he objected to was not so much private property per se as the insistence by its defenders that it is both natural and just and thus in no need of legitimation.

Mably, like the radicals of the previous century, was a passionate foe of private property, for, since it was unnatural, he felt it would inevitably corrupt, breed a taste for luxury and indolence, and encourage such vices as vanity and overweening ambition. But even worse than these things were the cruel inequality it spawned everywhere and the specious rationalizations that intellectuals like the Physiocrats concocted to justify its domination of the world. Few theorists who have dealt with these problems have been so convinced of man's natural goodness and of the evil nature of his socioeconomic institutions as Mably.

If Mably was confident about his diagnosis of the world's ills, he was even more certain about what the therapy should be. Briefly put, he prescribed a kind of authoritarian socialism within the framework of a "republican-monarchy." The abolition of private property, which was the heart of his prescription, was implicit in his diagnosis, and he did not hesitate to draw that "communistic" conclusion. Indeed, he made no bones about preferring equality to liberty, a preference he carried to the point of turning down numerous posts, honors, and rewards that would have significantly expanded his social and economic freedom.

Likewise he made no bones about the absolute necessity of rigid discipline in his ideal socialist or communist society, and he candidly took as his models the governments of the Jesuits in Paraguay, ancient Sparta, and Calvin's Geneva. In respect to the latter, however, he sharply criticized Calvin for not proscribing the acquisition of private fortunes. He, of course, was not a thoroughgoing disciplinarian, for he denied existing governments the right to coerce their citizens in the strict way he insisted upon for socialist commonwealths. As for other governmental policies he espoused, these included drastic cuts in state spending, a sharp restriction on land holdings, and all kinds of luxury taxes and other sumptuary legislation. All of these and still more policy prescriptions are detailed in his best known work, *Rights and Duties of Citizens,* which was published on the eve of the Revolution.[43]

Concerning the basis of his argument for equality, Mably did not rely on a common reason, as did most of the *philosophes,* and he certainly did not rely on the Christian premise of God's image existing in all humans. Instead he predicated his plea for equality on the assumption that all people are physically and psychologically identical in their needs, as exemplified by his assertion that Nature "has given us all the same needs to make us continually aware of our equality."[44] It is, therefore, quite correct to state that Mably carried the theory of equality well beyond that of the typical *philosophe* and, in fact, to the very brink of modern socialist and Marxian formulations of the ideal.

If Mably was a precursor of socialism, Morelly (his first name is unknown) was even more radical in his commitment to equality and was, in fact, a principal inspirer of twentieth-century proletarian revolutionary movements. Morelly's condemnations of eighteenth-century governments and economic systems were so impassioned that they made even Mably's pale by comparison. Like Mably and Rousseau, he believed that private property was the root of all evil, but as a therapist he went considerably beyond Rousseau and somewhat beyond Mably.

Basically, he believed that complete communism in production and ownership of property was the natural mode of existence, though he did not advocate a total abolition of ranks and hierarchies. Communism, indeed, was the major theme of all his theoretical works: *Essay on the Human Spirit* (1743); *Essays on the Human Heart, or Natural Principles of Education* (1745); and *The Law of Nature* (1755). These works, it should be added, were also among the very first books in the long literature of equality to propose unequivocally that every person in society should contribute to the community according to his abilities and receive according to his needs. Thus, if Mably is to be labeled a utopian socialist, as he usually is, it is only fair and proper to label Morelly a thoroughgoing egalitarian communist. That, at least, is the way modern communists look upon their acknowledged, if little known, forebear.[45]

Babeuf's great contribution to egalitarianism was his synthesis of theory and practice and his anticipation—to a degree that exceeded even Morelly's—of the later Marxian conception of equality. Unlike Rousseau and most of the other *philosophes,* Babeuf came to manhood during the French Revolution and thus lived to see the practical implementation (and perversion) of many of the basic ideals of the Age of Reason. His devotion to a radical vision of equality may first have been stimulated by the fact that he was the son of a tax farmer who, on the eve of the Revolution, was keeping accounts of estate property and the rights and privileges of nobility. He was eventually disillusioned by his connection with the much despised feudal agricultural duties, and so he walked off his job and in 1788 began an active career as a political journalist.

Babeuf, of course, hailed the outbreak of the French Revolution as a great step forward for the human race and, like Condorcet, saw it as a particular boon for the oppressed. Soon after its start, he made his way to Paris, where he established revolutionary journals, worked for a time in the government, and, on three or four occasions, suffered imprisonment.

It seems to have been during one of his prison terms that he for the first time clearly formulated his equality theories, centering them on his advocacy of an equal distribution of land and income. Then, upon his release from prison, he sought to put his theories into practice by becoming a full-time professional revolutionary, one of the first such people ever to exist. He started his revolutionary career by joining and becoming a leader in the Society of the Pantheon, which was seeking a much greater range of political and economic equality than that provided in the new French constitution. When the Society was dissolved in 1796, he proceeded to set up a secret inner Committee of Six to foment an insurrection, largely over the issue of the massive inequality that had survived the Revolution. Anticipating Marx and Engels by a little more than half a century, Babeuf, in April of 1796, published a Manifesto of Equals which espoused such radical tactics as a saturation propaganda campaign for reform; a strong central committee to plot an overthrow of the government; and a vast expansion of social, economic, and political equality. In addition, he envisaged that revolutionary agitators would be trained and dispersed into the field as part of a general strategy for the takeover of the state by egalitarians.

A month after issuing his anti-government Manifesto, Babeuf and his equality zealots convened a general meeting to raise a force of some 17,000 men that would pull off a coup d' état and return the country to the Constitution of 1793, considered by his group to be the most progressive as well as the most legitimate of the post-Revolution constitutions. However, two days later, after an informant squealed to the goverment's security forces, Babeuf and his fellow conspirators were arrested. Following an extended trial, he and one of his companions were convicted and, on May 27, 1797, guillotined.[46]

Although Babeuf's practical experiments in revolutionary violence turned out to be still-born, he initiated the first overt secular communist conspiracy in recorded history. Moreover, while not a systematic philosopher of equality, Babeuf, through his agitation and polemical works, summed up the earlier contributions of Mably and Morelly and thereby presented the nineteenth century with something close to a full-grown socialist conception of equality. Above all, he differed from the other apostles of the Revolution in really believing that it was possible to restore the natural egalitarian condition of the human race. But, as has been pointed out, "The goal of this restoration was not to take man back to the woods where he could rest quietly near a brook, but to provide him with four good meals a day, good housing, and whatever other amenities the progress of industry and agriculture could offer."[47]

The extraordinary, even bizarre career of Babeuf, structured as it was around his passionate quest for equality, dramatizes in a very special way a key fact about the history of social upheavals. That fact is that all the great crises of the modern world have been accompanied by egalitarian protest movements which have had more than a little in common with recent expressions of radicalism, and which have left a cumulative legacy of thought and practice to catalyze succeeding generations of reformers. Thus, during the Reformation the Anabaptists were the egalitarian avant-garde; in the English Civil War it was the Levellers and Diggers; and during the far more traumatic French Revolution it was Babeuf and his so-called Conspiracy of Equals.

All of the theorists whose writings have been analyzed in this chapter were, of course, egalitarians of one sort or another. But only Babeuf—perhaps the least systematic of all—dared propose a *revolution within a revolution* in order that the fundamental equality ordained by nature might be restored to the least of nature's children. Furthermore, it would appear that only Babeuf and the zealots comprising his Conspiracy fully appreciated the basic contradiction between the demands of the right to exist and the affirmation of the right of unlimited personal property. It was not surprising, therefore, that only they advocated the absolute community of goods and labor. However one finally evaluates Babeuf's egalitarian polemics, there can be no denying that he stands in an honorable tradition stretching from the jeremiads of the Hebrew prophets to the lamentations of Dr. Martin Luther King, Jr. He well and truly merited his title Tribune of the People.

Across the Channel, the English journalist and social philosopher William Godwin intensified the revolutionary *Zeitgeist* of the 1790s by publishing, in 1793, the remarkable if polemical *Enquiry Concerning Poltical Justice, and Its Influence on General Virtue and Happiness.* Unlike the French egalitarian extremists of that day, Godwin was basically an idealistic liberal who had committed himself about equally to the values of freedom and equality as essential components of social justice. On the other hand, his advocacy of an extreme, quasi-anarchistic form of individualism went beyond that advocated by most if not all of the French *philosophes,* who were generally more discipline-oriented. Of course, Godwin also believed in order and society and, in fact, proposed that future countries should be run by small self-subsisting communities in which freedom and equality would be simultaneously maximized. He likewise vigorously opposed the institutions of private property and social classes and insisted that, in the final analysis, human rights are reducible to one: private judgment.

Obviously Godwin, like most other theorists of the eighteenth century, was firmly convinced of the essential reasonableness of all people; and because of that basic conviction, he saw little if any need for centralized governmental coercion. Moreover, he believed that democracy, while obviously superior to autocracy in many respects, breeds demagogues no less than non-democratic polities, and he had no doubt that the tyranny of democractic demagogues would be as reprehensible as that exercised by oligarchs and absolute monarchs. He did not, however, agree with Babeuf that violet revolution is the remedy: he preferred to achieve redemption through education, complete religious freedom, and the absolute sovereignty of human reason to determine right choice. In this regard he was close to Condorcet and later liberals.

When all is said and done, Godwin probably had more similarities than dissimilarities with the French and continental egalitarian theorists. Certainly, opposition to private property and unlimited inheritance was a common theme in eighteenth-century thought; and his assertion that accumulated property was a source both of despotic social power and of economic inequality was a fundamental axiom among the radical *philosophes*. But he was anticipating the nineteenth-century utopian socialists when he predicted that the technological progress certain to accompany industrial development would eventually reduce the working time for everybody to half an hour a day and vastly accelerate the transition to a liberal, egalitarian society. Godwin's faith in the perfectibility of the human race, so different from the gloomy, unfashionable theories of Malthus, was exceeded only by the glowing optimism of Condorcet, and it remains to this day to color the thought of nearly all egalitarian theorists. If Godwin was not a systematic, scholarly political theorist, and he was not, he was something more highly-regarded by the disadvantaged: a courageous, idealistic man who opposed all kinds of injustice with every fiber of his being, and who literally burned to advance the common good. Finally, unlike the majority of eighteenth-century egalitarians, Godwin predicated his belief in freedom and equality not on natural rights or the social contract but on the doctrine of utilitarianism, and in so doing anticipated one of the most fundamental premises of modern liberalism. He was not the first utilitarian—Helvétius and Holbach were two of his ideological progenitors—yet there is no doubt he provided indispensable support for the moral and political doctrines of Bentham and the Philosophical Radicals and at the same time enormously strengthened the foundations of the democractic gospel of human equality.[48]

Since the American and French Revolutions, the theory of equality has become inseparably linked with the theory of constitutional democracy. In the following chapter, the details and ramifications of that fateful linkage will be examined in depth, along with an appraisal of the more important American equality theorists. In the remainder of this chapter, the principal post-Enlightenment political theories will be described in order to see what they have to tell us about the concepts of freedom, equality, and constitutional government.

The outstanding equality theorist of the early nineteenth century was unquestionably the French social philosopher, Alexis de Tocqueville, who was particularly concerned with the status and influence of the equality ideal in the United States. Descended from the lower French aristocracy, Tocqueville became a magistrate and came to the United States during the Jackson presidency to study our penal system. He studied far more than that; and after returning to France, he wrote the classic *Democracy in America,* which depicted our perfervid quest for equality as the quintessential core of U.S. democracy. He also believed that equality was the keynote of the new age of Western man.

It is clear today that Tocqueville was one of the first thinkers to perceive with crystal clarity that the quest for equality and the emergent ideology of democracy, both of which were accelerated by the eighteenth-century revolutions, were, together with the industrial revolution, creating an entirely new mass society in which the threats to social order were vastly increased. Although the word democracy in his day still conjured up visions of rapacious mobs—Elbridge Gerry, an American Founding Father, once called democracy the worst of all political evils—Tocqueville came to the United States as a chastened aristocrat, with a relatively open mind and a determination to get a grip on the exact relation between freedom and equality in the new republic. Strong libertarian that he was, he returned to France somewhat dismayed by what he discovered here but not despairing.

Tocqueville had no doubt that the American and French Revolutions, especially the latter, had made freedom and equality the cardinal goals of modern democracy; but since these ideals had turned out to be largely incompatible in post-Revolution France, he wondered if the same thing might not happen over here. He conceded that democracy was too powerful a movement to be stopped or thrown back. Still, because he believed democracy had been conceived in envy, and because he feared that equality was becoming an obsession, if not a disease with all Western peoples, he pinpointed the preservation of individual freedom as democracy's most difficult task and at the same time predicted that the complete realization of equality would be catastrophic for the world.

Tocqueville, moreover, was convinced that the homogenizing proclivities inherent in the equality ideal would lead inevitably to a tyranny of the majority, a conviction that put him close to John Stuart Mill, although Mill blamed this prospective tyranny not on equality but on industrialism. In any case, Tocqueville feared for the future of exceptional individuals in a fully democratic society, for he did not see how social, cultural, or other elites could long survive when the passion for equality challenged and then transvalued all hitherto existing value systems. The democratic masses, he believed, would invariably opt for more equality even if it meant less liberty for them and everybody else. Their envy, in short, would become irresistible.

Tocqueville, to be sure, was not the first theorist to express fears about the adverse effects of democratic equality on art, culture, and the general intellectual life of a nation. Nevertheless, he was one of the most perceptive commentators on the subject and his pessimistic views foreshadowed twentieth-century thought concerning the dangers of mass society. Not being a reactionary, he did not propose to turn the clock back to 1788 or 1774, even if that had been possible. Rather he chose to emphasize over and over the inherent difficulties involved in simultaneously maximizing freedom and equality, given a pre-existing inegalitarian social structure.

In this regard, Tocqueville was rather close to the famous French writer Stendahl, who argued that there was no likelihood of genius, in either art or politics, in an egalitarian society such as the United States was constructing, though Tocqueville was not quite so gloomy about the future as was Stendahl. Indeed, he believed that America's brand of egalitarian democracy was destined to be the wave of the future, and he discerned in that probable future both good and bad things. He predicted, for example, that the anti-equality institution of slavery would threaten the United States with disaster; and in foretelling the type of poetry a democracy would produce, he came close to delineating the art of Walt Whitman. He also made two famous predictions about the future that proved to be astonishingly accurate: that as the United State became more egalitarian, education would be valued less for its intrinsic content and more as a ladder to material success; and that the world of the future would be dominated by two giant powers—the United States, symbolizing equality and freedom, and Russia, symbolizing despotism and rigid stratification. He left no doubt that he himself preferred democracy despite its tendency to push equality too far and cut corners on essential freedoms, for only in democracy was there hope for either freedom or equality.

As a final point about Tocqueville's theory of equality, it should be noted that he viewed the reconciliation of freedom and equality in a dialectical sense well before Marx and Engels popularized that analytical concept. Thus, he predicted that the immediate aftermath of democratic revolutions would be a massive liberation of formerly oppressed groups. But then he went on to caution that as democratic governments become solidified, they will inevitably move toward greater centralization as a means of maximizing equality, and by so doing will bring the freedom-equality dilemma to a critical, even dangerous point.

This dialectical treatment of the problem was brilliantly set forth in the following famous passage from Tocqueville's *Democracy:*[49]

> I think that democratic communities have a natural taste for freedom: left to themselves, they will seek it, cherish it, and view any privation of it with regret. But for equality, their passion is ardent, insatiable, incessant, invincible: they call for equality in freedom; and if they cannot obtain that, they still call for equality in slavery. They

will endure poverty, servitude, barbarism; but they will not endure aristocracy.

Conservatives, here and abroad, have long doubted that the fruits of equality—growing conformity, centralization of government, distrust of excellence—are worth the price of complete liberation from authoritarian polities. Tocqueville, too, entertained such doubts and, in fact, often spoke of the drive for equality as an "irresistible passion."[50] Still, he believed there was a chance of keeping equality libertarian, and he would not concede that political equality had to lead to social leveling. The jury is still out on his apprehensions about democratic tendencies, which, incidentally, Kierkegaard, Stirner, and Nietzsche expressed even more forcefully in succeeding years. And though it would be hard to deny that democratic egalitarianism has strengthened conformity, mediocrity, and materialism in the Western world, and helped to subordinate the individual to the collectivity, one cannot dismiss the theories of egalitarians as patent nonsense without carefully weighing in the balance the positive side of the ledger.

Apprehensive though he was, Tocqueville offered no panaceas for reconciling freedom and equality in a democratic society. That therapeutic role was assumed by extremists of the Right and the Left: the continental reactionaries, led by Metternich, Bonald, and de Maistre; and the socialists, who took their cues from Marx, Engels, and certain lesser-known theorists. Since the reactionaries were unblushing antiegalitarians who hoped to see the French Revolution undone and the old order restored, their ideas of maximizing justice through hierarchy, tradition, and organic pluralism are beyond the purview of this analysis. Socialist theories, on the other hand, are intimately related to the quest for equality and must therefore be described in some detail.

Modern socialism is both a social and political movement that was founded in the first half of the nineteenth century as a humanitarian reaction to the technological and other concomitants of the industrial revolution which, it was felt, threatened the rights and personal dignity of the European masses. Egalitarian to the core, the early socialist theorists were among the first to suggest that the technological innovations of the industrial revolution had made it possible, for the first time in history, to maximize simultaneously equality, freedom, and affluence for all, provided only that the innovations were properly managed. The heart of the socialists' management proposals was the common ownership of all or most of the material forces of production.

The main differences between most earlier quasi-socialist doctrines, such as those of the Levellers and Diggers, and modern socialism are two:

the former were far more religious in orientation, and they required a degree of self-denying asceticism from their adherents that is unknown in most forms of contemporary socialism. The latter, indeed, quite often promise the faithful that they can have their cake and eat it too, which means they can be idealistic about the common good while still indulging their appetites for the benefits of material affluence. Human nature being what it is, it is hardly surprising that modern socialism has acquired a vastly greater following than any of its predecessors. Greed is contagious.

It may, in fact, be true that modern egalitarian socialism spread further in a shorter period of time than any ideal or doctrine since the rise of Islam in the seventh century A.D. This was the case despite the fact that the movement has never been a unified one. Indeed, in the nineteenth century, socialist groups arose and fragmented the way Protestant sects did in the Reformation era, which is to say with amazing rapidity. Some of the groups still exist, though the majority vanished from the scene after having made but little impact on their society. Best known of the groups were the Utopian, Cooperative, Christian, Marxist, Guild, Democratic, and Fabian Socialists.

The origins of the words socialist and socialism are of more than passing interest, and they have been extensively researched by modern scholars. Thus, we know today that in "1827 *socialist* was employed in the *Co-operative Manager* to denote the followers of Robert Owen's Co-operative doctrine; while *socialism* made its appearance in 1832 in the Saint-Simonian organ *Le Globe,* to characterize the Saint-Simonian doctrine. Thereafter both terms were commonly employed in France, England, Germany, and the United States."[51] The concept of socialism was apparently put forth in order to emphasize "the claims of man as a member of society rather than his claims as an individual."[52] It was also meant from the first to be in opposition to the kind of atomistic, dog-eat-dog individualism that proliferated in Europe after the rise of free enterprise capitalism. In its original Owenite form, socialism seems to have meant little more than communitarian cooperativism in the private sector, and because of that it is technically accurate to say that the modern European cooperative movement is the true heir of the earliest form of nineteenth-century socialism.

George Bernard Shaw often argued that socialism, reduced to its essence, simply signifies the conversion of private property into public property and the division of the resultant public income into equal shares among the entire population. This may, indeed, be the ultimate ideal that all socialists keep in their hearts and minds; but as a practical matter socialism has never meant precisely that, nor is there today a universally accepted socialist orthodoxy. Judging from the record, socialism may be either collectivist or libertarian, Marxian or liberal democratic, revolutionary or evolutionary, nationalist or internationalist.

The most meaningful distinctions among socialist theories are those that are based on differing attitudes toward equality, freedom, and democracy—the central concerns of this study. In terms of these criteria, one can argue quite plausibly that there really are but two fundamentally different socialist types: democratic socialists and Marxian socialists. Though, of course, it is true that neither Marxists nor democratic socialists constitute a homogeneous ideal type, it is clear that each type has certain attitudes and mythic doctrines that sharply distinguish it from the other. That is but another way of saying that the *intra*-group differences among socialist "sects" are less pronounced than the *inter*-group ones, and thus the democratic-Marxian division in the socialist movement is both analytically and empirically warranted.

The very early nineteenth-century socialists were dubbed "utopians" by Marx and Engels, and that pejorative epithet has remained as a stigma to this day. The leading theorists of utopian socialism, little appreciated today, were Saint-Simon, Charles Fourier, and Robert Owen, who held widely differing views on many subjects but who were united in advocating the reconstruction of capitalist society along more organically-integrated lines. They were likewise united in being non-Marxian reformers, and in rejecting both the natural equality of the radical *philosophes* and the social equality of communism, while espousing more limited forms of the equality ideal.

Saint-Simon, born of a noble family that traced its roots back to Charlemagne, was such a flaming idealist as a youth that he came to the United States at the age of 19 to fight with Lafayette in the American Revolution. After fighting bravely and being promoted to a full colonel at 23, he returned to France, full of admiration for the freedom and equality he had found in the New World. He began writing about the need for reform, and before long he became recognized as a leading social thinker. Saint-Simon, unlike the radical *philosophes,* was less interested in maximizing equality than in promoting efficiency in society and government. In order to achieve this, he proposed a kind of technocracy in which scientists, bankers, and expert administrators would supersede kings, aristocrats, and establishment politicians. He believed that such a transformation in the world's ruling elites would bring greater justice for all and allow the industrial revolution to ameliorate, not exacerbate, the condition of the lower classes. In proposing such a gadget-filled socialist utopia, Saint-Simon was, in effect, secularizing earlier radical utopian doctrines and at the same time advocating a new synthetic religion—a cult of Newton and the great men of science. His ideas were too abstract and technocratic to have much of an appeal to the oppressed of the world, though two of his themes would become part of socialist dogma: his view that industrial technology, if properly controlled, can provide affluence for all, and his belief that the capitalistic nation-states of Europe were incapable of promoting true justice and permanent progress. Perhaps even more important than Saint-Simon's role in advancing socialist egalitarian thought was the part he played in inspiring nineteenth-century positivism and the social science of Auguste Comte. In the final analysis, both he and the better known Comte were concerned with the same things: how to use the power of modern technology for the benefit of all, and how to find a moral substitute for the imperatives of Christian ethics. In grappling with both these issues, equality had a central role to play, but it was proportionate not pure communisitc equality.[53]

Charles Fourier was another utopian socialist who was a strong critic of nineteenth-century society, and who was even more certain than Saint-Simon that he knew the cure for the ills of the world. That cure, as he saw it, involved a back-to-the-land movement, decentralization in all areas of life, and a stress on communal harmony rather than competitive individualism. Like so many socialists of the past and present, Fourier was praised more for his social criticisms than for his therapies. In regard to the former, he made a scathing attack on the wastefulness of competitive capitalism that was full of prescient insights, and well before Marx he was urging his followers to adapt society to human needs. But unlike Marx and Saint-Simon, he was unable to accept the realities of industrial society, preferring—like Jefferson—to remain a nostalgic agrarian. This inability on his part to come to terms with the industrial revolution limited the practical impact of his somewhat romantic agrarian ideas.

Unlike the later Marxists, Fourier was amazingly concrete about the kind of ideal society he had in mind. Specifically he proposed that society should be fragmented into small, voluntary, agrarian communities—he called them *phalanstères* (phalanxes)—that would consist of about 5,000 acres and have a population of from 1,600 to 1,800 people. Commune members would have a free choice of work and would be allowed to change their jobs whenever they wished. As for the "dirty work," that would be handled by youth gangs, an arrangement that would keep adults happy and at the same time reduce juvenile delinquency. In effect, then, what Fourier was proposing was not an egalitarian commune but an organicist, functionalist society in which all people would be grouped according to the passional identities—a grouping that, presumably, would be far superior to the random competitive groupings of capitalism and certainly more humane. It was also rather monastic (Fourier was a religious man) and, for most people, quite depressing.

Fourier, no less than Saint-Simon, was both radical and conservative in his thinking. He was radical in his attacks on capitalism, his strictures on atomistic individualism, and his desire to humanize the industrial revolution. On the other hand, he was conservative in his organicism, his insistence on hierarchy, and his emphasis on the passions. His greatest contribution to social thought was the strong influence he exerted on the thinking of the young Marx. Of course, Marx rejected Fourier's decentralist agrarian utopia and his belief in reform through evolution, but he accepted three other key premises of the Fourier system. These were the conception of classes arising out of natural inequality; the doctrine of the inevitable exploitation of the lower classes under the competitive anarchy of capitalism; and the stress on the relations of production as the key focus of social reform.

Quite aside from his theoretical influence on later socialists, Fourier was an important thinker in the "Age of Ideology" for the practical reason that his *Treatise on Association* inspired the establishment of quite a few egalitarian communal settlements in the first half of the nineteenth century. Most of these were set up in France and the United States, and none of them turned out to be very successful. Fourier's leading disciples in the United States were Albert Brisbane, Horace Greeley, Charles A. Dana, Ralph Waldo Emerson, and George Ripley. It was these idealistic intellectuals who were responsible for the most famous of all the Fourierist experiments: Brook Farm (1841-46) located at West Roxbury, Mass. near Boston. Brook Farm eventually failed, like the other forty or so Fourierist phalanxes set up in the New World; but while it lasted, it had the benign blessing of New England's Transcedentalists (Emerson, Thoreau, Alcott, Hawthorne), whose good will, however, was insufficient recompense for the impracticality of the basic idea.[54] Whatever its shortcomings, Fourierism rendered a valuable service in graphically spotlighting once again that strain of sentimental utopianism that has, since the beginning, disfigured both the ideals of equality and socialism. It may also, unfortunately, have turned some otherwise well-disposed people away from the ideals.[55]

The most influential utopian socialist and the one best known to English-speaking peoples was the Welshman Robert Owen. To an extraordinary degree, Owen resembled the fabled heroes of the Horatio Alger books. He was the son of a saddler; he left school and went to work at the age of nine; he found employment in the big city of London with a linen draper, who allowed the young Owen to educate himself in his fine library; he borrowed a hundred pounds from his brother at the age of 18 to establish a small cotton spinning mill in Manchester; he later borrowed additional funds and bought the New Lanark cotton mills in Scotland, the largest then around; and, before he was out of his twenties, he was a self-made millionaire.

Owen may well have been the first of the industrial revolution's millionaires to acquire a guilty conscience in middle age and then become transformed from a capitalist obsessed with the acquisitive itch into a reformer literally thirsting after equality and justice. He was also one of the very few socialist theorists to practice what he preached, which is to say he genuinely tried in his daily life to implement the abstract doctrines of his social philosophy.

It was in the depressing mill town of New Lanark that Owen, so to speak, got religion and resolved to show the world that the acquisitive notions of the laissez-faire economists and their capitalist patrons were mythic, inhumane, and altogether unjust. Believing that men are born basically good and that bad environments make them evil, he sought to transform the town of New Lanark into a workers' paradise, particularly in such areas as housing, education, and infant care. Though, of course, there was a good deal of paternalism in his egalitarian "do-goodism," he succeeded in radically improving the lives of his workers, and to such an extent that people came from near and far to observe his experiment in humanizing the industrial revolution. He also, in the process, continued to amass healthy profits.

Owen's social philosophy was perhaps best expressed in his *New View of Society*, published in 1813. In that work and his other writings, he advocated such things as environmental determinism, greater equality in the distribution of goods and services, evolutionary rather than revolutionary reform, voluntarism not statism, interclass cooperation instead of class conflict, socially-conscious rather than competitive capitalism, and a worldwide expansion of cooperative communalism to coexist with responsible private property. In order to put his beliefs into practice, he also proposed a fusion of the cooperative and trade union movements, which for the first time would link all skilled and unskilled laborers; and throughout the later years of his life he pushed the creation of Villages of Unity and Cooperation. As a result, a number of Owenite communities were established, the most famous of which in the United States was New Harmony, Ind.; but like the Fourierist phalanxes, they flourished for a brief time and then disappeared. Today New Harmony is a thoroughly free-enterprise, conservative Middle American town, where middle-class freedoms are more highly regarded than equality for the disadvantaged.

Owen was by no means the only successful businessman to despair of his fellow capitalists and to seek ways of turning the West's new productive forces to the benefit of all mankind—Engels, for one, would later do the same thing. But, as noted above, he was one of the first to do this, and he was certainly one of the most zealous in his lifelong quest for social justice. Indeed, by the time he came to the United States, he was so famous that he was asked to address the Congress. In this regard it should be noted that In the United States, in contrast to Britain, Owen's egalitarianism was less influential in the cooperative and emergent trade union movements than in another field: that of popular education. His educational experiments at New Lanark particularly caught the Americans' fancy, with the result that he, along with Jefferson, became a principal inspirer of our egalitarian public school system.

Owen's theories, it is generally agreed, were shallow in numerous respects, and he appears to have been blind to the authoritarian possibilities of his ideal society. Nevertheless, though he was ultimately both a practical and a theoretical failure, he was enormously consequential in infusing a lofty ethical sense into nineteenth-century egalitarian thought. In fact, it was in large measure his and the Methodist influence on the British working class that kept England's disadvantaged masses from becoming as violent and revolutionary as their continental counterparts. Little wonder, then, that Marx would sardonically label Owen a "class collaborator." For while Marx agreed with his predecessor that the masses could increase their stature if only the stultifying effects of an inegalitarian environment were removed, he did not for one moment agree that cooperating with the bourgeoisie—as Owen had done—was the way to remove those effects.[56]

In England, toward the end of the nineteenth century, a different socialist movement arose that was destined to be far more consequential than the utopians, and whose doctrines would in time significantly affect the theory and practice of socialism, liberal democracy, and egalitarianism. That movement was known as the Fabian Society, and its members were called Fabians or democratic socialists.

The Fabian Society was created in London in 1883-84 with the avowed purpose of transforming Great Britain into an egalitarian, democratic socialist state. Like the earlier utopian socialists, the Fabians believed in the inevitability of gradualism toward the socialist state, and in the primacy of nurture over nature. Unlike the utopians, they stressed the reformist value of centralized government, if popularly controlled. Also, disillusioned by laissez-faire liberalism, they unblushingly called for state interference to abolish the appalling conditions causing despair among the masses. They did not, however, accept the apocalyptic Marxian doctrine of revolution, espousing instead a more soothing formulation of social change in which personal freedom was not sacrificed to the maximization of equality. Specifically, what they sought was a new order without breach of continuity or abrupt change in the overall social tissue.

The Fabian egalitarians named their society for the famous Roman general Fabius Cunctator, whose elusive tactics in avoiding pitched battles eventually led to his triumph over superior forces. It is unlikely that any egalitarian movement in history has ever had such famous leadership elites as the Fabian Society. Included among the early leaders of the society were George Bernard Shaw, Sidney Webb, Annie Besant, Edward Pease, Sidney Olivier, and Graham Wallas. For a number of years Shaw and Webb, later joined by Webb's wife, were the dominant personalities in the Society; in fact, it was Shaw who in 1889 edited the movement's best known theoretical statement, *Fabian Essays in Socialism.*

Initially, the Fabians hoped that their non-Marxian democratic ideas would appeal to both Liberals and Conservatives. When, however, that did not happen, they decided to implement their own doctrines by helping to form the Labour Representation Committee, which, in 1906, became the Labour Party. Convinced that their society could never become a genuine mass organization, the Fabians concluded that they could best maximize their influence on public policy by being the intellectual power behind the throne of the Labour Party's ruling elite. Since the early 1900s, that policy of "permeation" and "wire-pulling" has, in fact, been the Society's principal strategic weapon. It has worked amazingly well, most notably in the years since World War II.

The basic doctrines of the Fabians have changed little over the years. They have generally included nationalization of land and industry, redistribution of income through progressive taxation, abolition of the right of inheritance, majority-rule decisionmaking, socialized medicine and education, and universal cradle-to-grave security guaranteed by the state.

In the history of equality, the Fabians are justly famous for a number of reasons. They were among the first egalitarian socialists to attack Marx. They proved that there is a middle ground between laissez-faire capitalism and totalitarian Marxian socialism. They helped make equality popular with intellectuals and the middle class. And, most important, they were the chief prophets and architects of the twentieth-century's welfare states.[57]

By far the best known and most controversial of all egalitarian socialists are the Marxists or communists, who came to prominence in the middle of the nineteenth century, roughly equidistant in time between the utopians and the Fabians. Their philosopher-founders were a couple of bourgeois German "class traitors": Karl Marx and Friedrich Engels.

The principal theoretical works of Marxian or scientific socialism are today known everywhere and include the *Communist Manifesto, Critique of Political Economy, The Eighteenth Brumaire,* and *Das Kapital.* Though all of these develop the philosophical, social, and economic theories announced by Marx and Engels, the *Manifesto* is the most concise statement of the basic doctrines of scientific socialism. It is also the most powerfully argued and the most widely read.

By any criterion, the philosophy of Marxism is a many-splendored thing. Its ontology is dialectical materialism; its epistemology is modified empiricism; its axiology is an interest theory of value; its economic doctrine is centered on a labor theory of value; its philosophy of social change is historical materialism working through the class struggle; and its political ideology amounts to a total rejection of bourgeois capitalism and an espousal of state socialism. Marxism is, thus, at one and the same time a philosophy of being and reality, a new ethics, a diagnostic critique of capitalism and bourgeois democracy, a prescriptive therapy, and a prediction about the future. The prediction or eschatology, which seems to have been crucial in winning converts to the theory, holds that capitalism will inevitably decay, that victorious revolutions of the workers led by the Communist Party will erupt around the world, that an interim "dictatorship of the proletariat" will replace capitalism with state socialism, and that ultimately the state will *absterben* (die away), thereby ushering in the classless, self-regulatory societies of "pure communism."

The Marxian theory of equality is a highly eclectic one that was formulated less in opposition to conservative or aristocratic views than to the bourgeois liberal contention that equality should merely complement liberty. It includes elements of millenarian socialist thought of the sixteenth and seventeenth centuries; the anti-property bias of radical eighteenth-century thought; and a number of Hegelian and utopian socialist conceptions, such as the dialectical method of Hegel, the dialectical historicism of Saint-Simon, and the class antagonisms theories of Saint-Simon and Fourier.

From the Marxian perspective, nineteenth-century liberalism and the French doctrine of "liberty, equality, fraternity," were simply time-bound, superstructural ideologies that had absolutely no merit as scientific principles. The important thing, according to Marxists, is not to do away with social and political inequality piecemeal, but to attack head-on the real crux of the problem: the inevitable antagonisms bred by class differences. Furthermore, since equality, like all doctrines, is a product of the economic stage which society has reached at a given time, it has absolutely no intrinsic validity in and of itself. This means that scientific socialism is not derived from equality nor any other time-bound theory, but will instead be the ultimate source of both equality and justice.

Therefore, equality in the matrix of Marxian dialectics may be said to be the ultimate goal of history, the end toward which the dialectical juggernaut is tending. Whereas the nineteenth-century liberals transformed natural inequalities and individual competition into principles of justice, the final stage of history—pure communism—will be an era of perfect equality, in which the ruling principle will be: from each according to his ability, to each according to his needs. This final condition will be what Lenin meant by the change from formal to real equality, for the purely formal legal rights and equalities of liberal regimes will, at last, be transformed into genuine equality, resulting from the resolution of capitalistic contradictions and the abolition of all class divisions in society. Of course, before all this can come about and paradise be recaptured, there must have been a precedent development in the modes of production by which abundance will replace scarcity as the basic fact of everyday life. Finally, in pure communism, not only will property relations be radically altered but, equally important, the egoism and antagonisms of human character will be spiritually transformed, leaving all human beings better, more compatible, and restored to a state of natural equality. Marx and his followers seemed little worried by the possibility that pure communism might turn out to be a condition of compulsive conformism where equality leads to coerced homogenization. They were simply too busy attacking the equality ideologies of their liberal opponents to worry about logical or practical contradictions within their own formulations.

In terms of attitudes, the Marxian theory of equality might be described as a blend of radicalism, optimism, and a commitment to objective social science. It was radical in its scathing indictment of the inequalities and dehumanization that coexisted in bourgeois democracies with formal legal and political equality. It was optimistic—indeed utopian—in anticipating the recovery of paradise and the attainment there of perfect equality and perfect justice. And it was science-oriented in that it analyzed the problem of equality not in terms of ideological rhetoric but in terms of what were alleged to be universal, objective laws of social science, centering around the dialectical theory of human progress.[58]

Whatever one may think of Marxian socialism and its doctrine of perfect equality under pure communism, one cannot deny that it has given hope to millions of oppressed people around the world and greatly intensified the quest for equality in the twentieth century. The tragedy of Marxism is that it raises the hopes of the lower classes impossibly high and then cruelly dashes them on the rocks of dictatorship and totalitarian communism. This is true even though Marxist governments do usually increase equality of opportunity for the masses.

Few would deny today that the cost of pursuing the ideal of equality by way of Marxian socialism is a massive deprivation of personal liberty and human dignity, a truism that was not so obvious to nineteenth-century egalitarians. Indeed, for a century or more it was understandable that people around the world were highly impressed with the Marxian analysis of laissez-faire capitalism and its attendant inequalities, since that analysis was, for the most part, right on the mark. Where Marxism ultimately faltered and disillusioned its more conscionable adherents was in the areas of therapy and prognosis, which is to say in prescribing remedies for capitalistic ills and in predicting the shape of future events. All this, of course, is but another way of stating that Dr. Marx was an acute diagnostician, a merely fair prognosticator (partly because his predictions forced the ruling elites to make concessions), and an utterly unreliable therapist. Indeed, millions of people have discovered in the twentieth century that the Marxian cure for injustice and inequality is infinitely worse than the maladies it presumes to heal.

The twentieth century has seen the publication of scores of reformulations of equality theory, generally with an emphasis on its relation to such other ideals as freedom, justice, and democracy. The theorists responsible for these reformulations are generally liberals, radicals, or democratic socialists. A number of the theorists, it should be noted, are academicians intent on bringing objectivity and logical rigor to a subject too long confused by rhetoric and political polemics.

The most provocative refomulation of the equality ideal in recent years is that produced by John Rawls, professor of Philosophy at Harvard University. In his widely hailed *A Theory of Justice,* Rawls, like Plato in *The Republic,* is concerned basically with the primacy of justice in the good society and with the two most fundamental components of justice: freedom and equality. Seeking to establish justice, freedom, and equality on grounds more substantial than the doctrine of utility that has been the chief moral view for the past two centuries, Rawls returns to the egalitarian natural rights theory of the social contract tradition and posits principles of justice that free and rational persons would accept in an initial position of equality in the state of nature.

Like more conservative theorists, Rawls places a slightly higher value on freedom than equality. Yet in the closely-argued pages of Chapter II of his *Theory,* he makes clear that both freedom and equality, which he derives from the "Difference Principle," are essential parts of any system of well-ordered justice.

He writes in this regard:[59]

> First: each person is to have an equal right to the most extensive basic liberty compatible with a similar liberty for others.
> Second: social and economic inequalities are to be arranged so that they are both (a) reasonably expected to be to everyone's advantage, and (b) attached to positions and offices open to all.

In deciding where to draw the theoretical line between legitimate and illegitimate inequality, Rawls opts for a position that is much closer to liberalism than to conservatism. He explains his position by saying that "the higher expectations of those better situated are just *if and only if they work as part of a scheme which improves the expectations of the least advantaged members of society."* Then he emphasizes his egalitarian perspective by stressing that "the social order is not to establish and secure the more attractive prospects of those better off *unless doing so is to the advantage of those less fortunate."*60 Elsewhere in Chapter II, he leaves no doubt that his highly personal theory of justice is meant, first and foremost, to be "an egalitarian conception."61

Notwithstanding the considerable praise that has been heaped on the Rawls book by egalitarians, its formulation of justice has been vigorously criticized by spokesmen of a number of groups. Conservatives have denounced it for making equality an absolute natural right. Radicals of the Left have criticized it for an opposite reason: for not being egalitarian enough. And certain mainstream liberals have objected that utilitarianism is a far better foundation for the ideal of equality than the contractarian premise resurrected by Rawls. Rawls certainly did not say the last word on these or any other topics treated in his book; yet no thinker since Tocqueville has probed the freedom-equality problem with greater insight or with greater analytical objectivity.62 Finally, it should be stressed that Rawls, like Rousseau, is an egalitarian for the sake of independence, self-respect, and liberty rather than for the sake of equality.

If inequality is the most pervasive of social facts, as the theorists discussed in this chapter apparently believed, it is no less true that the doctrine of egalitarianism has today become one of the most popular and powerful of all social theories. No respectable theory denies the necessity of some degree of discriminatory inequality; and, because of this, equality has always been, in a certain sense, a doctrine in search of a legitimating rationale. In can therefore be said that the fundamental issue remains what it has always been: Given the legitimacy of equality as an abstract ideal of justice, which particular *de facto* inequalities must be rejected and which are capable of being legitimated? From this primary question, two ancillary ones arise. By what rationale do we legitimate those inequalities that we agree to accept? And when, if ever, may the disadvantaged "justly" overturn privilege, whether by peaceful or violet means?

This chapter has dealt chronologically and in overview fashion with the thematic development of the equality concept. A quick glance at the data might suggest that equality theorists, over the centuries, have become progressively more militant and radical. To some extent that is true but not entirely, since not all contemporary proponents of equality are by any means in an apocalyptic mood. Indeed, not since the late eighteenth and early nineteenth centuries has there been such confident optimism as there is today that human greed and self-interest can be controlled, that justice for all is a practical objective, and that the life of the average person need not forever be solitary, poor, nasty, brutish, and short. Though not universal, restrained optimism about these matters seems to be the order of the day.

In the Age of Reason and for some time thereafter it was fashionable for philosophers to look to science and technology as the keys to freedom, equality, and real social justice. This suggested that the West's intellectuals, most of whom were interested in at least some aspect of equality, truly believed that the achievement of freedom and equality was part of realizing the Baconian ambition of "effecting all things possible." Now it would appear that the proponents of equality are looking less to science and technology than in the past, and are increasingly embracing the view that most of the problems which beset the human race call not for techno-scientific solutions but for moral, political, and administrative approaches. Whether this represents an advance in the realism of equality thought can be determined only by what actual progress is registered in future years. In this regard it should be emphasized that though theory has utility for a number of reasons, it should never be viewed as an omniscient primer for instant problem-solving, as radical ideologues have sometimes viewed it.

Conservative theorists, of course, still regard as frivolously superficial, if not subversive, the belief that the "natural" inequalities of the human predicament are remediable save by totalitarian methods. On the other hand, there is probably nothing more superficial than failure to perceive that acquiescence in the notion that what exists is right and just is a major factor in freezing that notion as a canon of conventional wisdom. Egalitarian theorists have always insisted, and still insist, that the long-term welfare of human beings cannot be secured by timid public policies that promote the interests of ruling elites at the expense of the great mass of the people. Human equality, they argue further, is not an empty slogan nor a shallow symbol but a basic philosophical principle of justice, the importance of which is confirmed by a thousand revolutions and civil insurrections. Finally, most egalitarians would surely agree that the quest for equality has for too long been confined to the airy realms of speculative theory: it is time now to use the theory to change the world and save the conscience of the human race. The remaining chapters of this book will explore the degree to which this objective has actually been realized, particularly in the United States.

NOTES

1. Sanford A. Lakoff, *Equality in Philosophy* (Cambridge, Mass.: Harvard University Press, 1964), p. 1.

2. Lev. 24:22.

3. Gen. 1:27-9:6.

4. The story of Adam and Eve is found in Gen. 1:26-27, where *adham* (Adam) is used in a collective or generic sense, as well as in Gen. 3:20-24, where Eve is specifically named. In no other place does the Hebrew Bible mention the Adam and Eve story, save for the strictly genealogical reference in I Chron. 1:1. Some allusions occur in the noncanonical apocryphal books.

5. St. Paul introduced the Original Sin doctrine into Christian thought. Neither he nor any of the other early Christian leaders bothered to explain how Adam's sin could actually be transmitted to all his descendants, and so far as is known, no Jewish exegete ever added the *peccatum originis* idea to the Genesis account of the fall of Adam.

6. The Biblical ideal was that a man should cleave to one wife. Furthermore, though polygamy of the patriarchs is openly discussed in the Bible, special reasons are always adduced to justify it. Interestingly, the Biblical word used to designate the relationship between two wives of the same man is *Tzarah,* another meaning of which is "misfortune."

7. The clearest legitimation of slavery in the Old Testament is found in Lev. 24:44-55. For a good general survey of the subject of slavery, see *The New Encyclopaedia Britannica: Macropaedia,* 15th ed., s.v. "Slavery, Serfdom, and Forced Labour."

8. Lev. 25:10-17.

9. See Emanuel Rackman, "Judaism and Equality," in *Nomos IX: Equality,* eds. J. Roland Pennock and John W. Chapman (New York: Atherton Press, 1967), pp. 154-76. In this excellent study of various equality conceptions, Rackman also makes the interesting point that "In Judaic thought . . . freedom is more the means and equality more the end." Ibid., p. 176.

10. The most famous Scriptural passage dealing with this conception is that in Deut. 14:2: "For you are a people holy to the Lord your God, and the Lord has chosen you to be a people of his own possession, out of all the nations that are on the face of the earth." Reform Jews, downplaying nationality, have deleted references to a chosen people from their prayer book. Christians extrapolated the doctrine to apply to those who believe in Jesus Christ. See I Pet. 2:9: "But you are a chosen race, a royal priesthood, a holy nation, God's own people."

11. Rackman, p. 155.

12. Quoted in Lee Cameron McDonald, *Western Political Theory, From its Origins to the Present* (New York: Harcourt, Brace & World, 1968), p. 78.

13. Ibid.

14. Ibid., p. 79.

15. Lakoff, p. 22.

16. All the quotations in this paragraph are from Morris Stockhammer, ed., *Plato Dictionary* (New York: Philosophical Library, 1963), pp. 56-57, 78.

17. Ernest Barker, ed., *The Politics of Aristotle* (London: Oxford University Press, 1948), p. 240.

18. Marcus Tullius Cicero, *De Republica, De Legibus,* trans. Clinton Walker Keyes (London: William Heinemann, 1951), pp. 329, 333.

19. Lakoff, p. 21.
20. Gal. 3:28.
21. Augustine, *The City of God*, trans. M. Dods (New York: Modern Library, 1950), p. 693.
22. Lakoff, p. 22.
23. *International Encyclopedia of the Social Sciences*, s.v. "Equality as an Ideal."
24. Paul E. Sigmund, "Hierarchy, Equality, and Consent in Medieval Christian Thought," *Nomos IX*, p. 139.
25. See Majid Khadduri, *The Islamic Law of Nations* (Baltimore: The Johns Hopkins University Press, 1966).
26. Leo Strauss and Joseph Cropsey, eds., *History of Political Philosophy*, 2nd ed. (Chicago: Rand McNally, 1972), p. 200.
27. Quoted in Emil Brunner, *Justice and the Social Order*, trans. Mary Hottinger (London: Lutterworth Press, 1949), p. 46.
28. Among useful studies of Hobbes and his thought are Sir Leslie Stephen, *Hobbes* (London: Macmillan, 1904); Howard Warrender, *The Political Philosophy of Hobbes; His Theory of Obligation* (Oxford: Clarendon Press, 1957); and Leo Strauss, *The Political Philosophy of Hobbes, Its Basis and Its Genesis*, trans. Elsa Sinclair (Oxford: Clarendon Press, 1936).
29. Lakoff, p. 79.
30. Mulford Q. Sibley, *Political Ideas and Ideologies: A History of Political Thought* (New York: Harper & Row, 1970), p. 378.
31. Two excellent studies of Locke and his thought are Maurice Cranston, *John Locke; A Biography* (New York: Macmillan, 1957); and John Gough, *John Locke's Political Philosophy* (Oxford: Clarendon Press, 1950). A useful analysis of Locke's property ideas is C.J. Czajkowski, *The Theory of Private Property in Locke's Political Philosophy* (Notre Dame, Ind.: University of Notre Dame Press, 1941).
32. On the general subject of Anabaptism, see Peter James Klassen, *The Economics of Anabaptism, 1525-1560* (The Hague: Mouton, 1964); and E. Belfort Bax, *Rise and Fall of the Anabaptists* (London: S. Sonnenschein, 1903).
33. Quoted in Lakoff, p. 49.
34. The thought of the Levellers is aptly analyzed in G.P. Gooch, *English Democratic Ideas in the Seventeenth Century* (New York: Harper, 1959).
35. For an excellent appraisal of the Diggers, see George H. Sabine, ed., *The Works of Gerrard Winstanley* (New York: Russell and Russell, 1965).
36. Rousseau viewed Corsica as a kind of laboratory for the perfect society and in 1765 actually began work on a *Projet de constitution pour la Corse;* he died, however, before he could finish it. Two of the best scholarly studies of the Enlightenment are Ernst Cassirer, *The Philosophy of the Enlightenment* (Princeton; Princeton University Press, 1951); and Carl Becker, *The Heavenly City of the Eighteenth-Century Philosophers* (New Haven: Yale University Press, 1932). There are numerous good studies of Rousseau and his thought. One of the best is Alfred Cobban, *Rousseau and the Modern State* (London: George Allen and Unwin, 1934).
37. Jean-Jacques Rousseau, *The Social Contract and Discourses*, trans. G.D.H. Cole (New York: E.P. Dutton, 1946), p. 160. Rousseau also spoke of natural equality as physical equality.
38. Ibid., p. 192.

39. Ibid., pp. 203-05.

40. Ibid., p. 221.

41. Ibid., p. 3.

42. See Marie Jean Antoine Nicholas de Caritat Condorcet, *Outlines of an Historical View of the Progess of the Human Mind* (Philadelphia: Carey, Rice, Orwood, Bache, and Fellows, 1796), *passim*. Condorcet was, by all accounts, an important precursor of both nineteenth-century sociology and modern liberalism. In this regard, see J. Salwyn Schapiro, *Condorcet and the Rise of Liberalism* (New York: Harcourt, Brace, 1934).

43. For an excellent analysis of Mably's thought, see Kingsley Martin, *The Rise of French Liberal Thought,* 2nd ed. (New York: New York University Press, 1954), pp. 242-47.

44. Quoted in Lakoff, p. 117.

45. An interesting appraisal of Morelly's philosophy can be found in F.J.C. Hearnshaw, ed., *The Social and Political Ideas of Some Great French Thinkers of the Age of Reason* (London: Harrap, 1930), pp. 217-51. The appraisal there is by C.H. Driver and deals with Mably, too.

46. For a brief but excellent summary of Babeuf's career, see *The New Encyclopaedia Britannica: Micropaedia,* 15th ed., s.v. "Babeuf, Francois-Noel."

47. Lakoff, p. 122.

48. There are at least two first-rate studies of Godwin's career and political thought: Ford K. Brown, *Life of William Godwin* (New York: E.P. Dutten, 1926); and George Woodcock, *William Godwin* (London: Porcupine Press, 1946).

49. Alexis de Tocqueville, *Democracy in America,* ed. Richard D. Heffner (New York: The New American Library, 1961), p. 192.

50. Ibid.

51. Julius Gould and William L. Kolb, eds., *A Dictionary of the Social Sciences* (New York: The Free Press, 1964), p. 672.

52. Ibid.

53. Frank E. Manuel has written two excellent studies of Saint-Simon and his thought: *The New World of Henri de Saint-Simon* (Cambridge, Mass.: Harvard University Press, 1956); and *The Prophets of Paris* (Cambridge, Mass.: Harvard University Press, 1962).

54. Brook Farm had actually been established earlier by George Ripley, and was then converted to Fourierism mainly through the efforts of Albert Brisbane. It became the focus of Nathaniel Hawthorne's famous novel, *The Blithedale Romance.*

55. For an interesting analysis of Fourierism, see Jean Godin, *Social Solutions,* trans. Marie Howland (New York: Lovell, 1886).

56. Two of the best studies of Owen are Margaret Cole, *Robert Owen of New Lanark* (New York: Oxford University Press, 1953); and Arthur L. Morton, *The Life and Ideas of Robert Owen* (New York: Monthly Review Press, 1963).

57. The famed historian H.G. Wells left the Fabian Society after a personal falling-out with Shaw and the Webbs. He brutally caricatured the whole lot of them in his novel *The New Machiavelli* (New York: Duffield, 1927). Unlike the Marxians, the Fabians issued scores of tracts minutely detailing their thinking on every conceivable local and national issue. They, indeed, had a passionate faith in facts and appeared to believe that factual analyses

of specific social problems would inevitably lead to rational reform. Between 1884 and 1916 the Society published at least 181 *Fabian Tracts*. On this general subject, see George Bernard Shaw, *Essays in Fabian Socialism* (Edinburgh: Clark, 1932).

58. An excellent though brief analysis of the Marxian theory of equality is that contained in Lakoff, pp. 225-33.

59. John Rawls, *A Theory of Justice* (Cambridge, Mass.: Harvard University Press, 1971), p. 60.

60. Ibid., p. 75. Italics have been added for emphasis.

61. Ibid., p. 100.

62. One other fine twentieth-century work deserves passing mention here: R.H. Tawney, *Equality* (London: George Allen and Unwin, 1964). This work, the first edition of which appeared in 1931, is already on the way to becoming a classic. Professor Tawney was primarily concerned with Britain, and he indicted inherited wealth and the public schools as the twin pillars of inequality in that country. He looked upon both these institutions as hereditary curses.

3

EQUALITY, FREEDOM, AND

POLITICAL DEMOCRACY

For almost two centuries now, as noted in Chapter 2, the quest for equality has been linked to the larger quest for constitutional democracy, a fact that may well be the most significant development in the history of equality. As a practical matter, this means that equality concerns are now central to the broad issue of social reform and to such democratic questions as the meaning of justice, its scope and nature, and the means of its realization. Moreover, it now seems certain that neither equality, freedom, nor democracy can long survive without the other two, for they together form an integral trilogy of social justice.

In light of both the theoretical and empirical linkage of equality with democracy, it is appropriate here to sketch the highlights of the history of democratic government, with a view to underscoring the symbiotic relationship between these two bedrock ideals of Western civilization. Like the history of equality, the history of democracy goes back well beyond the Christian era, and specifically to the Athenian *polis* of the fifth century B.C. For it was there, under the inspired leadership of such men as Solon and Pericles, that the first democratic polity was established in the world. The label "democracy" seems to have been devised by the Greek historian Herodotus, who apparently first used it in his *History*.[1] It was derived from two common Greek words: *demos,* meaning "the people," and *kratein,* meaning "to rule." English as well as other modern languages have adopted Herodotus' word with only slight variations in spelling and pronounciation.

Athenian democracy reached its apogee in the Periclean or Golden Age of the fifth century B.C., and its principal goals seem to have been three: the secure maintenance of law and order; the promotion of justice for all; and the maximization of freedom and legal-political equality for all members of the citizen class. In order to realize these goals, a variety of institutional arrangements — some quite ingenious — were developed both before and during the Periclean Age. Included among these were short office tenure for public officials, direct participation of all adult citizens in the legislative process, majority-rule decisionmaking, a complex court and jury system, a prohibition on reelection to certain key offices, popular control of officials (including military ones), ostracism, and the lot system of election for certain government positions.

By twentieth-century standards, Athenian democracy, though noble in conception, was defective in a number of crucial ways. It was, for example, strongly anti-feminist since females, even wives of citizens, had no political rights. Moreover, though it endowed citizens with political and legal equality, it did not extend the equality concept to the educational economic, or other fields. One may say, therefore, that its general conception of citizenship was extremely narrow, with full citizenship being limited to adult males who were born in Athens of Athenian parents. The idea of acquiring citizenship through legal naturalization was not unheard of, though it seems to have been used only rarely.

There were other deficiencies. There were, for instance, numerous resident foreigners and freed slaves in Athens; and though an alien (*metoikos*) fared far better than slaves and non-residents, as shown by the status of Cephalus in Plato's *Republic,* he was subject to numerous restrictions on marriage and property ownership and was entirely excluded from politics and government. Still worse from the modern perspective is the fact that Athenian democracy rested on a system of human slavery, which, of course, was all but universal in the ancient world. Most of the slaves were acquired through trade or warfare in the Asia Minor and Black Sea areas, and they were owned by the Athenian government as well as by wealthy citizens. No doubt many, perhaps most, of the slaves were treated quite humanely, but those who did the backbreaking work in the government's silver mines must certainly have had a bleak existence.

Rather more surprising to modern minds is the lack of even a rudimentary state educational system in Athens, such as was pioneered in autocratic Sparta. It appears that the concept of a free, state education for everybody simply did not exist in the Athenian polity outside the books of Plato. This meant that only wealthy Athenians were able to assure their children an education, which they did by hiring for them one or more private tutors such as Socrates and the Sophists. The inegalitarian ramifications of this condition were enormous.

A final criticism of Athenian democracy from the modern standpoint is the charge that it viewed state and society as coterminous, and thus embraced a kind of "benign totalitarianism." It is certainly true that government and religion, which was neither doctrinal nor ethical, were fused in Athens, and all residents were required to pay nominal homage to the local deities. Furthermore no rights were recognized *against* the state. On the other hand, it is well known that the Athenians permitted private voluntary associations to exist and carry on their business relatively freely. But what is crucial here is that they did not regard such agencies, as we do today, as freedom-enhancing buffers between the isolated individual and the almighty sovereign state.

In the realm of political theory, it is somewhat surprising to find that most of the Greek philosophers who studied democracy in a systematic way were critical of both its premises and institutional structures. Indeed, among Athenian intellectuals, Pericles, who was more of a statesman than a contemplative egghead, was one of the very few who actually preferred democracy to minority-rule government. His famous funeral oration, delivered in Athens in 431 B.C. as a tribute to those who had fallen in the first year of the Peloponnesian War, is the clearest expression we have from the Golden Age of the exact nature and scope of Athenian democratic values. Pericles, if we are to believe the report in Thucydides, described the Athenian system in the following fashion:[2]

> It is true that we are a democracy, for the administration is in the hands of the many and not of the few. But while the law secures equal justice to all alike in their private disputes, the claim of excellence is also recognized; and when a citizen is in any way distinguished, he is preferred to the public service, not as a matter of privilege, but as the reward of merit. Neither is poverty a bar, but a man may benefit his country whatever may be the obscurity of his station. There is no exclusiveness in our public life.

Plato, unlike Pericles, was unmistakably hostile to Athenian democracy. An aristocrat who lived through the great civil war with Sparta, he viewed democracy, not as a fount of true justice, but as a mobocratic perversion of oligarchy. Thus in the *Republic* as well as in other works, he assailed not only the basic premises but also the institutional scaffolding of democratic polities. He argued, in the first instance, that governance is a highly specialized skill and that men differ innately in their abilities to exercise the various skills of life, especially including that of ruling. Given these major premises, it follows logically that those elites who exhibit, after training, the greatest capacity for ruling should be put in charge of their societies. Furthermore, in order to assure their maximal effectiveness, they ought to be entrusted with absolute authority to make and implement public policy. Egalitarian democracy might, indeed, be attractive to the masses, but Plato was sure it would produce less justice and worse policies than elitist government. Though Plato was not always specific about his political preferences, most of the time he appeared to favor a non-egalitarian, apolitical system that can perhaps best be described today as an intellectual meritocracy.[3] This comes out clearest in the *Republic*.

Aristotle, who was bourgeois rather than aristocratic and who spent several years at Plato's Academy, was somewhat less antipathetic than his master to democracy and equality. In his *Politics,* he argues that the best government ideally would be one run by an omniscient king or by a group of perfectly virtuous, public-spirited aristocrats. Since, however, monarchies and aristocracies are easily corrupted in the real world, he concluded that the best practical form of government is a mixed, carefully balanced constitutional state (*polity*) in which the middle class is the dominant force. It would appear that Aristotle had in mind something resembling the U.S. government of the late eighteenth century: a small agrarian state in which democratic, oligarchical, and aristocratic elements are counterbalanced against one another, and in which liberty is put above numerical equality, communalism above individualism.

Concerning Athens' particular brand of direct democracy, Aristotle considered that a perversion of *polity,* or, as he once put it, a system in which "not the laws are sovereign but the bulk of the unpropertied class." Believing in the superiority of the middle class as he did, he could obviously not accept such a derangement of values. Oversimplifying the matter, we may say that though Aristotle was deeply committed to constitutional government, he attacked classical democracy for five basic reasons. He believed it contrary to human nature. He thought it promoted an unwarranted brand of radical social and economic equality. He feared it would always display a partiality toward the untrained masses. He was sure it would seriously disadvantage the middle and upper classes. And, finally, he did not believe it could long survive without degenerating into license and mobocracy. Aristotle did, however, concede that democracy is the "least bad" of the perverted forms of government, among which tyranny is by far the worst.[4]

In the modern world, playwrights, more often than not, have tended to be both liberal and egalitarian, yet during the Golden Age of Athens that city's dramatists condemned the democratic ideal as sharply as did most of its philosophers. Euripides, for example, wrote a number of plays dealing with social problems in which he attacked tyranny and radical democracy alike. Furthermore Aristophanes, the greatest Greek writer of comedy, satirized almost every aspect of Periclean democracy in such witty plays as *The Clouds, The Wasps, The Birds, Lysistrata,* and *The Frogs.* It must, however, be stressed that the unusual freedom enjoyed by the Athenian dramatists is convincing evidence of the vitality of the city's democratic institutions. In Sparta, such freedom was not tolerated.

After the contributions of Pericles and his colleagues in the Golden Age, the Greeks who did most to advance the ideal of democracy were the Stoics. As suggested in the previous chapter, Stoicism rested on two related principles: universalism and equality. Nature, the Stoics argued, is the manifestation of a universal rationality roughly synonymous with the concept of God, and all men are therefore rational and equal and belong to one natural, universal community.

Also crucial to the theory of Stoicism was the concept of a universal Law of Nature, against which all political institutions are to be measured and, if found wanting, condemned. Few concepts affected the development of democracy more profoundly than this one. It became, in part, the basis of Christian ethics. It provided a key rationale for democratic revolutions in the post-Renaissance world. And, in the eighteenth century, it inspired the idea of a "law above the law" that served as a major premise of both the French and U.S. constitutional systems. Other "democratic" doctrines of Stoicism were the sanctity of the individual, belief in reason as the key to justice, and a strong stress on self-reliance that seemed to forecast Kant's categorical imperative. Although many of the Greek Stoics tended to be apolitical, like such other Hellenistic groups as the Cynics and Epicureans, their Roman successors were very much involved in public affairs, and some attained to high office. The belief of the Roman Stoics that every citizen is obligated to play an active role in public affairs is, of course, much closer to the democratic ideal than the standoffishness of their illustrious predecessors.

The era of the *Pax Romana* (roughly 27 B.C. to 180 A.D.) was far too authoritarian to permit much advance in either democratic theory or practice. Nevertheless, the Romans did show a certain regard for democratic values. Thus, in their political system there was at least theoretical control of the military by civilian authorities. Also, as in

Periclean Athens, there was a quite active assembly that was broadly representative of the Roman people. In addition, the Romans instituted one of the first non-patronage, "career systems" of public administration, and in the later imperial period virtually all class barriers to public office were dismantled. And, of course, it is well known that the Romans, as early as 449 B.C., received a written constitution, which was known as the Twelve Tables and distantly resembled the Hebrews' Ten Commandments. We may therefore say that if the Roman government was less "populistic" or egalitarian than the democracy of Athens, it was vastly more libertarian than most of the states in the classical age and never really became totalitarian, as Sparta did.

Rome's political theorists, most notably Cicero, were obsessed with the centrality of law in a just society, as modern democratic philosophers are; and Cicero in fact once defined the state as simply a community of law or *iuris societas.* Yet it was not until several centuries after Cicero's death that Roman law received its final systematization in the famous *Corpus Juris Civilis,* the vast collection of laws and judicial decisions developed under the sponsorship of the Byzantine emperor Justinian I in the sixth century A.D. Even a cursory glance at that collection reveals that Roman law was rather severe by modern democratic standards. Still, it included a number of egalitarian aspects, from Stoic and other sources, such as the mutuality of contracts, the relatively high status of married women, the limited control of the father over his family, and provisions facilitating the manumission of slaves.

In other areas besides the law, the Romans approached in theory, if not always in practice, the modern democratic conception of a commonwealth in which popular consent is the basis for legitimating government. This perhaps comes out clearest in the following passage from Cicero, in which Scipio is defining a *res publica:*[5]

> The commonwealth, then, is the people's affair; and the people is not every group of men, associated in any manner, but is the coming together of a considerable number of men who are united by a common agreement about law and rights and by the desire to participate in mutual advantages. The original cause of this coming together is not so much weakness as a kind of social instinct natural to man.

The Middle Ages saw the withering away of the great empires of the Western world and the emergence in their stead of a maze of small, decentralized agrarian governments. Although none of these governments could be labeled democratic, the democratic tradition, dormant like an underground spring, received certain theoretical and practical inputs in the transition period between the collapse of the Roman Empire and the advent of the Renaissance. One of the most important of these was the proliferation of local governments close to the people which, though formally authoritarian, kept alive the ideal of grassroots democracy that the Athenians had so cherished. And, more to the point, the conquest of medieval Europe by Judaic-Christian values, while not an unmixed blessing, infused a number of new concepts and practices into the Western political orientation that were destined to contribute significantly to the evolution of modern constitutional democracy. In one way or another, most of these concepts related to freedom, equality, and justice.

Among medieval analysts of politics, St. Thomas Aquinas, the synthesizer of Christianity and Aristotelianism, was preeminent. A Christian authoritarian rather than a democrat, St. Thomas nonetheless popularized several ideas and concepts that had more than a passing affinity to the ideals of democracy. His stress on the vital significance of law in the pursuit of justice is, of course, a basic ingredient of all democratic polities. He likewise had a conception of the state and government that was vastly more positive than that of the early Christians, and not too far removed from the views of modern liberal democrats. Reflecting his Aristotelian bias, he showed a lifelong preference for a mixed political system that combined aristocratic structures and popular consent in a positive guardianship of the social order. Moreover, in contrast to his predecessor Augustine, he maintained that political authority is wholly natural and not simply the fruit of man's sin.

In the socioeconomic realm, where democratic policy makers today confront the freedom-equality paradox in its sharpest form, St. Thomas clearly drew the line in favor of private over communal property. He did this for he believed that a person "is more careful to procure what is for himself alone than that which is common to many or to all." On the other hand, he drew the economic policy line in favor of the consumer when he argued against the legitimacy of usury and insisted both on fair prices and on the government's right to regulate business enterprise.[6] St. Thomas, in other words, was neither a Marxian socialist nor a Goldwater Neo-Spencerian.

In the later Middle Ages, a reform movement arose within the Christian Church that in many ways prefigured the recent agitation spawned by Vatican II. It was known as the conciliar movement, and it popularized certain ideas that had both democratic and egalitarian implications. The roots of the movement went back indirectly to the ideas of the thirteenth-century canonists who had tried to limit the autocratic power of the papacy, and more directly to the Great Schism that had scandalized Christendom in the 1300s.

Conciliarism attracted some of the brightest minds of the fifteenth century, among whom were bishops, cardinals, and the Chancellor of the University of Paris. These distinguished churchmen, while differing as to the best means of ending the Great Schism, agreed on a number of fundamental reforms. Specifically, they agreed on the necessity to constitutionalize (not democratize) church government by replacing papal supremacy with some form of governance by a representative council (*concilium* in Latin). The make-up and exact prerogatives of the proposed council were matters of dispute among the conciliarists; yet there was no disagreement that the Christian Church, if it was to survive as a united body, needed to put more emphasis on representation and consensus than had been the case in the past. The most brilliant theorist among the conciliarists was a German, Cardinal Nicolas of Cusa, who deserted the movement in the 1430s in order to become a papal diplomat.[7]

In the end, conciliarism utterly failed to destroy papal absolutism, a failure that may well have been one of the chief reasons for the triumph of the more radical Protestant movement in the succeeding century. Nevertheless, despite the movement's inability to alter the structure of the Catholic Church, conciliarism as an ideal definitely contributed to the emergence of modern democracy. It did that in the first place by affecting the thinking of sixteenth-century Protestant reformers, especially in such crucial areas as congregational democracy. Furthermore, over the next three centuries, the conciliarist ideals of representative government and consent slowly filtered into the secular realm and helped to inspire the gradual constitutionalization of most Western governments. The conciliarists, to be sure, did not invent either of these ideals, yet they tenaciously espoused and preserved them at a time when both seemed to be in eclipse.

In retrospect, it is now obvious that the Renaissance-Reformation period (roughly the 1400s and 1500s) was more critical as a seedbed of constitutional democracy than any period of Western history since the Periclean Age. Granted, the vast majority of governments remained absolutist or authoritarian, and there was little explicit theorizing as yet about democracy as a political doctrine. Still, in both theory and practice, certain trends were crystallizing that were inexorably, if slowly, advancing the underground river of democracy.

First of all, there was a substantial increase in personal liberty and individualism, resulting mainly from such phenomena as urbanization, decline of serfdom, spread of higher learning, and the split in Christendom.

Second, the rise of religious pluralism gradually prepared the way for a larger measure of religious toleration in the West and, eventually, for church-state separation through constitutional or statutory law. Third, the rise of empirical science in this era popularized one of the key ideals of the democratic orientation: conflict-resolution and problem-solving by reason instead of by blind reliance on authority and conventional wisdom. Fourth, the invention of printing made it possible to disseminate radical democratic ideas in printed form in quantities previously unheard of. Finally, the economic system we call capitalism, which has numerous affinities with democracy, arose in the Renaissance and a short time later received an added impetus from the so-called Protestant or Calvinist "work ethic."[8]

Viewed from the perspective of democracy, the Renaissance-Reformation era was also important for having witnessed the start of violent social protest as an almost normal feature of politics. Massive social protest really began in France in 1358 with the *Jacquerie,* an insurrection of the lower classes against the ruling nobility and the exorbitant taxes that came in the wake of the Hundred Years' War. Although the revolting peasants, nicknamed "Jacques" or "Jacques Bonhomme," were eventually crushed and then massacred by Charles II of Navarre, they made history by conceiving a new method of extra-legal change that has still not run its course, and that has served as an inspiration to countless generations of democratic reformers.

In 1381, masses of English peasants emulated their French counterparts by revolting against their landlords and going on an orgy of arson, assault, and murder. Indeed, in certain respects both the French and English peasant revolts were dress rehearsals for the Russian Revolution that erupted more than five centuries later. The English rebellion, like the *Jacquerie,* was soon suppressed, but not before the peasant-rebels had added yet another dramatic chapter to the legacy of justice-through-violence. Today, that legacy is an established part of the egalitarian democratic tradition, a fact that disturbs conservative and moderate democrats.

By far the most extensive popular revolt of the Reformation era was the German Peasants' Rebellion that took place in Swabia and Franconia in the 1520s. Inspired by Luther's attacks on the religious establishment, the oppressed peasants were seeking to extend his purely religious revolt to the socioeconomic realm. They articulated their demands in something called the "Twelve Articles," which resembled the way the U.S. Founding Fathers, more than 200 years later, would make their case against George III in the Declaration of Independence. Unfortunately for the peasants, Luther vehemently repudiated their revolt; and with his encouragement if not connivance, the autocratic princes soon crushed all resistance to their authority. Yet once again the "right of rebellion" had taken hold of the popular mind, so much so, in fact, that within a few centuries this right would become a moral imperative engendering a vast harvest of democratic revolutions throughout the Western world. The victims, in all cases, would be authoritarian governments and their supporters who denied any right of civil disobedience or tyrannicide.

As the preceding chapter demonstrated, it was in the seventeenth century that modern democratic theories first appeared, most notably in the doctrines of the Levellers, Diggers, and John Locke. It was not, however, until the latter part of the eighteenth century that these theories were put into practice to any significant degree, and then only in the United States and France. The attempts to implement democratic theory at that time stemmed from the victories of the American and French revolutionaries in the Revolutions of '75 and '89. But in both cases the attempts were partially aborted, in the United States by the aristocratic paternalism of the Federalists and in France by the Terror of the Jacobins and the military dictatorship of Napoleon.

If democracy did not spring full-gown from the heads of Washington and Robespierre, the political history of the Western world had been permanently altered in a number of key ways. Thus political democracy, which hitherto had been little more than a dream or an ideal, became after the French and American Revolutions a viable ideological movement with tens of thousands of adherents. Moreover the word itself now for the first time came into common usage and was increasingly employed in a honorific rather than pejorative sense. In addition, a number of philosophical treatises and state documents in the late eighteenth century advanced the theory, and indirectly, the practice of constitutional democracy. Chief among these were the U.S. Constitution of 1787 and the U.S. Bill of Rights. Also significant was the founding in the 1790s by Jefferson of the first overt political movement with the word democratic in its title: the Democratic-Republican Party. Of no less importance was the rise, at the end of the century, of emotional nationalism, which in a number of ways provided substantial new support to egalitarian democracy. And, perhaps most crucial of all, democracy finally received in 1789 a capsule definition and a talismanic motto: *Liberty, Equality, Fraternity*. That, of course, was the famous cry of the French revolutionaries, and it appears to have originated in an old Masonic ritual. In any event, that motto remains the official motto of the democratic French republic and is the implicit motto of all other democracies in the world.

The brief but protean motto of the French revolutionaries suggests what may well have been the most significant outcome of the American and

French Revolutions: namely, the fateful fusion of democratic republicanism with two of the most persistent dreams of Western people, freedom and equality. This fusion, to be sure, was not uniform in the Western world. And, indeed, out of the seedbed of revolution there emerged two (later three) distinct versions of democracy and social justice: one in the United States, the other in France. The former is usually referred to as the Jeffersonian version or model, the latter as the radical Jacobin model. The proponents of both models paid lip service to freedom, equality, republicanism, fraternity as essential components of true justice, yet they differed significantly in terms of priorities and tactics. The Jeffersonians put freedom first, particularly in the private sector; played down the communal concept of fraternity; and adopted a posture of moderate, instrumental pragmatism toward public affairs. The French radicals, on the other hand, preferred equality to freedom, though they put freedom first in their motto; emphasized fraternity far more than their American counterparts; and assumed an abstract, utopian attitude toward reform, best typified by their Declaration of the Rights of Man. One predictable consequence of these varying conceptions of democracy and social justics was that the United States developed more freedom and individualism, while revolutionary France, at least for a time, achieved more equality and fraternity.

One can discern the influence of these contrasting attitudes toward democracy not only in the different constitutional systems constructed by the Jacobins and the U.S. Founding Fathers, but also in the vast literature of democratic polemics and philosophy produced by writers in all Western countries. For the French version of democracy and equality, it is essential to read Rousseau, Morelly, Mably, and Babeuf. For the American version, one must turn to the Declaration of Independence, the Articles of Confederation, the Constitution of 1787, the Bill of Rights of 1791, the state constitutions, and the works of such theorists as Jefferson, Franklin, Patrick Henry, John Adams, and Madison. If one has time for only a single American theoretical work, that would have to be the *Federalist Papers,* authored by Madison, Hamilton, and Jay.

United firmly on a common goal — the maximization of freedom, equality, and justice — the American and French democrats differed throughout their lives on how this complex goal could best be achieved. Today their ideological descendants still disagree on the crucial issue of means. And to complicate matters further, a new version of democracy has been added to the original two, which is most often referred to as the Whig or conservative model. On the democratic continuum, it stands somewhat to the right of the Jeffersonian model.

The Federal Constitution, written in 1787, is of course the revered Bible of U.S. democracy; yet in its original form it did not include the concept of equality nor did it provide directly for twentieth-century mass democracy. The concept of egalitarian democracy is implied in the phrase "We the people" that begins the Preamble, and the whole document is a glowing tapestry spun with equal parts of rhetorical gold and practical realism. But for all its liturgical intensity, the Constitution was even less explicit about equality than the Declaration of Independence. Indeed, the concept of "equal protection of the laws" did not get into the Constitution until 1868 when the Fourteenth Amendment was adopted, and even that vital addition to the nation's basic law did not guarantee Indian or female rights. It is therefore correct to state that neither liberty for all nor equality was really maximized by the American Revolution, and fraternity had to await the conquest of the wild frontier.

One of the little-known results of the revolutionary ferment that closed the eighteenth century was the creation of a radically different justification for the egalitarian ideal after its *de facto* fusion with constitutional democracy. From Hebraic and early Christian times, the rationales for equality have been essentially moral, religious, and metaphysical, all of which lacked clarity and precision. What was needed was the clearing away of useless, obfuscatory theoretical debris in order that genuine progress might be made toward conceptual clarification. In the late eighteenth century, the French and American revolutionaries thought they had achieved just that by depriving equality of its metaphysical mystique and outfitting the bare bones with new naturalistic garments. The new outfitting involved, among other things, secularizing, legalizing, constitutionalizing, ideologizing, and politicizing both equality and freedom within a democratic or quasi-democratic context. The consequences of this transformation in equality's basic rationale were enormous, though it took quite a while for that fact to become widely perceived.

In this regard, it is often argued that the French *philosophes* were mainly responsible for the "naturalization" of man and his values that occurred in the Enlightenment. One can make a plausible case for that argument, yet it can just as easily be demonstrated "that the naturalization of man was only a specific application or concomitant of the general modern notion that nature can serve as an autonomous standard for human life, divorced from religion or philosophy. Once one treats himself as part of nature, subject to laws which he can only discover and not create or will, then analytic knowledge supplants philosophical knowledge and manipulative activity is loosened from purposive activity."[9]

In the old Christian conception of equality, people were deemed equal because all had been created in the image of God. But along came the *philosophes* and their American counterparts with a preference for nature over religion, and they insisted on grouding equality on the "scientific" fact that all human beings are animals, albeit more rational and vocal than the beasts of the jungle. Moreover, being instrumentalists, they tended to view men as a means rather than an end and, in the opinion of critics, they denigrated both humanity and the equality ideal. To be sure, much progress toward equality was made by the more secular, more instrumental orientation of constitutional democracy, but the price was high in terms of the diminution of our moral sense and the growing homogenization of opinions, attitudes, values, and manners. With the advantage of hindsight, we know now that there "is something imperialistic in the equalitarian temper: it refuses to stay within the borders originally set for it."[10] That has no doubt always been true, though it was not so obvious in the eighteenth century as it is today.

Another little-known result of the new naturalistic, democratic conception of human beings was that the mandated equality, being almost wholly legal and political, was confined strictly to the public sector, leaving the private sector to operate on the principle of near-absolute freedom. Hence, we may say that while equality was being advanced in the political and governmental systems of the West, the freedom to discriminate in the private sector was actually being enhanced by the abolition or diminution of the old authoritarian, mercantilist controls.

The significance of this aspect of the freedom-equality paradox has been perceptively underscored in the following observations:

> Liberty, which expresses men's inequalities and diversities, resides within the zone of privacy. The fundamental convention, then, is that all men shall be treated as equals in the public realm, in order that they will be able to express their inequalities in the private realm. By assigning the principle of equality to one territory and the principle of inequality to another, the constitutionalists thought that both could be preserved without conflict.[11]

This radical separation of public and private equality standards, for which Madison was as much responsible as anybody, was an integral part of one of the most fateful developments of the post-Renaissance world: the separation of political theory from private ethics. In the days of Plato and Aristotle, the theory and practice of politics were one with the theory and practice of ethics, whether in the public or private sector. However, beginning with Machiavelli in the sixteenth century, a sharp distinction came to be made between the realms of public action and private morality, and between ethics and political theory. In the eighteenth century that distinction, now hallowed with time, became a matter both of ideology and of law. To be sure, the U.S. Supreme Court, in recent years, has substantially eroded the private-public distinction in constitutional law, yet this binary conception continues to authorize what it authorized in the Age of Reason: maximal public equality coexisting with minimal private equality.

The quasi-democratic polity constructed by the U.S. Founding Fathers in 1787, though more coercive and interventionist than the Confederation government it replaced, was actually not far removed from pure laissez-faire. But the economic individualism of the Founders gradually fell into disrepute, and during the past century or so the public sector has steadily grown at the expense of the private sector. The ramifications of this have been substantial for the freedom-equality dilemma; and though they were perceived but dimly in the nineteenth century, they are now apparent to almost everybody as they complicate and exacerbate every public issue that arises in the U.S. democracy.

Few doubt that the proponents of both equality and freedom have benefited from the expansion of the public sector, yet it is just as certain that a number of key liberties have been set back rather than helped by this development, most particularly the liberty to be left alone in one's private world. Only now are we beginning to appreciate the full import of the old axiom that the price of equality is fraternity — something about which not everybody is enthusiastic.[12] Of course, Madison and Jefferson cannot be blamed for all our current problems stemming from the ideologization of equality in the eighteenth century. The lesson in all this, if there is one, is that social change, no matter how popular and persuasive, inevitably brings in its wake hidden, long-run consequences which may, in the end, turn out to be more permanent and fateful than the original change itself.

Of all the consequences of the rise of modern political democracy, few were more significant than the legal and constitutional separation of religion (God) and government. Moreover, about the time that church and state were being formally separated, the egalitarian fiction of popular sovereignty was being introduced into the Western world, leading to its apotheosis in the Rousseauean myth of the General Will. If the radical democrats of the Enlightenment had not slain God, they had at least eliminated his authority in matters political, social, and economic. As for the ramifications of all this, it hardly matters whether the fusion of secular constitutional democracy and equality that occurred at the end of the eighteenth century is genuine truth: what matters is that this intellectual and political development was a dramatic naturalistic vision that had (and still has) an almost obsessive power to command belief and sacrifice.

Skeptics have always maintained that the moment democracy and equality were fused, without benefit of clergy, the resulting hybrid was a pathological ideology. Egalitarians, on the other hand, deny that anything pathological resulted and insist that the fusion was actually the beginning of real progress both for equality as a basic social norm and for democracy as a legitimate and preferred form of governance. But conservatives will doubtless continue to argue that the French Revolution and most of the revolutions that followed it were, in reality, revolts aginst reason and against that traditional wisdom that held inequality to be both natural and generally benign.

Though it is true, as Chapter 2 showed, that egalitarian theory goes back to the classical age, it cannot be too strongly emphasized that the organized pursuit of equality as an ideal of justice by large sovereign governments is a modern phenomenon that does not antedate the French and American Revolutions. Before the eighteenth century, the pursuit of equality was something confined for the most part to messianic individuals and groups operating, without assistance, in the private sector. It is therefore quite accurate to say that it was not until the French and American revolutionaries seized control of their governments that equality was officially integrated with the core ideal of justice and recognized as one of the basic end-values pursued by all genuine constitutional democracies. A different way of looking at this matter is to say that eighteenth-century democracy did not so much mature the idea of equality as ferment it, creating in the process an intoxicating brew that ever since has brought the world to recurring frenzies of hope and anguish. Liberty, equality, and democracy — when fused together — do, indeed, make an extraordinarily heady concoction.

More than is generally recognized, equality has also turned out to be an embarrassment to democratic theory: the skeleton in the democratic closet. Everybody agrees it is one of the fundamental dogmas of modern democracy, and yet nature screams on every hand that men are *unequal*. One may go even further and argue that the whole value system of democracy has always seemed to go against the facts. Democracy assumes, for example, that most people are basically rational most of the time, but are they? Furthermore, it assumes people will do the right thing when enlightened, but will they? Finally, it assumes majority rule by versatile amateurs will, in the long run, be more effective than minority rule by qualified experts, but will it? And so it goes on and on.

In the nineteenth century, democracy, along with its libertarian and egalitarian components, became linked with several social, intellectual, and other phenomena that proved to be critical in promoting what Tocqueville liked to call the democratic revolution. Among these linked phenomena were Jacksonianism, laissez-faire capitalism, Social Darwinism, mythic nationalism, the anti-slavery movement, the opening of the U.S. West, and the Social Gospel. Following democracy's link-up with these diverse movements, striking progress toward equality was registered in a number of key societal areas. Thus, the British Empire and the United States abolished black slavery. Russia emancipated her serfs. The British Reform Act was passed, transforming Britain from an aristocratic oligarchy into a quasi-democratic, bourgeois polity. And, after the U.S. Civil War, the Congress, with the concurrence of the states, added to the Federal Constitution the Thirteenth, Fourteenth, and Fifteenth Amendments, which respectively freed the slaves, conferred citizenship upon most of them, and guaranteed them protection from state discrimination at the ballot box.

In the intellectual realm, a variety of forces were likewise at work advancing the increasingly popular cause of egalitarian democracy. Bentham's utilitarianism became the *de facto* ethical principle of democratic societies, supplanting the old natural law-natural rights doctrine that stemmed from the contractarian "state of nature" concept. John Stuart Mill's espousal of liberty, feminism, and radical individualism, along with proportional representation, added vital new dimensions to the democratic dogma. In the arts, Walt Whitman's dithyrambic hymns to the democratic man dramatized as never before the appeal of egalitarian ideals. And most important of all symbolically was Lincoln's Gettysburg Address, delivered at the height of the Civil War, which provided a capsule definition of democratic government that is still one of the best ever conceived. It ranks with the French revolutionaries' motto.

The advent of the twentieth century witnessed a fundamental transformation in both the scope and nature of constitutional democracy, as well as in the relative weights assigned to the ideals of freedom and equality. As noted earlier, Westerners in the eighteenth and nineteenth centuries generally favored freedom over equality, especially in the private sector. But in the present century, there has been a steadily rising tendency, in the United States and abroad, to draw the policy lines in favor of equality over freedom when one must give. That is true in both the public and private sectors, as Tocqueville predicted.

Several factors have clearly been responsible for this historic reorientation of democratic theory and practice. Foremost among these have been Marxism, Fabian Socialism, liberal religion, technological innovations in the communications and transportation fields, Keynesian economics, anti-racism, anti-imperialism, feminism, the recent so-called "liberation" movements, U.S. Supreme Court decisions, executive and legislative initiatives, the creation of the League of Nations and the U.N., and the sudden emergence in recent years of "creative violence" as an instrument for transforming the status quo to the benefit of the disadvantaged.

Today there appear to be at least five distict categories of democrats who can be distinguished by the relative priority they assign to equality and freedom. For the sake of easy reference, these categories may be labeled liberals, centrists, conservatives, radicals, and socialists. Most U.S. democrats would probably fall into the first three of these categories, while Europe and the Third World would have a somewhat larger percentage of radicals and socialists. Marxists, of course, consider themselves the quintessential democrats and socialists, though their opponents regard them as totally authoritarian. One man's label, in short, is another man's lie.

The crucial turning point in the world's attitude toward egalitarian democracy seems to have come in 1917, when President Wilson took the United States into World War I with the imperative, "Make the world safe for democracy." Before the start of that historic, and ultimately disillusioning crusade, it is probable that democracy was as often a pejorative as an honorific term. However, since then, with the exception of fascists and Birchites, just about everybody has come out for at least the theory of democracy and for its congeries of revered symbols and icons. And even the fascists, in some of their less intransigent moments, have argued that fascism is actually "the purest form of democracy."[13]

By the end of World War II, the ideal of equality had achieved such an exalted place in democratic dogma that it was viewed by many as a sort of vaccine which, if injected into the masses in moderate amounts, would forever blunt the appeal of more radical egalitarian ideologies such as communism. But things have recently changed; and as subsequent chapters of this study will show, equality by the mid-1970s had suffered an erosion of its former exalted position that seemed to threaten its future advance. It must be stressed, however, that this reduction in status has occurred more in the intellectual realm than in the field of public policy. In any event, equality is viewed by more and more critics today as a serious *threat* to freedom rather than its handmaiden and, indeed, as a danger to all the basic values and institutional hierarchies hitherto tolerated by constitutional democracy. This intellectual derogation of equality, coinciding as it does with tremendous egalitarian victories in the social and governmental realms, is surely one of the most extraordinary ironies in the history of the equality ideal.

Since the operative conceptions of democracy before the twentieth century entailed little more than maximal freedom in the private sector and a formal commitment to equality for all male citizens before the ballot box and the law, it was not especially difficult to realize these limited goals of the democratic ideology. Thus, the first of these goals was attained, until recently at least, simply by having the government follow a policy of non-intervention in the economy. The goal of political equality was chieved primarily by institutionalizing universal suffrage. The third goal, that of equality before the law, was also rather easily accomplished, theoretically at least, by setting up a network of state and federal courts that would impartially adjudicate controversies arising under the Federal Constitution, English common law, and state and federal statutory law. However, the realization of true equality before the law for *all* classes and groups of people has, in practice, turned out to be enormously difficult in the United States. And because of the complex, far-reaching problems raised by this critical freedom-equality issue, the following chapter will be devoted exclusively to that subject.

Until the twentieth century, it was not uncommon to qualify the noun "democracy" with the adjective "political" in references to the constitutional systems of the Western world. Such a qualification made sense, for democratic governments did, indeed, seem to emphasize personal freedom and citizens' *political* equality above other values. Political democracy particularly entailed a steady extension of the franchise, a process that has reached a point where today most democracies grant the right to vote to everybody save minors, resident aliens, and persons institutionalized for criminal or mental reasons. Furthermore, since there is no weighting of ballots, each person's vote counts the same as every other person's.[14] That, at least, is the theory.

Since the late eighteenth century, political democracy has also been defined first and foremost in terms of popular sovereignty, which is simply a shorthand phrase for resting the ultimate ruling power in a society with the people.[15] Among the most important components of this mythic phrase, political equality would have to be placed near the top. Yet, despite the fact that popular sovereignty seems to imply universal adult suffrage, all the major democracies of the world have, at one time or another, placed restrictions on the right to vote. That has been especially true in the United States. In colonial days, for example, there were religious and property criteria for voting. Until the Civil War almost all blacks were excluded from voting, and until the 1920s most women, of whatever race, were disfranchised. Other groups disfranchised until recently were Indians, illiterates, and non-payers of the voting poll tax in those states that used the poll tax as a prerequisite for voting. In the United States the suffrage issue was also complicated by the fact that the Founding Fathers, perhaps unwisely, chose in 1787 to leave suffrage requirements to the states. The result of that decision was, of course, to let stand all the various statutory limitations on the right to vote then existing in the states.

Political equality, it must be noted, entails far more than the legal right to vote in free elections. It also involves the right to campaign for public office, the right to hold office if elected, the right to participate freely in political parties and pressure groups, the right to be active in every aspect of the candidate-nomination process, the right to freedom of speech and association throughout the political system, and the right to be free from such legislative attacks on equality as malapportionment and gerrymandering.[16] Though it is not always realized, these egalitarian aspects of political democracy are by no means as universal as the right to vote, and in some places the battle over them is having to be constantly refought. Until the battle for truly equal citizen's participation in the political process is everywhere won, the democratic concept of popular sovereignty will be something less than a perfect bulwark of freedom and equality. For expanded popular participation, on a basis of equality for all citizens, is a vital check on government power and the authoritarianism of ruling elites. Popular sovereignty and its concomitant of universal suffrage may not be the panacea or sure road to justice that the eighteenth-century radicals viewed it as being. But it is at least a *sine qua non* of any liberal and viable democratic tradition.

Following the Civil War, which brought about the emancipation of some four million slaves and the enfranchisement of black males, there seems to have emerged a general consensus in the United States that at long last the nation had maximized both freedom and political equality and in the process had learned how to keep those two ideals in a state of healthy equilibrium. As part of that consensus there was also a widespread belief that the nation had become a truly just pluralistic society, in which governmental authority rested upon the similarities rather than the differences among people, and in which any poor boy with spunk and tenacity could easily rise from rags to riches. This extraordinary, somewhat naive belief that the United States was, indeed, a wide-open, free, egalitarian society where opportunity was unlimited was perfectly encapsulated in the popular novels of Horatio Alger, the stereotyped heroes of which always had their just reward in the end as a result of a combination of virtue, cheerful perseverance, hard work, and a little bit of luck. It is doubtful if any other myth save that of the western frontiersman had so powerful an influence on nineteenth-century U.S. culture as did the myth of the Alger hero.

What are we to make of this cockeyed optimism, so radically different from the gloomy *Zeitgeist* of the present day? Had the advent of political democracy, popular sovereignty, and near-universal adult male suffrage really brought about a condition of unequalled freedom and equality, or was the consensus on that point merely an illusion fostered by the ruling elites to rationalize and perpetuate their vested interests? Certainly the majority of U.S. citizens must have embracd the consensus, or it would not have been possible for a mediocre writer like Horatio Alger to sell tens of thousands of his novels to the nation's reading public.

But there were, of course, dissenters from the consensus, as there always must be. They included, among others, disillusioned small farmers of the South and Midwest, racial and ethnic minorities, some embittered Catholics in New England, militant women, and political radicals such as socialists and Marxists. Though they never quite stated it in so many words, these groups, by their dissent and alienation, seemed to be saying that the adoption of near-universal adult male suffrage no more made all citizens equal than did the invention of the Colt .45. While conceding that political democracy, however imperfect, was a giant step forward in the right direction, spokesmen for the disadvantaged minorities gradually began to evolve something approaching a seamless web theory of equality, according to which genuine social democracy and justice require not only universal suffrage and popular sovereignty but also the removal of gross inequalities from every aspect of public and private life.

The critics were saying, in other words, that only the first steps had been taken toward true equality for all in a context of real freedom, and that far more would have to be done — and quickly — if dreams were to become realities. As Horatio Alger was the quintessential apologist for the U.S. establishment in the late nineteenth century, Edward Bellamy was perhaps the leading dissenter from the Gilded Age view that made a gospel of wealth and portrayed the United States as a near-perfect political democracy. Using the utopian novel as the vehicle of his dissent, Bellamy condemned his fellow countrymen both for their smugness and their crass materialism, saying that "selfishness was their only science." He also argued that their much vaunted "competition . . . is the instinct of selfishness," and should be replaced by brotherhood through equality in cooperative association.[17] Other well known dissenters who agreed with Bellamy that popular sovereignty alone was not enough to establish social justice and human dignity were Henry George, Brooks Adams, Laurence Gronlund, Lester Ward, and Thorstein Veblen.[18] They all agreed on the need for constitutional democracy and the positive, reform state, but they disagreed about the question of power. Some had a strong anti-institutional bias, while others exalted the technical scientific or administrative expert. In any event, they were all utopians of a sort, who anticipated the Kingdom of God on earth and who, like eighteenth-century radicals, looked forward to continuous, universal progress.

The dissenters likewise raised, directly or indirectly, a number of vital questions that would plague the nation for years to come. How, for example, would the courts and the executive branch implement the Reconstruction Amendments to the Federal Constitution? What, if anything, would be done about franchise restrictions and other kinds of inequality that were *de facto* rather than *de jure*? More particularly, would blacks *really* be allowed to vote and run for office in the South? Who in the future would determine the fundamental problem of social allocation? What principles would henceforth determine the reallocation of scarce resources? And, most important of all, how could full equality for disadvantaged groups be achieved without at the same time infringing the liberty and privileged perquisites of the dominant white middle-class males? Merely to list these questions is to suggest the scope and nature of the tasks that confronted the political democracy of the United States as the nation entered its second century of existence as a free republic.

However much radicals and utopians might protest, the issues implied in the above questions would have to be resolved — if they were to be resolved at all — within the framework of the traditional U.S. constitutional system. And here it is important to point out that the United States differs from most other democratic polities in two key ways: it is federal rather than unitary, and it is characterized by the tripartite separation rather than fusion of basic governmental functions. Because of these structural differences, the problem of maximizing freedom and equality in the United States has almost always involved nasty jurisdictional conflicts that pit the states against Washington and each branch of the federal establishment against every other branch. Out of this ongoing, almost dialectical conflict, the federal judiciary, at least until recently, seemed to be the principal ally of egalitarians as the activist judges stepped into a vacuum left by the political branches to become the spearhead of social change.[19] This development, generally applauded by egalitarians, obviously would have been quite impossible except for the radical diffusion of power in the U.S. government and the frequent periods of near-paralysis in the political process.

Whether a polity is federal or unitary, it is generally preferable in a democracy for elected legislative and executive officials to initiate social, economic, and political change rather than non-elected judges, a point often stressed by the late Justice Frankfurter. There are many reasons why this is so, not the least of which is the fact that the courts cannot even consider an instance of inequality wherever found unless somebody brings a "case" or "controversy" before the judges with full standing to sue.[20] Furthermore, contrary to what radical reformers often think, it is quite difficult for isolated judges to fashion effective remedies for inequalities that go deep into the roots of a culture and society. This, of course, is not to say that the courts should never act to correct blatant inequality: only that they should act cautiously, with a sense of their own vulnerability, and with a recognition that not all inequality problems are susceptible of judicial solution. Perhaps in an ultimate sense it matters little whether freedom and equality are advanced by executive, legislative, or judical action, since the victories of these ideals are generally cumulative and all but impossible to reverse.

As this chapter has sought to show, there has been a fairly steady progress toward political democracy in the Western world since the late eighteenth century, accompanied by the emergence of three models of constitutionalism: the liberal contractarian model, the radical revolutionary model, and the conservative Whig model.

The liberal contractarians, since the days of Locke and the U.S. Founding Fathers, have sought to put an equal emphasis on individual liberty and political-legal equality, both of which they derive from the mythical social contract and a secularized, individualized view of natural law. They accept the legitimacy and benevolence of private property so long as it is regulated in the public interest, and they rate politics and economics about equally high. In recent times they appear to have become somewhat more utilitarian than contractarian, and in a broad sense they are all practitioners of political economy.

The radical revolutionaries, taking their cue from theorists like Mably and Morelly, unequivocally place equality above freedom and do so on the basis of some such absolutist ideology as socialism or Marxism. As for private property, they would abolish all or most of it; and like the Maoists today, they assert, at least implicitly, the primacy of revolutionary politics over economics. This means that they often, unwittingly, turn Marx on his head.

Whiggish conservatives, while calling themselves nominal democrats, give a clear preference to freedom over equality because, in their view, the former is prescribed by nature and tradition and the latter is not — except to a modest degree. They perceive private property not as the root of all evil but as one of the greatest of all positive goods, and one that should be only minimally regulated. Unlike the radicals, they prefer the "laws" of free market economics to the murky waters of democratic politics.

These models, which are models of equality, justice, and democracy as well as of the constitutional system, are all replete with logical, philosophical, and empirical complexities. Moreover, none is as yet supported by anything like a universal consensus, and none has satisfactorily shown how the practical and conceptual dilemma posed by the simultaneous pursuit of freedom and equality can be resolved through the democratic process. One thing, however, does not admit of dispute: the dominant political aspiration of the post-Enlightenment era is clearly equality, and statesmen who ignore the fact do so at their peril. Finally, whichever model one embraces, it should be kept in mind that all of them are, in a sense, theories of moral obligation and forms of moral intuition. They are, therefore, justified by their proponents both on the grounds of ethical absolutism and of pragmatic efficiency. All of which makes them doubly difficult to attack.

In terms of political practice, each of these models legitimates constitutional democracy and rejects any form of authoritarianism. Each of them also supports, at least implicitly, the strengthening of formal institutions of government and heightened popular participation therein. Both of these things are clearly basic to democratic modernization, yet to a certain extent they stand in contradiction to each other. Thus, greater equality in political participation invariably means greater pressure on public institutions to do their job more equitably, whether by guaranteeing economic well-being to all or providing essential social services. This is but another way of saying that while heightened popular participation increases the legitimacy of constitutional authority and widens political democracy, it at the same time puts additional serious strains on all public institutions. The greatest danger in this regard comes, of course, when mass participation in politics and government is extended by a single explosive moment, as after a revolution. The problem here, as in other areas of democratic policymaking, is a balancing one: how to strengthen democratic institutions without doing so at the expense of popular participation or official accountability.

From the perspective of history, we can see today that the post-Enlightenment development of constitutional democracy has gone through three stages, which, though they overlapped to a degree, can be analytically distinguished. The first of these was the legal-political stage, in which the emphasis was on basic political and legal liberties for all citizens. That has been the focus of this chapter and will be continued in the next. The second was the economic stage, in which efforts were made by egalitarians to expand political democracy into the economic sector. Chapter 5 deals with that development. The third stage is that of sociocultural democracy, in which the thrust of egalitarian reform is in such diverse areas as race relations, feminism, education, and housing. Chapters 6 through 8 will concentrate on those explosive issues.

It does not seem an exaggeration to state that the first stage of democracy was consummated when universal suffrage became a reality. And though it has been the fate of egalitarian movements for reform, both here and abroad, to be oversold, it would be hard to rebut the view that the culmination of the suffrage crusade in the one man, one vote concept and the elimination of fetid, rotten boroughs through legislative reapportionment were monumental landmarks in the continuing definition of the constitutional right of equality in freedom. As could have been predicted, these events — decisive though they were — merely whetted the appetites of aspiring egalitarians, with the result that the apocalyptic undercurrent that ran through primitive democracy in the eighteenth century became, over the next two hundred years, increasingly harsh, strident, and overpowering — sometimes to the detriment of freedom. But that, it would seem, is the price society must pay to purge itself of ancient injustices. Reformers insist the price is not exorbitant. Conservatives, on the other hand, argue that the price is indeed exorbitant, and that the decline of true liberal democracy can be correlated with the steady advance of the militant, leveling equality movement.

Be that as it may, the remaining chapters of this book will deal with the public docket of contemporary democracy or what might be called the dynamics of democratic agenda-building. More specifically they will deal with the way that the freedom-equality paradox has been politicized into a series of public policy issues by means of a cluster of systemic and institutional factors. The entire discussion that follows is premised on the assumption that freedom and equality have become increasingly competitive, and that out of their ongoing competition will arise a growing stream of procedural and substantive conflicts, pitting individuals and groups against one another as they scramble for scarce resources or scarce positions.[21]

So, in the final analysis, all of the problems analyzed in this book are systemic issues, which, by any definition, lie at the very heart of constitutional democracy as it has evolved since the American and French Revolutions.[22] They are all the more compelling in this age of mass communications, because television has transformed the living room into a public arena and thereby acquainted the most ordinary citizen with problems and issues he would otherwise have known or cared little about. Of course, to view the freedom-equality dilemma surrounding these issues as an either-or matter in all circumstances would be to display a weakness for melodrama. But the dilemma has undeniably bred a host of conflicts, daily exacerbated by the media, and never again will the people of the West be able to view the compatibility of freedom and equality as a self-evident truth. For that myth, like so many others relating to democracy, has given way to a heightened sense of the incredible complexity of the democratic way of life. The loss of innocence is all to the good.

NOTES

1. See M. Rejai, *Democracy, The Contemporary Theories* (New York: Atherton Press, 1967), p. 2.

2. Quoted in Otto Butz, *Of Man and Politics, An Introduction to Political Science* (New York: Holt, Rinehart and Winston, 1963), p. 24. The original source of the Funeral Oration is Thucydides, *History of the Peloponnesian War* (Chicago: Great Books Foundation, n.d.), pp. 100-08. At the peak of his power, Pericles' authority was roughly comparable to that of the U.S. President, Secretary of State, and Chief of Staff combined. His most important elective office was that of *strategos,* a key position that combined executive and military responsibilities.

3. Plato belonged to a distinguished Athenian family, and it is quite likely that he inherited from them a bias against Athenian democracy. In recent years, political scientists have spent an inordinate amount of time and energy debating whether Plato was a "democrat" or a "totalitarian." For a summary of selected essays relating to this controversy, see Thomas Landon Thorson, ed., *Plato: Totalitarian or Democrat?* (Englewood Cliffs, N.J.: Prentice-Hall, 1963).

4. Aristotle, *The Politics,* pp. 162-65.

5. Quoted in McDonald, p. 85. Cicero got many of his ideas about popular government from the Greco-Roman historian Polybius, who favored such things as mixed government, separation of powers, and strict integrity in public affairs.

6. See Dino Bigongiari, ed., *The Political Ideas of St. Thomas Aquinas: Representative Selections* (New York: The Hafner Library of Classics, 1963), pp. 127-58.

7. Cusa's greatest theoretical work was *De Concordantia Catholica.* For a superb appraisal of Cusa's life and writings, see Paul E. Sigmund, *Nicholas of Cusa and Medieval Political Thought* (Cambridge, Mass.: Harvard University Press, 1963). A useful general survey of the ideals of the conciliarists is Brian Tierney, *Foundations of the Conciliar Theory* (New York: Cambridge University Press, 1955).

8. On this subject, see Max Weber, *Protestant Ethic and the Spirit of Capitalism,* tr. Talcott Parsons (London: Allen & Unwin, 1930). In this famous work Weber sought to show how the Calvinists' absorption in otherwordly concerns and their strict discipline facilitated capitalist accumulation and a high degree of materialistic success in this world.

9. John H. Schaar, "Some Ways of Thinking About Equality," *The Journal of Politics* 26 (1964) : 878 (footnote). This is an unusually insightful essay about some of the difficult philosophical and practical problems involved in the equality issue.

10. Ibid., p. 895. Two additional essays are also valuable for their insights: George H. Sabine, "The Two Democratic Traditions," *The Philosophical Review* 61 (1952) : 451-74; and Bernard Williams, "The Idea of Equality," in Peter Laslett and W.G. Runciman, eds., *Philosophy, Politics and Society,* Second Series (Oxford: Blackwell, 1962), pp. 110-32.

11. Schaar, p. 886.

12. On this general subject, see Wilson Carey McWilliams, *The Idea of Fraternity in America* (Berkeley: University of California Press, 1973). In this fascinating book Professor McWilliams, in effect, revives a key argument made by Rousseau: that the highest virtue of a polity is fraternity among its citizens pursuing a common ideal of justice.

13. Mussolini, "The Doctrine of Fascism," in William Ebenstein, ed., *Great Political Thinkers: Plato to the Present,* 4th ed. (New York: Holt, Rinehart and Winston, 1969), p. 627.

14. There are several fine works dealing with the right to vote in the United States. Among the best are Harold F. Gosnell, *Democracy: The Threshold of Freedom* (New York: Ronald Press, 1948); Dudley O. McGovney, *The American Suffrage Medley: The Need for a National Uniform Suffrage* (Chicago: University of Chicago Press, 1949); Kirk H. Porter, *A History of Suffrage in the United States* (Chicago: University of Chicago Press, 1918); and Chilton Williamson, *American Suffrage from Property to Democracy, 1760-1860* (Princeton: Princeton University Press, 1960).

15. On the subject of popular sovereignty, see Robert A. Dahl, *A Preface to Democratic Theory* (Chicago: University of Chicago Press, 1956), pp. 34-62.

16. See Sidney Verba and Norman H. Nie, *Participation in America: Political Democracy and Social Equality* (New York: Harper & Row, 1972).

17. Edward Bellamy, *Looking Backward* (Boston: Houghton Mifflin, 1888), pp. 201, 244.

18. George's panacea for the problems of inequality was a single-tax on the unearned increment of land. Adams proposed replacing laissez-faire capitalism with a centralized planning state. Gronlund proposed a transition from capitalism to Marxian socialism, but he preferred to see the transition occur not through revolution but by evolution. Ward espoused a post-democratic "Sociocracy," in which science would replace politics and in which social scientists would be the drafters of solutions to public problems. Veblen, who joined satire to his scholarship, advocated the development of democratic commonwealths which, if properly constructed, would downplay pecuniary motives and turn power over to engineers and technicians. A brilliant summary of the views of these dissenters is contained in A.J. Beitzinger, *A History of American Political Thought* (New York: Dodd, Mead, 1972), pp. 426-47.

19. The best single example of this judical activism is the U.S. Supreme Court's decision in *Baker* v. *Carr,* 369 U.S. 186 (1962). In that judicial landmark the Warren Court held that federal courts have jurisdiction over apportionment controversies, that the issue is definitely justiciable, and that voters have standing to challenge state apportionments. Then, two years later, urban egalitarians were particularly delighted when the Court held, 6-3, that as far as possible *congressional* districts must contain an equal number of people. This was the genesis of the one man, one vote concept that carried the doctrine of political equality to its logical conclusion. The case was *Wesberry* v. *Sanders,* 376 U.S. 1 (1964). For a good analysis of this addition to the equality gospel, see Calvin B.T. Lee, *One Man, One Vote: WMCA and the Struggle for Equal Representation* (New York: Charles Scribner's Sons, 1967). Also useful is Richard C. Cortner, *The Apportionment Cases* (Knoxville: University of Tennessee Press, 1970).

20. *U.S. Constitution,* Article III, Section 2.

21. On this general subject, see Roger Cobb and Charles Elder, *Participation in American Politics: The Dynamics of Agenda-Building* (Boston: Allyn and Bacon, 1972).

22. The following are among the best general studies of democracy: Robert A. Dahl, *A Preface to Democratic Theory* (Chicago: University of Chicago Press, 1956); Charles Frankel, *The Democratic Prospect* (New York: Harper, 1962); Hans Kelsen, *Vom Wesen und Wert der Demokratie* (Tuebingen: Mohr, 1929); William Kornhauser, *The Politics of Mass*

Society (Glencoe, Ill.: Free Press, 1959); A.D. Lindsay, *The Modern Democratic State* (New York: Oxford University Press, 1943); and Henry B. Mayo, *An Introduction to Democratic Theory* (New York: Oxford University Press, 1960).

4

EQUALITY AND CRIMINAL
JUSTICE

If after the U.S. Civil War the achievement of universal adult suffrage was only a moderate political problem save in the case of women and blacks, the realization of full equality before the criminal and civil law, another of the basic imperatives of political democracy, became an extremely controversial issue both in the United States and abroad. Indeed, it was (and is) so controversial that it remains, to a dismaying degree, part of the unfinished business on democracy's agenda.

Equality before the law especially means equality before the criminal law, the purposes of which are the protection of lives and property, the preservation of community peace, and the prevention of crime. The actual implementation of this ideal takes place in what is now called the criminal justice system, a catch-all term embracing law enforcement agencies, judicial bodies, prosecutorial staffs, prisons and jails, as well as legal, constitutional, and other institutional protections for the accused. As has previously been indicated, a number of our ideas about equality and law came from the ancient Greeks. Thus, as the Greek word *isos,* often used by Aristotle, means both "equal" and "fair," the concept of equality before the law, at least in democracies, has become identified with fairness and equal treatment for all in the entire legal process.

To define equality before the law is simply a matter of stipulation; to implement it effectively in a society less than perfectly egalitarian is vastly more difficult. This is true because implementation involves the cooperation of numerous executive, administrative, legislative, and judicial agencies, all of which have their own bureaucratic values, along with differing conceptions about how constitutional and legal mandates should be executed in a given case. If, as often happens in the best of countries, a particular criminal justice system produces inequality instead of equality, that will almost always be the result of one of three things: blatant prejudice against certain groups, bureaucratic inefficiency, or a general cultural indifference to minority problems. Each of these factors is itself caused by a host of big and little things; and of the three, the first may well be the easiest to remedy.

When one surveys the history of criminal justice, one quickly discovers that, in practice, the concept of legal equality has generally not precluded a judicial process that advances one interest against another, nor has it prevented a particular group of interested specialists from effectively controlling a given legal system. Indeed, until well into the present century, the concept meant only that equality must be equal for equals, to use a phrase popularized by Aristotle. To be sure, middle-class white males have usually got their due in the United States and other countries with similar legal systems, but the same can scarcely be said for women, blacks, Indians, Chicanos, political non-conformists, sex "deviates," young people, or the poor. As noted above, there are several reasons why this has been so, but certainly a major one is the fact that most of these groups did not receive political equality, as symbolized by the franchise, until the twentieth century. That is a crucial datum, for history has shown that when people do not enjoy political equality with their neighbors, they are not likely to have legal equality either.

The pre-twentieth century conception of legal equality unequivocally justified the division of society into first- and second-class citizens. The former, of course, wrote the laws, and their position toward the latter was assumed to be that of *in loco parentis*. This quaint (to our minds) view of equality persisted well into the present century; and though it denied the masses genuine legal or political equality with the upper classes, it did include the ideal of *noblesse oblige*. The masses, in short, were not to be treated under the law as fully responsible adults, but were rather to be dealt with paternalistically, as parents deal with children. The conception of citizenship implied in this attitude is obviously unacceptable to most people in our egalitarian age, even though its paternalism was not entirely devoid of compassion or humane treatment. Perhaps its most lasting harm to the lower classes and minorities was not physical but psychological, particularly its insidious inculcation of feelings of inferiority and unworthiness among the disadvantaged. Some of the indoctrination is still felt.

With the maturing of egalitarian democracy in the present century, equality before the law has come to mean far more than a mere paternalistic concern for the subsistence welfare of "lesser breeds." Concretely, it has come to mean equal status before both the criminal and civil law of all citizens, whatever their race, creed, color, sex, or politics. Indeed, equality before the law in this inclusive sense has come to be viewed as the quintessence of democracy's definition of citizens' rights.

Today, the democratic view of this lofty ideal is best encapsulated in two simple phrases in the U.S. Constitution: "due process" and "equal protection of the laws." Both phrases have had a long history in Anglo-American jurisprudence, and both denote substantive as well as procedural equality. These imperatives and the other postulates of democratic justice to be examined in this chapter are derived from seven principal sources: constitutional provisions, statutory enactments, common law, judicial case law, tradition, utility, and the so-called "higher law." Legal equality in the democratic sense is not an absolutely rigid transcendent principle, nor is it a legal moralism that wholly rejects pragmatic compromise. It is, nevertheless, a fundamental commitment of democratic societies and carries with it the corollary assumption that people have no real freedom in the criminal justice system unless they have equal status before every law and law enforcement agency.

If legal equality, like political equality, is a necessary though not sufficient condition for democracy, due process is an absolute *sine qua non* for the realization of equal justice under law. This follows from the fact that due process establishes the democratic principle of limited government and, if properly implemented in the courts of the land, protects the lowliest citizen from governmental discrimination at all levels. When you have due process in all its manifestations, you have justice. When you do not have it, you have tyranny. It is as simple as that.

Historically, the Anglo-American concept of due process was derived from the "law of the land" doctrine in Chapter 39 of Magna Carta. It was inserted into the Fifth Amendment of the Bill of Rights by the first U.S. Federal Congress as a guarantee of equal treatment under national law. Then, after the Civil War, it was made binding on state and local governmental agencies by being incorporated into the Fourteenth Amendment. Madison did most of the drafting of the Bill of Rights, and was also responsible for substituting an imperative "shall" for the weaker "ought" and "ought not" in those sections spelling out individual rights. The due process clause provides that "No person shall be . . . deprived of life, liberty, or property, without due process of law . . . ." The corollary of this is that any citizen *may* be sent off to die in wartime, *may* be incarcerated for criminality, or *may* have his property taken by taxation or eminent domain proceedings, *provided* he gets the same due process accorded every other citizen when dealing with state authorities. The courts will decide, when asked, whether a given person did indeed get due process.

As the pursuit of equality in freedom gradually culminated in the modern democratic state, the concept of due process was undergoing an enormous transformation. Today, as any student of government knows, the due process clause of the U.S. Constitution imposes extremely strict substantive limitations upon governmental power. Yet, in the pre-Civil War period, and more especially in the eighteenth century, the concept meant little more than a guarantee that white adult male citizens would be processed in the criminal justice system with fair, standardized, and known procedures. Originally, in other words, it was neither egalitarian nor very libertarian. Hamilton once described this limited original conception of due proecess in this way:

> The words "due process" have a precise technical import, and are only applicable to the process and proceedings of the courts of justice; they can never be referred to an act of the legislature.[1]

With the continued intermingling of freedom, equality, and social justice in nineteenth-century thought, and the concomitant decline of natural law as the chief bulwark of human rights, the U.S. courts began gradually but firmly expanding the scope of the due process concept. The first landmark decision in this expansion process was handed down in 1856 in a court in New York, a state that has often pioneered libertarian as well as egalitarian reform. The decision was announced in the case of *Wynehamer* v. *People,* and it may well have been the first instance in which a U.S. court unequivocally supported the notion that individual rights are protected by due process from a substantive as well as procedural point of view. The case itself grew out of a New York prohibition statute. The court, in its widely hailed decision, held that the statute at issue, while containing no procedural defects, fell "certainly within the spirit of a constitutional provision [due process] intended expressly to shield private rights from the exercise of arbitrary power." It is also important to note that the *Wynehamer* court's rationale, "particularly its substitution of substantive due process as a check upon arbitrary governmental power for the prior natural law approach, was to be that ultimately adopted by American courts, including the highest bench in the land after ratification of the Fourteenth Amendment."[2]

Ironically, the immediate results of *Wynehamer* were to strengthen slavery rather than freedom or equality. This was shown by the fact that in the very next year the U.S. Supreme Court invalidated that part of the

Missouri Compromise Act of 1820 which forbade slavery in the northern part of the Louisiana Purchase by holding that "the act of Congress which prohibited a citizen from holding and owning property of this kind [slaves] in the territory of the United States north of the line therein mentioned, is not warranted by the Constitution, and is therefore void."[3] According to Chief Justice Taney, Congress' power to regulate the territories was restricted by the *substantive* protection given property rights through the due process clause of the Fifth Amendment, and rights of property are definitely identified with the rights of a person. In the face of such reasoning as this, it is not improper to state that the Taney Court in this instance maximized the property rights of the southern slaveocracy while concomitantly minimizing the freedom and equality claims of black people. Even more important, the decision helped to bring on the holocaust of the Civil War, which, though ultimately a democratic blessing in disguise, came periously close to destroying the nation, along with its libertarian and egalitarian ideals.

The "perversion" of substantive due process into an inegalitarian instrument for shoring up corporate vested interests continued after the Civil War and reached its apogee in the Age of the Robber Barons. Strongly influenced by conservative Justice Stephen J. Field, the post-bellum Supreme Court handed down a number of critical decisions which, by construing the due process clauses of the Fifth and Fourteenth Amendments to be primarily bulwarks of property rights, effectively insulated big corporate business from governmental interference. That was the period, of course, of galloping capitalism, when the democratic revolution appeared to have been shunted aside by the all-consuming crusade to dominate nature and conquer the continent under the rugged banner of Social Darwinism. It is highly probable that the majority of U.S. citizens approved their judiciary's enshrinement of substantive due process as a crutch for business, unaware as most of them were of the damage being done to the common man's liberties and equality hopes. Even had they known, many might not have disapproved.

The nation has still not fully grasped the extraordinary irony that lies at the heart of the checkered history of due process, especially Fourteenth-Amendment due process. That Amendment was added to the Federal Constitution by the Radical Republicans who controlled congress during Reconstruction primarily to nationalize most, if not quite all, of the civil liberties included in the Bill of Rights. Those liberties, at that time, were considered by the courts to be applicable solely to federal agencies. What followed, however, was one more example of how laws and constitutional enactments in democracies often have consequences that are quite different from those originally intended.

Thus, the Fourteenth Amendment, intended by the Reconstruction Radicals to be a Great Charter of personal rights, was converted almost overnight into a virtual Magna Carta for corporate business — all by a strained process of judicial construction. Indeed, one may say that the post-Civil War Supreme Court in effect read laissez-faire into the Fourteenth Amendment and thereby gutted what had been designed to be the heart of the congressional Reconstruction program. The gutting was accomplished through a series of "judicial review" opinions that all but ignored the intent of the Amendment's framers to elevate the concept of equality to the constitutional plane via the due process and equal protection clauses and in so doing advance the rights of the black minority. Rarely in legal history have intentions and consequences been so far apart, and not until the 1890s would the drive for equality suffer comparable setbacks at the hands of the judiciary.

Obviously equal status before the law for black people was quite impossible so long as the Constitution and congress tolerated and legitimated slavery; hence Lincoln was right to insist, as he often did, that "all men are created equal, except Negroes."[4] After the death of Lincoln, the Reconstruction congresses made a massive effort — critics said too massive — to provide real legal and political equality for almost all the nation's inhabitants. In making this effort they were reflecting the views of egalitarians like Senator Charles Sumner of Massachusetts who asked in 1866, "What is Liberty without Equality? One is the complement of the other . . . . They are the two vital principles of republican government."[5] While not all democrats today see liberty and equality as harmoniously linked as Sumner did, there can be no denying that the history of the modern drive for legal equality in the United States really began with the Reconstruction Amendments he so zealously supported.

Notwithstanding the clear intentions of Sumner and his radical colleagues, the U.S. Supreme Court continued for almost three-quarters of a century to interpret due process as a substantive protection for corporations against government regulation. As though that were not bad enough, the Court also began paying less and less attention to the original meaning of due process, which was guaranteeing fair procedures to all defendants in the criminal justice system. And since the majority of defendants were poor people and racial or ethnic minorities, the judiciary's eccentric construction of due process resulted in a significant retardation of progress toward full legal equality for the disadvantaged. In fact, it was not until after the Court Revolution of 1937 that the quest for legal equality resumed its forward march, as the Roosevelt Court threw out economic substantive due process and again showed a solicitude for the procedural rights of poor defendants at every stage of the legal process.

Throughout much of the nineteenth century, and especially in the immediate post-bellum period, the judiciary was not in the forefront of the flight for legal or any other kind of equality, and, indeed, it was often a substantial obstacle to that fight. The reverse has been true, of course, for much of the present century, which is to say that the federal judiciary has usually been ahead of congress and the executive branch as well as the people in giving flesh-and-blood meaning to the egalitarian ideals of the U.S. legal system. As noted earlier, this situation poses a number of philosophical and practical problems for U.S. democracy, but it perhaps became inevitable when the other branches of the federal government could not or would not take remedial action in the criminal justice and other fields.

All of the initiatives taken by the judiciary in this century to advance the legal rights of minorities have been highly controversial. Besides the rejection of economic substantive due process, they have included the following: excision of laissez-faire from the Constitution; rehabilitation of procedural due process; a stricter, more pro-individual reading of the Bill of Rights; judicial "activism" when basic civil liberties are alleged to have been abridged by some agency of government; a particularly tight construction of that part of the Bill of Rights known as defendants' rights Amendments (Four through Eight); near-total nationalization of the Bill of Rights through a new interpretation of the Fourteenth Amendment; and a general shift of emphasis in court decisions from property concerns to personal rights. As a result of these and other judicial initiatives, almost all forms of equality have been pushed forward in the United States, but that has been particularly true in the case of legal equality for minority defendants.

Because of the near-nationalization of the Bill of Rights via the Fourteenth Amendment, the U.S. Supreme Court today exercises an extraordinarily close supervision of state and local criminal justice systems, as well as of state civil and administrative proceedings. A corollary of this is that neither state nor federal economic legislation is scrutinized as closely now as it was during the heyday of substantive due process, all of which has meant a reduction of the freedom of corporations to do as they wish without regard for the rights of workers or consumers. Though corporations deeply resent this seeming derogation of property rights, the Supreme Court remains firm in its insistence that the due process clause of the Fourteenth Amendment applies to the states only those provisions of the Bill of Rights that are "so rooted in the traditions and conscience of our people as to be ranked as fundamental."[6] Laissez-faire is not among these, though most of the freedom guarantees in Amendments One to Eight definitely are. And when state or local acts on their face seem to regulate any of these constitutionally-guaranteed rights, the Supreme Court will employ the strict "compelling interest test" in its scrutiny of them. Simply put, this means that unless a compelling reason can be shown for the state law or regulation depriving somebody of a certain liberty, it will be invalidated as violative of the due process clause of the Fourteenth Amendment.

Certainly the most striking innovation of the Warren Court in the field of criminal justice was its resolve, confirmed by a long string of criminal law decisions favoring defendants, to make Fourteenth-Amendment due process ever more inclusive. Naturally this development was greeted by civil libertarians and minorities as a resounding victory for both liberty and equality, and criticized by conservatives as being subversive of true liberty and orderly justice. But even more important than the Court's inclusive reading of due process was its expansion of the substantive content of the entire Bill of Rights by giving the guarantees embedded therein a far broader meaning than they had hiterto had in U.S. law and jurisprudence. This was most notably true in the case of the First Amendment and the defendants' rights Amendments. The key decisions involving the latter were *Mapp* v. *Ohio,* 367 U.S. 643 (1961); *Gideon* v. *Wainwright,* 372 U.S. 335 (1963); *Escobedo* v. *Illinois,* 378 U.S. 478 (1964); *Miranda* v. *Arizona,* 384 U.S. 437 (1966); *Katz* v. *United States,* 389 U.S. 347 (1967). The holdings in all these historic cases advanced the equality of every defendant involved in a criminal proceeding, but they were particularly beneficial to poor and minority defendants who earlier had received something less than equal treatment before the law.

A brief summary of the holdings in these cases will suggest the scope of their importance. *Mapp* held that evidence obtained in violation of the search and seizure provisions of the Fourth Amendment is not admissible in any state court, and thereby overruled *Wolf* v. *Colorado,* 398 U.S. 25 (1949).[7] *Gideon* held that an indigent defendant must be provided counsel even in a noncapital case, for "reason and reflection require us to recognize that in our adversary system of criminal justice, any person haled into court, who is too poor to hire a lawyer, cannot be assured a fair trial unless counsel is provided for him. This seems to be an obvious truth."[8] *Escobedo* held that when the investigatory process becomes accusatory then our adversary system begins to operate and the accused must be permitted to consult at once with counsel. *Miranda,* the most controversial of all the Warren Court criminal law decisions, held that an individual undergoing interrogation must be clearly informed that he has a right to consult counsel and to have his lawyer present during questioning. The prosecution, furthermore, "may not use statements, whether exculpatory or inculpatory, stemming from custodial interrogation of the defendant unless it demonstrates the use of procedural safeguards effective to secure the privilege against self-incrimination." Finally, *Katz* held that the seizure of evidence obtained by a warrentless wiretap is a violation of the Fourth Amendment. This decision overruled *Olmstead* v. *United States,* 277 U.S. 438 (1928) and *Goldman* v. *United States,* 316 U.S. 129 (1942).[9] There were other decisions during the Warren era that pushed forward the equality required by Fourteenth-Amendment due process, but none had a greater or more lasting impact on the criminal justice system than did these.[10]

The other part of the Fourteenth Amendment that has had an impact on the drive for legal equality is the equal protection clause. This clause, which directly follows the due process clause in section 1 of the Amendment, does not forbid the legislative classification of persons nor does it require identical treatment of all citizens. Moreover, it does not prevent strictly private organizations, unsupported by public funds, from treating different groups of people unequally. According to the U.S. Supreme Court, the equal protection clause requires four things: that state-local laws not arbitrarily discriminate against persons; that legal classifications be reasonable and related directly to the end sought; that all persons falling within a given classification be treated in roughly the same way; and that classifications not be normally established on the basis of color, religion, ethnicity, or social class.

Equal protection, like due process, derives from the democratic doctrine that all persons ought to enjoy equal status under the law as well as share the right to equality of opportunity. For a long time it was somewhat neglected by the courts, but in recent years it has been particularly useful to egalitarians in such fields as housing, public eduction, racial and sexual liberation, voting, and legislative apportionment. Due process has always been, and continues to be, of more practical benefit to poor people and minorities entrapped as defendants in the criminal justice system.

Still, in at least two famous criminal cases, equal protection proved to be a strong bulwark for minority defendants. In the first of these,[11] a black person by the name of Strauder was convicted of murder in a West Virginia state court which, by state law, was required to exclude all persons of his race from both grand and petit jury duty. The Supreme Court, in reviewing Strauder's conviction, held that the state's discrimination against blacks through its jury laws violated both the privileges and immunities and the equal protection clauses of the Fourteenth Amendment. Justice Strong, speaking for the Court, wrote that the laws in every state must "be the same for the black as for the white; that all persons, whether colored or white, shall stand equal before the laws of the States, and, in regard to the colored race, for whose protection the amendment was primarily designed, that no discrimination shall be made against them by law because of their color." Then, sounding like a modern egalitarian, he went on to add that

The very fact that colored people are singled out and expressly denied by a statute all right to participate in the administration of the law, as jurors, because of their color, though they are citizens, and may be in other respects fully qualified, is practically a brand upon them, affixed by the law, an assertion of their inferiority, and a stimulant to that race prejudice which is an impediment to securing to individuals of the race that equal justice which the law aims to secure to all others.[12]

Two justices dissented from the Court's decision in this case, and conservatives, ever since it was announced, have sharply criticized its logic and reasoning. They agree with the West Virginia authorities of the time in maintaining that Strauder's right to equal protection was in no way denied. And why not? For five reasons basically. One, the West Virginia jury law was no more inconsistent with the spirit of the Fourteenth Amendment than jury laws elsewhere which based jury selection on intelligence and educational qualifications. Two, West Virginia had a perfectly "rational basis" for the jury law its legislature had adopted. Three, nowhere was it demonstrated that the all-white jury failed to render Strauder an impartial verdict. Four, the logical extension of the holding in this case would be a plan for proportional racial representation for all juries. And five, whatever the merits of the Court's opinion, reversing convictions is surely not the only effective method of preserving blacks' equal protection right to jury service.[13]

As though listening to the arguments of its critics, the Supreme Court, in the very same year, held that the mere absence of blacks from a jury did not of itself mean a denial of constitutional rights.[14] To prove the latter, a litigant would have to show that blacks were deliberately and systematically excluded from all juries trying black defendants. Unfortunately for the caue of legal equality, the South paid more attention to the second of these cases, thus paving the way for the exclusion of blacks from most southern juries until quite recent times.

The other important equal protection criminal case was decided in 1948.[15] In this instance, a black man was indicted for murder by an all-white Mississippi grand jury, convicted by an all-white petit jury, and then sentenced to death in the electric chair. On appeal, the defendant introduced evidence that in 30 years no black man had served on a grand or petit jury in the county involved; hence, he argued, he had been denied equal protection in the selection of jurors. The Supreme Court unanimously agreed, holding, as in *Strauder,* that the exclusion of blacks from juries solely because of their race denies black defendants equal protection of the criminal laws as required by the Fourteenth Amendment.

Clearly, in this instance, the Court had no trouble finding that there had been a systematic, not merely accidental, exclusion of blacks from the county's juries and for the obvious purpose of perpetuating white supremacy in the state's criminal justice system. Finally, it is interesting to note that Justice Black, a native of Alabama and former member of the Ku Klux Klan, wrote the opinion in this case.

In their drive to achieve full equality before the bar of justice in all U.S. courts, twentieth-century egalitarians, encouraged by favorable rulings by the Supreme Court, have demanded several related types of legal equality: equality between rich and poor defendants, equality between popular and unpopular defendants, adversary equality between prosecution and defendant, equality between races from the start to the end of the legal process, and equality between religious and ethnic groups. This drive (really a crusade), in the words of former Supreme Court Justice Abe Fortas, is "the most profound and pervasive revolution ever achieved by substantially peaceful means."[16] That it has largely been a judicially inspired and led revolution is somewhat strange, given the judiciary's record for foot-dragging on the issue of equality during Reconstruction.

Aside from the crucial Fourteenth Amendment, the most important sections of the U.S. Constitution dealing with criminal justice are Amendments Four, Five, Six, and Eight, which, as noted earlier, are usually referred to as defendants' rights Amendments. They were put into the Bill of Rights for one simple reason: to minimize the likelihood of innocent persons being sent to prison. Moreover, since they require that strict procedures of fairness be adhered to at every stage of the criminal justice system, they are in a certain sense handcuffs on law enforcement personnel. Precisely for that reason, accused persons and egalitarians admire their provisions, while police and prosecutors generally dislike them, though without always saying so publicly. Be that as it may, these Amendments are even older than the Fourteenth, and they are what most clearly distinguish the U.S judicial process from the criminal justice systems of authoritarian and totalitarian countries. Equally important, the defendants' rights Amendments are literally steeped in the ideals of freedom and equality and the corollary ideal of distrust of big government.

The Fourth Amendment declares "The right of the people to be secure in their persons, houses, papers, and effects, against unreasonable searches and seizures, shall not be violated, and no warrant shall issue, but upon probable cause, supported by oath or affirmation, and particularly describing the place to be searched, and the persons or things to be seized." This vital guarantee, which was generally neglected until the prohibition era, protects all U.S. citizens, however unpopular, from *unreasonable* search and seizure of criminal evidence by police. But implementing it is another matter.

Justice Powell has noted that "Searches and seizures are an opaque area of the law,"[17] and he is certainly right. The equality-minded Warren Court took the view that, with a few exceptions, any search without a warrant is unreasonable.[18] But despite or because of that "hard line," the justices have recently been sharply divided on this issue, though most would no doubt insist that they use the criterion of common sense in deciding when a search is reasonable and when there is probable cause for the issuance of a search warrant. They simply disagree as to what is commonsensical.

In this regard, it must also be emphasized that the ban on unreasonable searches and seizures is interpreted in conjunction with the Fifth Amendment's prohibition against forced self-incrimination and its requirement of due process for all defendants. Practically speaking, this means that the Supreme Court, in order to enforce the provisions of the Fourth Amendment, insists on the so-called *exclusionary rule,* which was first adopted in 1914 to apply only to federal courts.[19] Later, in 1949, the Court held that the Fourth Amendment's ban on unreasonable searches and seizures applies to state and local police.[20] However, as mentioned earlier, it was not until the *Mapp* case of 1961 that the Court held that state courts must likewise exclude "tainted" evidence obtained in violation of the Fourth Amendment, a holding opposed by Chief Justice Burger.

The Fifth Amendment significantly advanced the concept of equal justice for all by guaranteeing to every defendant, as well as to citizens generally, five basic procedural rights. The first of these is the right to a grand jury screening and formal indictment before being subjected to trial in a federal criminal court. Before Watergate, the grand jury was a rather obscure element of the U.S. criminal justice system; today it is one of the most talked about and most controversial aspects of that system. If the Watergate grand jury promoted egalitarianism by bringing indictments against some of the highest officials in the land, it is also true that some grand juries, on occasion, have acted in a harassing manner and persecuted unpopular groups. Such harassment is facilitated by the secrecy and minimal restraints that surround the grand jury.

The second procedural guarantee of the Fifth is the provision that no person shall "be subject for the same offense to be twice put in jeopardy of life or limb." This means that defendants shall not be tried before a federal or state court more than once for exactly the same statutory crime, assuming there is no hung jury, no interruption in the original trial, and no appellate court's grant of a new trial at the request of a convicted defendant. In other words, if a trial is finished and ends with an acquittal, the defendant concerned is free of all charges against him, though, of course, he may still be tried in another jurisdiction under a different statute for actions realted to the original charge. This suggests, among other things, that double jeopardy is not involved when a single criminal act violates both federal and state laws and the defendant is subsequently exposed to prosecution in both federal and state courts. Furthermore, the ban on double jeopardy does not foreclose the filing of a civil suit for damages after a criminal prosecution.

The third guarantee is a person's right not to be "compelled in any criminal case to be a witness against himself." The claiming of this right is popularly known as "taking the Fifth," a pejorative epithet that apparently has diminished the Fifth Amendment's merits in the popular mind. As indicated earlier, the Supreme Court, to the dismay of conservatives, has held that the failure of the police to warn arrested persons of their right to remain silent automatically renders any statements obtained by questioning inadmissible in later criminal proceedings. True, an accused person may voluntarily waive his right of silence and thus save the police and taxpayers time, money, and trouble; but he must clearly know what he is doing and must never be forced to confess. On the other hand, the courts have held that handwriting samples, blood tests, and police lineup appearances do not violate the ban on coerced self-incrimination.

The fourth procedural guarantee is due process. As previously noted, this became particularly meaningful after the Civil War, when it was incorporated in the Fourteenth Amendment and thereby made binding on all state and local governmental agencies. Nothing further need be said about this vital guarantee except that it affords everybody — rich and poor, black and white — full protection against arbitrary and unfair procedures (as defined by the courts) in either judicial or administrative proceedings.

The last guarantee of the Fifth Amendment, which is of more concern to middle-class propertied people than to poor defendants, is the provision that no private property shall "be taken for public use, without just compensation." The egalitarian aspect of this pro-property clause is the implicit premise that the public interest takes precedence over any property-holder's individual material interests, and any private property may be "socialized" to advance the general welfare of the citizenry if basic standards of fairness are observed in the "taking" process. This, of course, is nothing more nor less than the old doctrine of *eminent domain,* which was popularized by such seventeenth-century natural-law jurists as Hugo Grotius and Samuel Pufendorf.

The Sixth Amendment guarantees every accused person seven fundamental rights: a speedy trial, a public trial, a trial by an impartial local jury, precise advance information about "the nature and cause of the accusation," confrontation with opposing witnesses in open court, compulsory process for obtaining witnesses in his favor (subpoena right), and "the assistance of counsel for his defense."

A few comments about these procedural rights are necessary to underscore their significance. Concerning the first, the Supreme Court has held that intentional or negligent delay by the prosecution that prejudices the defendant's right to defend himself is grounds for dismissal of the charges. It must, however, be stressed that a trial may be "speedy" in a legal sense and still be long-delayed, if the delays are caused by counsel for the accused with concurrence of the judge.

As for the right to a public trial, that is a guarantee belonging to defendants and not to television cameramen, photographers, or newspaper reporters — unless, of course, they themselves are the accused. Aslo, it is permissible, in rare circumstances, for the presiding judge to exclude the general public from the courtroom. But generally speaking, the courts have been bothered by too much rather than too little public involvement in trials. Well aware of this, the Supreme Court has held that "Trial courts must take strong measures to ensure that the balance is never weighed against the accused."[21]

The right to an "impartial jury" supplements the earlier jury trail guarantee contained in Article III of the U.S. Constitution. The requirements that a jury must have twelve members and must reach a unanimous verdict were derived from the common law and are not specifically mentioned in the Constitution. These requirements are absolute for federal but not for state courts, since the Supreme Court has held that state juries need not necessarily be composed of twelve members nor need jury verdicts in state courts be unanimous if state law provides for other arrangements. Of course, state variations in this area must not violate the Court's conception of due process.

Although young adults, women, and racial-ethnic minorities were often totally excluded from trial jury service in the past, that is no longer permissible. It should be noted, however, that the jury trial requirement does not apply to petty offenses, deportation or loyalty proceedings, or to cases in which the accused is subject to military jurisdiction. Finally, it is possible for a defendant, with the judge's permission, to waive his right to a jury trial. But even if he does not do that, he may petition for removal of the trial (change of venue) to a more distant area where, presumably, the required impartial jurors will be easier to find. The judge, of course, has the discretion to grant or reject such petitions. Though there is room for disagreement, most minority defendants would doubtless agree with Sir William Blackstone's statement in his famous *Commentaries* that "the trial by jury ever has been, and I trust every will be, looked upon as the glory of the English law."[22]

Of all the guarantees of the Sixth Amendment, the right to counsel is probably the most indispensable, for an accused person who goes to trial without a lawyer is patently being denied equality before the law and will most likely end up deprived of his freedom. Yet, despite the plain language of the Sixth Amendment's final clause, the U.S. Supreme Court until the early 1960s held that only in capital cases did a state have the constitutional duty to furnish counsel for indigent defendants. Since most defendants are not involved in capital cases, and since most tend to be poor, the majority of U.S. defendants before the 1960s went to trial without counsel and, not surprisingly, most were convicted and sentenced to jail or prison. Today, as the result of Supreme Court holdings, judges must appoint attorneys from the local bar to represent poor defendants shortly after their arrests, with city and county taxpayers footing the bill. In a few major cities, public defender offices have been set up and staffed by full-time attorneys, who are paid on the same basis as those employed in the offices of prosecuting attorneys. In any event, it seems safe to say that "No Sixth Amendment right has been more strengthened or expanded by recent court decisions than the right to professional legal advice."[23] The landmark cases in this area, as noted earlier, were *Gideon* v. *Wainwright, Escobedo* v. *Illinois,* and *Miranda.*

The last of the defendant's rights Amendments, the Eighth, has recently become extremely controversial, principally because of its direct relation to the issue of capital punishment. The wording of the Amendment seems simple enough: "Excessive bail shall not be required, nor excessive fines imposed, nor cruel and unusual punishments inflicted." In practice, however, these three requirements have raised a host of egalitarian and libertarian questions, while at the same time placing an enormous interpretive burden on the appellate courts.

Fines, of course, are pecuniary punishments imposed upon convicted persons, and the ban on excessive fines has caused the least problem for appellate courts. As a general rule, such courts have shown a willingness to accept almost any fine, not clearly violative of a statute, that a trial judge may assess. Moreover, it is unlikely that indigent or minority defendants have been much discriminated against in the matter of fines in comparison to the treatment accorded well-to-do persons. For it is the former who are usually imprisoned and it is the latter who are fined.

The ban on excessive bail is a far more serious matter,[24]for the simple reason that throughout U.S. history poor people have generally fared worse than rich people under the traditional bail system. Indeed, the bail system was long one of the biggest scandals in the entire criminal justice process, and in some jurisdictions it still may be. The scandalous nature of the system arises from three interrelated facts: middle class people are more often released on their own recognizance, without putting up any bail money, than poor people; when monetary bail is set, poor people are often required to pay more than upper class persons charged with comparable offenses; and even when the bail is the same for rich and poor arrestees, the financial burden on the latter proportionately is much greater. As a result of these inescapable realities, "nice" people almost never spend more than a day or two in jail before trial — if that — while poor people historically have had to resign themselves to spending the entire time between arrest and trial locked up in an overcrowed jail cell. This is so notwithstanding the nation's commitment to equality before the law and to a presumption of innocence of everybody before trial and conviction. This tradition of selective jailing also ignores the fact that a jailed person has a far more difficult time preparing an adequate defense than a defendant allowed to go free on bail. A few years ago it was probably true that more than half the people incarcerated in the U.S. criminal justice system were simply awaiting trial and had not been tried on the charges made against them, let alone convicted.

Conservatives like to point out that the Eighth Amendment does not expressly provide that citizens have a *right* to bail, and, of course, that is true. But what such a statement ignores is the fact that the institution of bail is a deeply ingrained part of the criminal justice system and has been recognized by statute in the United States since at least 1791. In 1966, egalitarians scored a ringing victory for their cause when they pressured congress into enacting a Bail Reform Act, the purpose of which is to facilitate the pretrial release of persons accused of noncapital crimes. The reform was a long time coming; but once enacted, it dramatically advanced legal equality by reducing, if not quite ending pretrial imprisonment of indigent defendants who could not afford to post moeny bail and who were, in effect, being confined because of their depressed economic status. The provisions of the law discourage the use of money bail by requiring judges to seek other means of insuring a defendant's appearance for trial.

The 1966 Bail Reform Act, of course, applies strictly to federal courts, and was, in fact, the first significant federal bail legislation since the Judiciary Act of 1789. But within a short time state and local governments began to enact similar reform statutes to remove the invidious discrimination against poor persons in their jurisdictions. State-local action in this area is even more vital than federal action, since the great bulk of criminal litigation in this country is handled not in federal but in state and local courts. In the case of capital crimes, accused persons of whatever socioeconomic class are normally denied bail in most U.S. jurisdictions. It is also true that judges, in the past, have often enforced an extra-legal form of "preventive detention" for dangerous defendants by deliberately setting an extremely high bail with no expectation of its being paid. Though intermediate appellate courts sometimes strike down high bail as excessive, the U.S. Supreme Court has rarely had occasion to do this.[25]

Four years after passage of the Bail Reform Act, Congress shocked egalitarians by passing a law that authorized judges in the District of Columbia to detain prior to trial persons accused of dangerous crimes of violence if, after a hearing, the judge concludes that release could endanger the safety of the community. Although preventive detention has rarely been used, its authorization poses serious equality questions, especially since it seems to have been aimed at the large black youth population in the nation's capital.[26] Speaking of an earlier version of the District of Columbia Crime Control Act proposed by President Nixon, Senator Sam J. Ervin of North Carolina insisted it was blatantly "unconstitutional and smacks of a police-state rather than a democracy under law."[27] Egalitarians fully concurred.

The last clause of the Eighth Amendment, forbidding "cruel and unusual punishments," has in recent years become one of the most controversial provisions of the defendants' rights Amendments. Everybody apparently agrees that such punishments as drawing-and-quartering and other forms of torture would clearly violate this clause. But what about "clean" capital punishment where the methods of execution are hanging, asphyxiation, electrocution, or shooting? Is society also to be denied these forms of punishment?

In all its history, the U.S. Supreme Court has but rarely struck down court-imposed punishments as "cruel and unusual" and thus violative of the Eighth Amendment. In 1910 the justices held invalid a law that authorized twelve years in chains at hard labor,[28] and in 1962 they overturned a California statute which made drug addition a crime.[29] Beyond these holdings, they have seldom ventured.

Then on June 29, 1972, while some 600 men and women waited in death row cells around the country, the Supreme Court held by a five-to-four vote that the death penalty, as then administered, constituted cruel and unusual punishment and was thus unconstitutional.[30] All four Nixon-appointed justices dissented. Of the majority, only Justices Brennan and Marshall declared capital punishment in all cases to be unconstitutional *per se.* According to Justice Brennan, the rejection of capital punishment "by contemporary society is virtually total, and there is no reason to believe that it serves any penal purpose more effectively than the less severe punishment of imprisonment." Justice Douglas did not go that far, but chose instead to rest his opposition to capital punishment on the fact that, as then imposed, it fell more heavily on the "poor and despised." Justices White and Stewart restricted their holding to conditions in which judges and juries have such wide discretion in imposing or not imposing the death sentence that "erratic and arbitrary" actions result. Justice Stewart added that the death penalty is "so wantonly and so freakishly imposed . . . that these death sentences are cruel and unusual in the same way that being struck by lightning is cruel and unusual."[31]

The dissenting justices, while expressing personal distaste for the death penalty, accused the majority of usurping the role of state legislatures and of ignoring almost 200 years of historical precedent. They also suggested that the principles of federalism had been overriden by the majority decision. Chief Justice Burger went further by counseling that "legislative bodies may seek to bring their laws into compliance with the Court's ruling by providing standards for juries and judges to follow in determining the sentence in capital cases or by more narrowly defining the crimes for which the penalty is to be imposed."[32]

In order to appreciate the reasoning behind the majority opinion, which was strongly supported by egalitarians, it is necessary to recall a few simple facts about capital crimes and capital punishment in the United States. Capital crimes are those offenses for which execution may be the punishment; and though they differ from state to state, the most common in recent times have been first degree murder, rape, and certain kinds of arson. As is well known, large numbers of murders and other capital crimes are never solved, which means the police make no arrests. Of those arrested in capital cases, by no means all are tried for their lives. Plea bargaining quite often results in a reduction of the charges to a noncaptial offense. Of those actually tried on capital charges, many are never convicted. Of those convicted, a certain number will be sentenced to prison instead of to death. Furthermore, of those who do get the death sentence, a significant number have in the past had their sentence commuted to life imprisonment by executive action. In other words, of the thousands of murderers, rapists, and arsonists who traditionally have wreaked their violence on Americans every year, only a tiny percentage have actually been executed for their crimes — perhaps no more than one or two percent at the very most.

Even more shocking to egalitarians concerned about legal equality is the well-documented fact that the overwhelming majority of capital felons who have been executed in the United States in modern times have been lower class minority and poor white males, even though women and middle class whites have done their share of murdering through the years. These facts therefore do, indeed, make capital punishment highly "unusual" and inescapably "cruel" for that tiny handful of convicted felons who, for whatever reasons, missed every one of the many detours from the execution chamber with which the U.S. criminal justice system has long been studded. Quite obviously the more intelligence, money, and social standing a capital felon has, the less likely he is to be executed.[33] Justice

Stewart was clearly on the mark when he observed that being executed in the United States is rather like being struck by lightning — utterly unpredictable.[34] In only one way was his comparison invalid: lightning does not discriminate on the basis of race or class. It strikes all classes and races with about equal, if unpredictable, frequency.

Not too surprisingly, state legislators around the country were more impressed by Chief Justice Burger's dissent than by the 1972 majority opinion, and by the mid-1970s more than 30 states had passed new capital punishment laws, all of which seemed tailored to meet the standards suggested by the Court's dissenters. Though the new statutes differed widely, they generally restricted the death penalty to such crimes as killing a prison officer, mass murder, kidnapping, and hijacking. After the new laws were passed, prison death rows began filling up once again, and before long there were nearly 600 convicted felons awaiting execution, with a majority being black and all but a few men. As the death rows in those states with new capital punishment laws continued to expand, the nation held its breath and waited for the Supreme Court to review and uphold or overturn the new statutes. Executions, meanwhile, were held in abeyance.

The Supreme Court's judgment on the new laws was rendered in five related cases, announced in early July 1976. Voting seven-to-two, the justices held in the cases of *Proffitt* v. *Florida, Gregg* v. *Georgia,* and *Jurek* v. *Texas,* that the new capital punishment laws enacted by the legislatures of Florida, Georgia, and Texas did not violate the Eighth Amendment and were thus constitutional. At the same time the Court held by a five-to-four vote in the cases of *Woodson* v. *North Carolina* and *Roberts* v. *Louisiana* that the revised North Carolina and Louisiana laws were unconstitutional because they were too rigid in requiring death for certain crimes. As in the 1972 decision, the justices differed widely in their reasoning, but the central issue for all of them was whether the death penalty could be reconciled with the constitutional ban on cruel and unusual punishment. Obviously the majority thought it could be in certain cases.

All five cases decided in 1976 were brought by men convicted of murder. In requesting a review by the Supreme Court, they were not actually challenging the trial court findings of guilt but the sentences of death imposed under the post-1972 state laws. Justice Stewart, writing in the Georgia case, took a somewhat different tack from that taken in 1972 when he voted to strike down the old capital punishment laws. He observed that

> There is no question that death as a punishment is unique in its severity and irrevocability . . . . But we are concerned here only with the imposition of capital punishment for the crime of murder, and

when a life has been taken deliberately by the offender, we cannot say that the punishment is invariably disproportionate to the crime. It is an extreme sanction, suitable to the most extreme of crimes.[35]

Stewart and the majority were able to distinguish and uphold three of the new state laws. This was largely because the laws provided for considering aggravating and mitigating factors, and because they established an elaborate two-part proceeding, in which the death penalty could be imposed only after extensive hearings, and with compulsory review by state appellate courts. The justices were also obviously impressed by the fact that roughly two-thirds of the nation's state legislatures had enacted new capital punishment laws since 1972.

The first execution under the Supreme Court's new dispensation occurred not in the South but in Utah, and involved not a black man but a ne'er-do-well white man. That case, which was highly sensationalized in the press, was atypical because the felon, Gary Gilmore, expressed a strong wish to die and bitterly denounced civil libertarian organizations that tried to delay his execution. He finally got his wish when he was executed by a firing squad at 8:07 a.m. on January 17, 1977. He was the first capital felon to be executed in the United States since 1967.

Capital punishment was again in the news in the summer of 1977 when the Court held that a unique Georgia law providing capital punishment for adult rape was grossly disproportionate and excessive and thus violative of the Eighth Amendment. It is possible that the Court will eventually invalidate all capital punishment laws that do not actually involve the taking of human life, but it has not yet done so. Egalitarians would, of course, roundly applaud such a step if it comes. In the meantime, they remain convinced that capital punishment as historically administered is indeed cruel and unusual, while conservatives are just as certain that it is a proper expression of society's moral outrage at particularly offensive crimes. Conservatives also still believe that it is both an individual and a general deterrent to serious crime.

Though this analysis has so far concentrated on the Fourteenth Amendment and those sections of the Bill of Rights spelling out the rights of accused persons, it should be stressed that Article I of the U.S. Constitution also made a significant contribution to the cause of legal equality. That contribution was contained in sections 9 and 10, which forbid suspension of the writ of habeas corpus (save in cases of rebellion or invasion), and ban the passage, either by congress or state legislatures, of bills of attainder or ex post facto laws.

Habeas corpus is a particularly valuable guarantee, for it enables a person whose freedom has been restrained by a governmental agency to petition a federal court for an order testing whether such restraint was imposed in violation of the Constitution or laws of the United States. In recent years it has been especially helpful to minorities, since the Warren Court instructed federal district judges to carefully scrutinize the allegations of persons claiming they have been imprisoned as a result of constitutionally invalid trials. State judges generally resent the use of habeas corpus to investigate the validity of state judicial proceedings, and the Burger Court has restricted habeas corpus applications to federal courts by state prisoners, thereby somewhat reducing the business of federal courts. Egalitarians criticize this development as leaving the door open to an increase in cases of unlawful imprisonment in state jurisdictions. It is too soon to say if they are correct.

A bill of attainder is a legislative punishment imposed upon an individual or group without recourse to a judicial trial. The most recent example of this was a congressional enactment that made it a crime for any person to serve as an officer or employe of a labor union, save in a minor clerical capacity, who was a member of the Communist Party or had been within the previous five years. On reviewing the issue involved in this statute, a majority of the Supreme Court held the provision complained of to be unconstitutional as a bill of attainder. In speaking for the majority, Chief Justice Warren noted that Congress had not simply set forth a category of persons deemed ineligible to perform certain acts but had also designated certain individuals who possessed "the feared characteristics" in question. Four members of the Court (White, Clark, Harlan, and Stewart) rejected the majority's holding that the provision in litigation was a bill of attainder.[36]

An ex post facto law, also proscribed by Article I, is a statute that retrospectively changes the legal consequences or relations of a given act or deed, to the disadvantage of persons committing the act. It is, in other words, a law that aggravates a crime by making it greater than it was when committed, or that criminalizes an act that was innocent, legally speaking, when performed. Retroactive tax and other civil laws are not defined as ex post facto laws, nor are criminal laws that retroactively mollify, instead of strengthen, the rigor of the criminal law. Though formerly quite common in Europe, ex post facto laws have not been a significant threat to freedom or equality in the West in modern times. The Supreme Court's classic exegesis of the meaning of the ex post facto provision of the Constitution was made back in 1798. The crux of the Court's holding in that case was that there is a definite distinction between retrospective civil laws, which are permissible, and ex post facto criminal or penal statutes, which are not.[37]

Of all the constitutional and extra-constitutional doctrines underpinning the U.S. criminal justice system, seven are generally regarded as absolutely fundamental. Most of these were described in the preceding discussion, but all seven will be summarized here for the sake of emphasis:

All persons accused of criminal acts are deemed to be innocent unless and until they are convicted in a court of law, in accord with the requirements of due process and equal protection.

The homes and offices of private citizens are not to be searched for criminal evidence unless there is "probable cause" to justify such a search.

Grand juries shall not return true bills of indictment against persons except in cases where they are satisfied there is "probable cause" that the crime under investigation has been committed by a given suspect and that a trial to determine his guilt or innocence ought forthwith to be held. Although grand juries shall be entrusted with the subpoena power, prosecutors and the FBI shall not be.

All criminal trials must be conducted in accord with the accusatorial or adversary procedure, rather than the inquisitorial system, which means that each of the opposing parties shall be represented by counsel and shall have full opportunity to establish its opposing contentions in open court.

Every accused person is entitled to acquittal if, in the minds of the trial jury, his guilt has not been proved beyond a "reasonable doubt."

In all federal criminal trials, the guilt or innocence of a defendant may be determined solely by a formal and unanimous verdict of a twelve-person jury, reported to the court and accepted by it.

Finally, the U.S. Supreme Court has discretionary review power over all lower court cases in which a federal issue is raised, as well as over the actions of the executive and legislative branches of government, provided somebody with proper standing institutes a "case or controversy."

These doctrines are obviously crucial to any criminal justice system that seeks to maximize freedom and equality along with social order, but it is up to the courts, today as always, to infuse them with flesh-and-blood meaning. It is therefore necessary now to examine a few of the interpretive concepts or rules employed by U.S. courts in order to assist judges in delineating the outer bounds of such procedural guaranties as due process, equal protection, and so on.

It is quite clear that at the present time most U.S. courts, taking their cue from the Supreme Court, rely mainly upon the "balancing doctrine of competing interests" to determine the exact scope and nature of a defendant's rights when these are disputed in a case or controversy. This means that the defendant's right to a fair trial and to equal status before the law will be weighed against the state's legitimate interest in the speedy, efficient, and economic enforcement of society's criminal laws. In certain cases the adjudicational line may be drawn slightly in favor of the defendant; at other times, in favor of the prosectuion as the representative of the sovereign people. In any event, contrary to what happens on such television programs as *Perry Mason,* neither side in real life wins them all.

Although this balancing interpretive doctrine is adhered to as a kind of absolute by U.S. courts, its specific results in a given case are relativistically determined. The doctrine, therefore, is actually a kind of situational ethic, since the courts refuse to say precisely what the procedural guaranties of the accused mean in all situations and circumstances. Obviously such a doctrine, short as it is on general principles and long on case-by-case analysis, makes for a mountain of litigation as well as for much unpredictability about the outcome of a particular criminal appeal. In addition it makes enormously difficult the task of ascertaining the weight of competing interests in any given case. On the other hand, it provides a certain flexibility and variety in the adjudication process and thereby diminishes the likelihood of ideals hardening into doctrinaire absolutes in the field of law enforcement.

Egalitarians, though strong supporters of the utility principle in most other areas, have never been happy with the Supreme Court's utilitarian interest-balancing in the field of criminal justice. They long for a more principled attitude toward defendants' rights and for rather less relativism in judicial constructions of the Fourteenth Amendment and Bill of Rights. They are particularly concerned that interpretations of the rights of the accused which focus on relative costs may not properly protect unpopular defendants charged with serious criminal or administrative offenses. More important, they believe that when courts insist on balancing the basic right of defendants against the putative needs of society and the state, the former will eventually cease to be accepted as a fundamental prerogative which individuals can assert against the power of government and will instead be downgraded to just another check and balance in the separation of powers scheme. They feel, in other words, that when due process and related guaranties cease to be taken seriously as quasi-absolute rights, there is a very real danger that all the defendant's protections designed to assure procedural fairness and equity will ultimately be diluted. At the same time, they fear that continued judicial use of interest-balancing in due process and other litigation will lead to an abandonment of any effective limits on the power of big government to injure the isolated individual.

Egalitarian theorists have long been fond of pointing out that when Congressman Madison was drafting the Bill of Rights, he proposed that the due process clause should be inserted into Article I of the original Constitution where, as was noted above, there are express prohibitions on ex post facto laws and bills of attainder. In explaining the purpose of his Amendments, Madison observed that

The prescriptions in favor of liberty ought to be levelled against that quarter where the greatest danger lies, namely, that which possesses the highest prerogative of power. But this is not found in either the executive or legislative departments of Government, but in the body of the people, operating by the majority against the minority.

It may be thought that all paper barriers against the power of the community are too weak to be worthy of attention . . . . [Yet] it may be one means to control the majority.[38]

The interest-balancing doctrine is not, of course, the only method courts may use, or have used, to guide them in delineating the rights of the accused; nor, indeed, do all flexible methods of interpretation necessarily involve explicit balancing procedures. Thus, before judicial confidence in the concept of natural law waned, jurists often interpreted due process and other procedural guaranties as perforce imprecise but still mandated as precious rights under a higher law.[39] Another mode of interpretive analysis involving flexibility but not interest-balancing was the use of conventional morality notions in lieu of natural law abstractions to evaluate the fairness and equity of criminal justice procedures.[40]

Proponents of legal egalitarianism not only want the courts to drop their interest-balancing analysis in criminal justice litigation, they go further and argue that the judiciary should quit viewing itself as little more than one of several policy-planning institutions within the political process. In their view, the judiciary ought to be a kind of ombudsman for the citizenry, policing the limits of governmental power against the individual, rather than simply reviewing the quality of public policies. This, they feel, can best be accomplished by shifting from interest-balancing in criminal law litigation to a more fixed standard of interpreting defendants' rights.

Egalitarian theorists clearly fear the encroachment of big government upon the rights and freedoms of the isolated, non-conformist individual. And all of them believe, moreover, that the Fourteenth Amendment and the Bill of Rights, properly interpreted, are the greatest guaranties of freedom and equality in the U.S. criminal justice system. But despite general agreement on these basic points, they often sharply disagree when specifics of interpretation are the issue.

The more absolute among egalitarian theorists would probably be happy if the courts tied defendants' rights closely and firmly to either natural law or conventional morality standards. Others, like the late Justice Black and the distinguished political philosopher Alexander Meiklejohn, would be satisfied if the Supreme Court would at least concede that there are a few near-absolutes in the Constitution and then conclude that interest-balancing in Bill of Rights litigation is improper because inconsistent with the text of the first Ten Amendments.[41] More moderate and realistic egalitarians maintain that while due process and other defendants' rights must be flexibly interpreted, "there are modes other than interest balancing in which judicial power can be exercised flexibly yet in a fashion more congenial to the judicial function of specifying the requirements of constitutional rights."[42]

In recent years, those who argue for greater equality before the law for disadvantaged defendants generally have been less concerned with interest-balancing per se than with the way the Burger or Nixon Court seems, in their view, to be using the doctrine to tip the balance in criminal cases against defendants — especially unpopular ones — and in favor of "law and order." They appear to be convinced that the Supreme Court of the 1970s is both pro-prosecution and regressive in its construction of the Bill of Rights. As one spokesman for this view recently put it, the Bill of Rights requires "an ardently sympathetic" Court, and there "is no way for the guarantees of the Bill of Rights to have real meaning if not enforced by unstinting judicial affirmations that keep restraints upon government."[43]

It is still too early to say how far the Burger Court will go in overturning pro-defendant precedents in criminal justice cases, but two things seem certain about the present Court. It shows every intention of holding fast to the balancing approach, and it is most unlikely to retreat from its oft stated view that all constitutional rights are limited in nature. This means that there will be no absolute rules for explicating the meaning of due process; and, if present trends continue, there will be no expansion of either liberty or equality and, indeed, there may be some contraction. The Burger Court is particularly unsympathetic toward defendants they view as hard core professional criminals, and the justices—or most of them—are not about to restrict judicial discretion in order to defer to unbending rules of fairness so beloved by egalitarians. On the other hand, given the number of moderates and switchers on the Court, Professor Levy seems to be indulging in conspiracy thinking when he charges that "Richard M. Nixon now and for an indefinite period in the future casts four votes in criminal-justice cases decided by the Supreme Court."[44]

Egalitarian critics of the jurisprudence of the Burger Court do not, of course, oppose anti-crime campaigns nor do they believe in coddling vicious criminals. It is true, however, that they attach relatively little significance to the criminal law as a guarantee of public safety and generally oppose judicial opinions that make concessions to law enforcers when the Constitution is being construed. As for the approach of people like Levy to the escalating crime problems, they would try to rejuvenate our cities, our schools, and our economy, and in the future send only dangerous felons to prison. They believe, in other words, that the most efficient as well as the most egalitarian way to fight crime is not through the forces of the criminal law but through basic socioeconomic reform. In this respect they are essentially utilitarians and environmental determinists.

At this point it may well be asked what precisely is the relevance of the freedom-equality dilemma to the field of criminal justice? Do freedom and equality advance hand-in-hand when reforms are made in this vital area of democracy, or must freedom sometimes be sacrificed to obtain greater legal equality for disadvantaged groups?

As might be expected, egalitarians maintain that in this field, even more than in most others, freedom and equality do indeed advance together, with the former rarely if ever having to be sacrificed in the interest of the latter. Most conservatives, on the other hand, flatly and often vociferously disagree with that conclusion. It is their general view that the ancient democratic problem of reconciling freedom and equality is just as visible here as in other public policy fields and has, in fact, recently become more acute.

It seems to be the view of mainstream conservatives that minorities in the United States of whatever race or ethnicity today have genuine equality before the civil and criminal law. But many would go further and insist that some disadvantaged groups, especially blacks, actually have more than their share of legal equality because the courts, trying to rectify past injustices, now bend over backward to give defendants from such groups every possible advantage in criminal litigation. This, they argue, is un-American, unfair, and unconstitutional. Indeed, Judge Arlin M. Adams of the U.S. Court of Appeals recently warned that judicial activism to advance egalitarian goals "erodes the legislative process, because it tends to relieve legislators from accountability for social reconstruction and constitutional propriety."[45] In that sense, the judiciary is becoming the primary lawmaker of the United States, or so it is alleged.

If letters to the editors of newspapers are a reliable indication of popular thinking, it would appear that the number of conservatives who feel that minorities are getting more equality than they deserve is growing. People who take that view invariably argue that there has been a concomitant diminution of the freedom of other groups in the criminal justice system, most notably the freedom of police officials, prosecutors, grand and trial juries, officials of correctional institutions, and victims of violent crimes. The more militant conservatives maintain that since these groups represent in a very direct way the sovereign people, society as a whole has lost valuable freedoms as the courts become ever more solicitous of criminals' rights. Therefore, they say, it is time to think more about the freedoms of nice people and less about the equality claims of punks and hard core criminals.

One of the prime movers in the conservative campaign to tip the balance more in favor of the police and prosecution is Americans for Effective Law Enforcement (AELE), which was founded in 1966 by Northwestern University Law Professor Fred Inbau. Though much smaller in staff and resources than such egalitarian groups as the American Civil Liberties Union (ACLU), AELE in the early 1970s was starting to make a definite impact on the criminal justice system. Disdaining any connection with the far Right, Professor Inbau has declared that "We're not out to put the ACLU out of business. But we want to make sure that the courts hear the law-enforcement side of arguments."[46] Although AELE says it seeks to avoid the equality vs. law-and-order issue, it probably showed its ideological bent when it opposed a petition to dismiss contempt charges against the Chicago Seven.

In the 1970s, conservatives quite openly suggested that the nation's concern with legal equality, which reached a crescendo of solicitude under the Warren Court, was causing an inflation of the murder rate and thereby endangering the freedoms of all law-abiding citizens. They also seemed to take a certain delight in pointing out that the groups most involved in criminality were the very same racial and ethnic minority groups that had benefited most from the recent democratization of the U.S. criminal justice system.

It is obviously not possible to prove that egalitarian advances have been a major factor in the rising murder rate; yet conservatives, as well as many other people, believe that to be the case. Their point is that as society becomes increasingly egalitarian, poor and disadvantaged people have a tendency to blame their troubles not on themselves, as in the past, but on the corrupt world around them. Moreover, as they resort to violent crime to rectify their allegedly unfair plight, they do so with a bitterness and a feeling of self-righteousness that rarely accompanied criminal acts in the past. As a result of this ongoing phenomenon, all crimes become in effect political or sociological, and the safety and freedom of society's non-criminal elements inevitably decline.

This kind of reasoning assumes, of course, that the freedoms and rights of the nice people in a country are more worthy and needful of protection than those of the not-so-nice people. Such an attitude is quite understandable for, indeed, there has always been at least an implicit assumption in conservatism that "quality people" merit more consideration from the law than "non-quality people." Naturally, conservatives deny that they are opposed to due process or equal protection for accused persons: they simply disagree with their critics about the nature of these constitutional guaranties.

Reflecting rising conservative concerns about the threat to freedom from criminals, Dr. Donald T. Lunde, a Stanford University professor of

Law and Psychiatry, recently made the following perceptive comments:

> When traditional values and the Protestant ethic reigned, people felt responsible for themselves. If they were frustrated, as they were in the Great Depression, when banks were failing, they took it out on themselves and jumped out windows. What is happening now, during our bad economic situation, is that we are experiencing an incredible increase in the murder rate — not only the highest ever recorded in this country but one of the highest in the world. We are in the midst of a murder epidemic [sparked by young adults of the post-World War II generation]. That generation is much more likely to blame others than themselves, because of the way they were reared and because they've grown up in a time when there is much more governmental control.[47]

Conservatives have likewise taken the lead in advocating more aid for crime victims as a kind of couterpoise to the constant pressure of leftists for more equality for poor defendants. As two experts in the field have recently noted, "There is something almost obscenely hypocritical about the way in which public figures bewail and deplore criminal violence . . . and yet contrive to ignore the plight of the victims of that violence," which falls disproportionately upon the uninsured poor.[48] By 1977, a total of nineteen states had adopted laws to compensate innocent victims of crime, while five more states had laws providing for partial compensation. Great Britain and New Zealand appear to have been the pioneers in providing such state aid to crime victims in order that they would not have to bear their own losses.

The main objection to victim compensation laws seems to be the potentially high cost. But most states have been able to get around this by simply setting a limit on compensation, with limits ranging from around $10,000 to $50,000. In some states only needy victims are compensated. Among the large states, California has a $23,000 limit, while in New York the relevant legislation does not put a dollar limit on compensation.

For some time now, Representative Peter Rodino of New Jersey has been pushing in Congress a bill that would grant states fifty percent of the cost of compensation to innocent victims of crime at an estimated cost of $29 million per year. The bill was approved by Rodino's House Judiciary Committee in 1977. Rodino and others have pointed out that, contrary to popular belief, compensating victims of crime is not new. In fact, they say, the principle was embedded in the ancient Babylonian Code of Hammurabi. An alternative proposal is "to make it a requirement of the allocation of federal funds to states for crime control purposes, that all states in receipt of such funds should set up schemes for the compensation of victims of crimes of violence."[49]

Perhaps the most graphic intrusion of the freedom-equality dilemma into the criminal justice system is the issue of reconciling the right of the accused to a fair trial with the guarantee of freedom of the press. Here there is a potential conflict between two of the most vital provisions of the Bill of Rights: the First and Sixth Amendments. The Sixth, it will be recalled, assures all defendants an impartial jury trial, and the First proscribes all laws that abridge the freedom of the press.

This dilemma becomes particularly acute when the media insist on the freedom to publish absolutely everything about a sensational crime and, at the same time, the person charged with the crime argues that such unrestrained freedom destroys the possibility of his getting an impartial jury trial. Such collisions between First and Sixth Amendment rights seem to be occurring with growing frequency these days, largely because of the increase in crime and because of the extraordinary advances made in mass communications in this century.

Theoretically, there are three basic ways of handling this dilemma. Officials can more or less ignore it and simply refuse to admit its existence. Alternatively, they can restrict the freedom of the media in order to maximize the likelihood of a completely fair trial for the defendant, as Britain does. Or they may follow the traditional way of giving full scope to the First Amendment's free press guarantee and hope for the best when the defendant's trial day arrives. As the Supreme Court has aptly observed, "Free speech and fair trials are two of the most cherished policies of our civilization, and it . . . [is] a trying task to choose between them."[50] It is, indeed, and the choice officials have to make is essentially one between press freedom and equality for all defendants.

After intense and prolonged pressure by egalitarians and defense lawyers, U.S. judges some time ago stepped up their efforts to assure an impartial trial for all defendants by stressing such techniques as voir dire, trail postponement, sequestering of juries, and changing trial venue. But in the more sensational criminal trials, these techniques did not seem entirely adequate; so courts have recently begun "gagging the press" in order to do everything possible to maximize the rights of the accused. As expected, this provoked an outcry from media spokesmen and certain civil liberties groups, who demanded, in effect, that the judiciary finally decide whether free press and fair trial are, in most contexts, complementary or competing values, and whether the United States shall go all the way to the draconian British system in making certain that all defendants, infamous or noninfamous, have equal access to an absolutely fair trial. The media, of course, reject Britain's way.

Until recently, the most significant U.S. Supreme Court decision in this controversial area was that handed down in the *Sheppard* case in the mid-1960s.[51] The Court, in that landmark case, reversed a murder conviction of a prominent doctor because of prejudicial pretrial publicity, which, in the view of the majority, catered to "the insatiable interest of the American public in the bizarre" and thereby created the atmosphere of a "Roman holiday." The Court, moreover, stressed in dictum that "reversals are but palliatives" and recommended that trial courts, in future, adopt "remedial measures that will prevent the prejudice at its inception."[52] Among the remedial measures suggested by the Court were the regulation of the release to the press by police of case leads and gossip and the flat prohibition of extra-judicial statements of a prejudicial nature by court officials, witnesses, or parties to a criminal case. Although *Sheppard* did not actually propose direct prohibition of publication by the press, it seemed to move in that direction; and in the aftermath of the decision, "trial courts began to gag participants in trials to prevent prejudicial information from reaching the media."[53] Inevitably, the media protested and insisted on their right to publish anything relevant to a pending trial.

In the summer of 1976, the Supreme Court handed down its most important "fair trial-free press" decision since *Sheppard.* The case arose in Nebraska, where a judge had issued a "gag order" that severely restricted the publication of news about a sensational murder trial, pending selection of a jury. Among other things, the order provided that the press could not report that the accused had confessed, even though that information had come out in an open hearing.

After reviewing the case, the Court held unanimously that judicial gag orders, under most circumstances, are invalid, and that the judge in this instance could have provided the accused with a fair trial without fettering the press. Chief Justice Burger, writing for the Court, acknowledged that pretrial publicity can seriously threaten an individual's right to a fair trial, but emphasized that "Prior restraints on speech and publication are the most serious and least tolerable infringement on First Amendment Rights." However, the Chief Justice also stressed that "the guarantees of freedom of expression are not an absolute prohibition under all circumstances," and thus the Court did not go so far as to ban all pretrial press restraints. It is possible, therefore, that future gag orders may be held permissible in exceptional cases, even though Justices Brennan, Marshall, and Stewart declared that gag orders should never be imposed on the press. Justices Stevens and White expressed grave doubts that exceptions could be made.[54]

Whatever the future may hold, the Nebraska decision was clearly a victory for the freedom of the press and perhaps only indirectly a defeat for the equality claims of "infamous" defendants. The press, to be sure, is not totally out of danger; but then it never will be. Freedom, like equality, is always in danger. The "fair trial-free press" issue may well be one of those eternal problems that have no pat solutions in a society that places a lofty value on both fair trials and a free press. Crime and publicity, in short, seem inevitably linked in democratic states.

A new and growing concern of egalitarians is what they regard as unfair discrimination against persons in correctional institutions. Until recently, prisoners in the United States were regarded as having virtually no legal or constitutional rights. Whatever "rights" they enjoyed—and they were precious few—were privileges extended to them by paternalistic prison administrators. Appellate courts rarely listened to prisoner complaints, since courts assumed that few if any constitutional rights followed the convict through the prison gates. But, as a result of mounting pressure by a variety of egalitarian groups, that situation of non-benign neglect is rapidly changing, and today the argument is not about whether prisoners have constitutional rights—all courts now agree that they do—but about which rights they have and to what degree they have them.

The prisoners' "rights" now being advanced by egalitarian reformers include conjugal visits in privacy, freedom from search and punishment without due process, freedom from censorship, protection from racial discrimination, freedom to practice one's religion and to express one's political beliefs, the assurance of decent living conditions, and liberty in matters of personal grooming and appearance. Furthermore, some egalitarians are now saying that depriving prisoners of the suffrage right is a grave defect of the U.S. penal system, since it neither advances the rehabilitation of inmates nor enhances the physical security of correctional institutions. Generally speaking, egalitarians want the courts to tip the balance in favor of prisoners' rights when adjudicating inmate challenges to institutional authority. Some judges, though probably not a majority, agree with that view, as does the influential American Civil Liberties Union.

In late 1975, conditions at a jail in the nation's capital got so bad that U.S. District Judge William B. Bryant, in a widely-publicized decision, held that the situation there constituted cruel and unusual punishment of the inmates. Among other things, he forbade the use of shackles for more than 24 hours at a time and required officials to report promptly to doctors any use of physical restraints on inmates. At about the same time, several state prison systems were becoming so overcrowded that they were having to release prisoners early and, in some cases, were refusing to take additional ones.

One much discussed report of the prison overflow included the following grim facts:[55]

Louisiana's department of corrections is thinking of bringing a World War II troopship out of mothballs to serve as an auxiliary prison. The Florida State Prison at Starke has 646 inmates living in Army tents and converted warehouses. Georgia's maximum-security prison at Reidsville is so overcrowded that 119 prisoners are forced to double up in 8-ft. by 5-ft. cells . . . State prison systems around the country are backing up like flooded sewers, particularly in the South.

Since the great majority of U.S. prisoners are poor people and minority males, and since prisons are more jammed than ever, egalitarians argue that the nation's disadvantaged are bearing an ever greater share of prison inequities. They were particularly shocked to learn in the spring of 1975 that the Federal Bureau of Prisons had decided to reduce its stress on rehabilitation and give more weight in the future to punishment and deterrence. Proponents of equality, while agreeing that rehabilitation has been oversold and never really implemented, opposed the Bureau's decision on the ground that rehabilitation programs do often help the disadvantaged and provide a rational purpose for incarceration. They also recommended that prison be limited to those persons who are truly dangerous, a policy which, if adopted, would significantly reduce the Bureau of Prisons' problems. The Bureau, however, seemed uninterested.

It is scarcely an exaggeration to state that among criminal justice egalitarians the issue of prisoners' rights has become an Archimedean point for assessing progress toward full legal equality for all individuals and groups. Although this issue has been pushed by reformers for more than a century, it was not until September 1971 that the question of prisoners' rights became headline news, indelibly engraved upon the public consciousness. For that was the date of the tragedy at Attica Prison in New York State, which ultimately took 43 lives and revealed extraordinarily oppressive conditions within the prison walls.

The following year an official report was issued about the bloody tragedy, complete with dramatic photographs of the riot.[56] But despite the massive amount of publicity that attended the Attica uprising, conditions there had apparently not greatly improved five years later. Attica is a maximum-security institution where only hardened criminals are normally sent, and reformers have long despaired of doing much about such structures. Not enough money is available to improve physical facilities; legislators and judges are reluctant to intervene; and there is as yet no popular consensus demanding reform. The poor and minority groups that people such "warehouses" are truly the pariahs of society. The only kind of equality they enjoy is that of a common misery.

Egalitarians have lately been emphasizing an issue that conservatives prefer to softpedal—namely, the gloved-hand treatment given white collar criminals, before and after incarceration. It has been widely estimated that some $40 billion a year are taken from U.S. citizens by white collar or economic crimes; yet few of the people responsible for such crimes ever wind up at Attica or similar prisons. Such institutions continue to be primarily the destination of blacks, Chicanos, Puerto Ricans, and other ethnic minorities.[57]

Egalitarians have likewise decried the criminal justice inequities stemming from Watergate. Thus, former acting FBI Director L. Patrick Gray III admitted destroying FBI files and evidence, but was not indicted for that or any other offenses in connection with Watergate. Former Attorney General Richard Kleindienst pleaded guilty to a charge of refusing to answer pertinent questions before the Senate Judiciary Committee, which is only a misdemeanor. Satisfied, U.S. District Judge George Hart gave him a suspended prison term of 30 days and a suspended $100 fine. On October 10, 1973, Vice President Spiro Agnew, facing a federal income tax charge, resigned from the second highest office in the land, pleaded no contest to the charge, and received a suspended prison sentence and a $10,000 fine. True, Agnew's troubles were not Watergate-related. But they occurred during the "Watergate Administration," of which he had been one of the most enthusiastic boosters until his own political demise.

Finally, on September 8, 1974, the biggest shocker of all came when President Ford granted former President Nixon a full pardon for all federal crimes he "committed or may have committed or taken part in" while in office.[58] The pardon came in the nick of time, for, as was later revealed, the Special Watergate Prosecutor's office was giving serious consideration to indicting Mr. Nixon for his part in the Watergate coverup. Despite the pardon, he, of course, remained subject to civil action and to prosecution for state crimes.

Egalitarians, as well as civil libertarians generally, never tire of pointing out the sharp contrast between the leniency shown the higher-ups in the Nixon Administration and the prison sentences meted out to such minor Watergate figures as Herbert L. Porter, Dwight Chapin, and Donald Segretti. The court records show quite clearly that Judges John Sirica and Gerhardt Gesell, as a matter of principle, took a position of giving the heaviest sentences to those entrusted with the greatest responsibility. Judge Hart, on the other hand, not only did not do this but publicly praised Kleindienst as a man of great integrity in both private and public life, and characterized his false witness before the Senate Judiciary Committee as a mere technical violation of the law. Little wonder that civil libertarians began charging, with a good deal of plausibility, that the Watergate sentencing record demonstrated conclusively that justice in the United States is, indeed, unequal and that the scales are sharply tilted in favor of the rich and well born, not the poor and disadvantaged.[59] Conservatives generally deny such allegations and argue that if much more is done by government to rectify past inequities against minorities, legitimate liberties of business and professional people will inevitably be impaired. Additional legal equality bought at such a price, they maintain, would imperil the very foundations of the U.S. criminal justice system and establish an equality-mad imperial judiciary that would intrude into people's lives in a manner unparalleled in U.S. history.

A final area of criminal justice in which egalitarians are making a major push toward greater equality involves the field of substantive criminal law. In this instance, the objections of reformers focus on what they call "victimless crimes": non-violent actions engaged in by consenting adults in private, which have been criminalized—often with severe penalties— because of pressures brought on legislators by puritanical moralists. These include such "crimes" as prostitution, fornication, adultery, public drunkenness, obscenity, statutory rape, gambling, marijuana use, juvenile delinquency, homosexuality, and vagrancy.[60]

Critics of such statutes attack them both on libertarian and egalitarian grounds. They allegedly proscribe behavior that does little if any direct harm to society. They represent an undesirable intrusion of religious morality into strictly secular issues. They open the way to blackmail by hardened criminals and by unscrupulous law enforcement personnel. They lead to a false allocation of scarce resources in the crime-fighting field. They have criminogenic effects since they invariably lead to a black market in the forbidden commodity, thereby bringing organized crime into the forbidden area. They are inept instruments for coercing people toward virtue. And, most damaging from the equality perspective, they are usually enforced in a selective, discriminatory manner, very much as capital punishment laws are enforced. Thus, arrests are made of prostitutes but rarely of their "scores," of male homosexuals but not of lesbians, and of lower-class but not upper-class drunks.

Today the great majority of egalitarians support John Stuart Mill's philosophy of criminalization, which he expressed in the following way:[61]

> . . . the sole end for which mankind are warranted . . . in interfering with the liberty of action of any of their number, is self-protection. . . . The only part of the conduct of any one, for which he is amenable to society, is that which concerns others. In the part which merely concerns himself, his independence is, of right, absolute. Over himself, over his own body and mind, the individual is sovereign.

Egalitarians were especially pleased when the American Law Institute's 1955 *Model Penal Code* embraced Mill's basic premise that the power of the state should not be used to enforce purely moral or religious standards.[62] Two years later, they were likewise heartened by the even more "Millian" *Wolfenden Report*, which asserted that "It is not . . . the function of the law to intervene in the private lives of citizens, or to seek to enforce any particular pattern of behavior . . . Unless a deliberate attempt is made by society, acting through the agency of the law, to equate the sphere of crime with that of sin, there must remain a realm of private morality and immorality which is . . . not the law's business."[63]

It may not be altogether true that "Nobody knows a damned thing about crime,"[64] but one thing is certain: every time a legislative body criminalizes something that was formerly permitted it increases crime, simply because if there were no criminal laws there would be no crimes in the legal sense. But quite aside from being the formal cause of crime, criminal law is also an efficient cause of crime in the sense that certain statutes, notably those defining victimless crimes, have been shown to foster, encourage, and sustain crime. That is why egalitarians oppose such statutes, not only for the ideal reasons just cited but also for utilitarian reasons. Moderate egalitarians would probably settle for decriminalization of victimless sex, gambling, and drug offenses, while militants would go further and legalize most if not all such activities. Conservatives, of course, oppose both decriminalization and legalization on the ground that they would diminish the freedom of society as a whole and interfere with the liberties of persons living in areas patronized by gamblers, prostitutes, and drug dealers. More important, they deny that "victimless" crimes are truly victimless, though they concede that there have been inequities in police arrest practices. But the remedy for that, they say, is to tighten up enforcement, not repeal the laws.

As the crusade of legal egalitarians intensifies, there is always a danger that the zealots who demand total equality before the law will vent an indignation so extreme as to lack moral discrimination. Surely not all inequalities in the legal process are grossly immoral, nor are all its admitted shortcomings maliciously contrived by upper class people who hate poor people and racial minorities. Here as elsewhere, if passions get out of hand, there is a very real danger that the unfortunate may suffer at the hands of their self-proclaimed messiahs, something conservative libertarians say is already happening.

To summarize, egalitarians believe that equality and freedom, most of the time at least, advance together in the criminal justice field. But they insist that we still have a long way to go before we achieve genuine equality before the law for everybody. Conservatives, on the other hand, argue that freedom and legal equality, far from always moving forward together, often move in contrary directions. They also maintain, in opposition to their opponents, that the poor and the disadvantaged are now roughly equal—and sometimes more than equal—to everybody else in the criminal justice system. They have both freedom and equality.

In respect to the future, egalitarians seem to be saying that full legal equality will never become an accomplished fact unless and until a half-dozen basic reforms are everywhere implemented.

Thus, they argue that the Warren Court's pro-equality interpretations of the Bill of Rights and Fourteenth Amendment must be sustained and expanded by every court in the land. There can be no retreat from justice.[65]

The policy of selective arrest adhered to by most police forces in the country, which disadvantages poor people and minorities, must be totally abolished. Of course, there has to be some discretion in the criminal justice system, they concede, but not the kind that discriminates against blacks, radicals, "troublemakers," and other non-conformists. With police discrimination must also go the myth, carefully nurtured by law enforcement people, that the police have been dangerously "handcuffed" by the courts and thereby deprived of essential freedoms. Nothing could be further from the truth, egalitarians claim.

The concept of procedural and substantive due process must be extended to prisoners in all correctional institutions, and the machinery of the grand jury must be radically overhauled to make it less of a tool of prosecutors.

The entire bail, punishment, and parole system must be revamped in order to remove the institutionalized racism and classism that now taint it.

The judicial system must begin punishing white collar and political criminals with the same severity it has traditionally used against perpetrators of street crime.

And, finally, all victimless crimes must be decriminalized both to advance equality and to more rationally allocate our scarce law enforcement resources.[66] Once that is done, some legalization might follow.

So, the tension between liberty and equality remains unresolved in the criminal justice system, as in most other areas of the nation's life. Theoretically, both conservatives and reformist egalitarians support the ideal of full equality before the law, and both are well aware that big government is at one and the same time a major friend and foe of this ideal. Here as elsewhere, they continue to disagree about the nature of freedom and equality, about current realities, and about the best instruments for maximizing the two. Ironically, conservatives, who are the strongest supporters of economic laissez-faire, are authoritarians in their advocacy of laws proscribing victimless crimes. Egalitarians likewise are inconsistent when they demand maximal judicial activism in support of minority rights, while espousing judicial restraint in regard to the rights of corporations and the well-to-do. Both want to have their cake and eat it too.

Freedom and equality in the criminal justice system may perhaps best be compared to the ends of a large candle, horizontally and delicately balanced in the scales of the blindfolded goddess Justitia. In a democratic society, both ends of the candle are lit, and each gives off a brilliant light. If, however, one end is permitted to burn more rapidly than the other, the balance will be upset, the candle will fall from the scale, and its light will be extinguished. This metaphor, imperfect though it is, aptly underscores the perennial problem of democratic justice: how, through the democratic process, to strike a proper balance between competitive and equally legitimate values.

NOTES

1. Quoted in Bernard Schwartz, *The American Heritage History of the Law in America* (New York: American Heritage Publishing Co., 1974), p. 69. It appears that a 1692 Massachusetts law was the first U.S. statute to use "due process of law" instead of the "law of the land" phraseology found in Magna Carta.
2. Ibid., p. 71.
3. *Dred Scott* v. *Sandford*, 19 Howard 393 (1857).
4. Quoted in Schwartz, p. 119.
5. Ibid.
6. *Palko* v. *State of Connecticut*, 302 U.S. 319 (1937). Since *Palko*, the Supreme Court has decided that all the guarantees of the Bill of Rights are "implicit in the concept of ordered liberty" and thus binding on states via the due process clause of the Fourteenth Amendment, except for the right to a grand jury indictment and the right to a jury in civil cases involving over twenty dollars (Seventh Amendment). Though the specific issue of *Palko* was overruled by *Benton* v. *Maryland*, 395 U.S. 784 (1969), the decision, written by Justice Cardozo, stands as a landmark in the judiciary's egalitarian "modernization" of the Federal Bill of Rights.
7. The *Wolf* Court had refused to apply the federal "exclusionary rule" to the states, thus allowing "tainted" evidence, inadmissible in federal courts, to be admitted at state trials. The decision was six to three.
8. An excellent journalistic account of the *Gideon* case is that contained in Anthony Lewis, *Gideon's Trumpet* (New York: Random House, 1964).
9. A sharply-divided Court in *Olmstead* held that criminal evidence acquired by wire tapping does not constitute a violation of the Fourth or Fifth Amendments. In *Goldman* the court reconfirmed the *Olmstead* decision by holding that the use of a "detectaphone" that did not require trespass on defendant's property was not a violation of the Fourth Amendment.
10. The literature on due process is voluminous, especially in law journals and reviews. One of the best recent articles on the subject is "Specifying the Procedures Required by Due Process: Toward Limits on the Use of Interest Balancing" (Notes), *Harvard Law Review* 88 (1975):1510-43. As noted in this analysis, due process adjudication "involves two analytically distinct issues: whether the right to due process is applicable; and, if so, what procedures must be provided. . . . Under present doctrine the form of due

process depends upon a utilitarian balancing of the conflicting interests in which the individual's need for requested procedural safeguards is weighed against the governmental interest in summary or informal action." Ibid., p. 1510.

11. *Strauder* v. *West Virginia*, 100 U.S. 303 (1880).
12. Ibid.
13. See William B. Lockhart, Yale Kamisar, and Jesse H. Choper, *The American Constitution: Cases and Materials* (St. Paul: West Publishing Co., 1964), pp. 830-31.
14. *Virginia* v. *Rives*, 100 U.S. 339 (1880).
15. *Patton* v. *State of Mississippi*, 332 U.S. 463 (1948).
16. Quoted in Schwartz, p. 291.
17. *Schneckloth* v. *Bustamone*, 412 U.S. 218 (1973), and quoting from Justice Harlan in *Ker* v. *California*, 374 U.S. 23 (1963).
18. See *Chimel* v. *California*, 395 U.S. 752 (1969); *United States* v. *Harris*, 403 U.S. 573 (1971)
19. *Weeks* v. *United States*, 232 U.S. 383 (1914).
20. *Wolf* v. *Colorado*, 338 U.S. 25 (1949).
21. *Sheppard* v. *Maxwell*, 384 U.S. 333 (1966).
22. Quoted by Justice Black, *Reid* v. *Covert*, 354 U.S. 1 (1957).
23. Charles P. Sohner, *American Government and Politics Today: A Concise Introduction* (Glenview, Ill.: Scott, Foresman and Company, 1973), p. 97.
24. This provision of the Eighth Amendment was copied from a similar clause in the English Bill of Rights of 1689. Technically, bail is the pledge of money or property by an arrestee or his sureties in order to guarantee his appearance for trial.
25. See *Stack* v. *Boyle*, 342 U.S. 1 (1951) and *Carlson* v. *Landon*, 342 U.S. 524 (1952).
26. See Ronald Goldfarb, "A Brief for Preventive Detention," *New York Times Magazine*, 1 March 1970, p. 73.
27. *New York Times*, 12 July 1969, pp. 1, 40.
28. *Weems* v. *United States*, 217 U.S. 349 (1910).
29. *Robinson* v. *California*, 370 U.S. 660 (1962).
30. *Furman* v. *Georgia*, 408 U.S. 238 (1972).
31. Ibid.
32. Ibid.
33. One of the best analyses of capital punishment from an egalitarian perspective is Chapter 20 in Ramsey Clark, *Crime in America* (New York: Simon and Schuster, 1970), pp. 330-37.
34. As far back as the late 1950s the Supreme Court, wrestling with the concept of "cruel and unusual," concluded that its meaning must be deduced from— "the evolving standards of decency that mark the progress of a maturing society." *Trop* v. *Dulles*, 356 U.S. 86 (1958).
35. "Major Decisions End Supreme Court Term," *Current American Government, Spring 1977* (Washington, D.C.: Congressional Quarterly Inc.), p. 120. (Quoted).
36. *U.S.* v. *Brown*, 381 U.S. 437 (1965). The enactment at issue in this case was a section of the Labor-Management Reporting and Disclosure Act of 1959, which had been adopted to replace the affidavit provisions of the Taft-Hartley Act. The purpose of the enactment was to protect the national economy from the threat of sabotage and politically inspired strikes.

37. See *Calder* v. *Bull*, 3 Dallas 386 (1798).
38. *Annals of Congress*, 1st Cong., 1st sess., 1789, pp. 454-55.
39. See *Twining* v. *New Jersey*, 211 U.S. 78 (1908); *Hurtado* v. *California*, 110 U.S. 516 (1884); *Bank of Columbia* v. *Okely*, 17 U.S. (4 Wheat.) 235 (1819). The last of these held that the due process clause protects citizens from any "arbitrary exercise of the powers of government, unrestrained by the established principles of private rights and distributive justice."
40. See Justice Frankfurter's concurring opinion in *Louisiana ex. rel. Francis* v. *Resweber*, 329 U.S. 459 (1947), in which he wrote that due process inquiry involves not the "application of merely personal standards but the impersonal standards of society," and courts should thus inquire whether the procedures in question comport with the "concensus of society's opinion."
41. See Justice Black's dissenting opinion in *Konigsberg* v. *State Bar*, 366 U.S. 36 (1961). See also Alexander Meiklejohn, *Political Freedom: The Constitutional Powers of the People* (New York: Harper & Row, 1960).
42. "Specifying the Procedures Required by Due Process," *Harvard Law Review*, p. 1536 (n. 112).
43. Leonard W. Levy, *Against the Law: The Nixon Court and Criminal Justice* (New York: Harper & Row, 1974), p. 440.
44. Ibid., p. 421.
45. Quoted in *Des Moines Sunday Register*, 9 January 1977, p. 5B.
46. "The Other Side," *Newsweek*, 4 December 1972, p. 31.
47. Quoted in *Moneysworth*, 13 October 1975, p. 3.
48. Norval Morris and Gordon Hawkins, *Letter to the President on Crime Control* (Chicago: University of Chicago Press, 1977), p. 70.
49. Ibid., p. 75. Many aid programs are coordinated by a little-known conservative organization in the criminal justice field, the National District Attorneys Association (NDAA) of Washington, D.C. The NDAA has a special Commission on Victim-Witness Assistance, one purpose of which is to untangle bureaucratic tie-ups. Such groups as the NDAA obviously believe that we ought to be stressing equal opportunity for victims instead of equal opportunity for criminals.
50. *Bridges* v. *California*, 314 U.S. 252 (1941). In this famous case, a five-four Supreme Court majority reversed a conviction for contempt of court imposed upon several newspaper editors and labor union leaders as a result of their published comment upon litigation in progress before the California courts. The majority held that the convictions violated the First Amendment's guarantee of free speech made applicable to the states by the Fourteenth Amendment. Speaking for the Court, Justice Black noted that to imply that adverse editorial criticism would "have a substantial influence upon the course of justice would be to impute to judges a lack of firmness, wisdom or honor—which we cannot accept as a majority premise." Also related to the issues of free speech, editorial comment, and criminal justice is *Pennekamp* v. *Florida*, 328 U.S. 331 (1946).
51. *Sheppard* v. *Maxwell*, 384 U.S. 333 (1966).
52. Ibid.
53. Andrew M. Schatz, "Comments: Gagging the Press in Criminal Trials," *Harvard Civil Rights-Civil Liberties Law Review* 10 (1975): 618. Judges prefer to call their restrictions on the press "protective orders." In dealing with contested gag orders, courts "have differed primarily on the question of the applicable standard, whether a clear and present danger of interference

with a fair trial or only a reasonable likelihood of prejudice must be found for a gag order to be permissible." Ibid., pp. 620-21. Judges, of course, can use the traditional contempt of court citation against anybody involved with a criminal case regardless of whether a gag order has been issued and violated.

54. *Nebraska Press Association* v. *Stuart,* 427 U.S. 539 (1976).

55. *Time,* 10 November 1975, p. 43.

56. *Attica: The Official Report of the New York State Special Commission* (New York: Bantam, 1972). The best popular study of Attica is Tom Wicker, *A Time To Die* (New York: Quadrangle, 1975). See also Jessica Mitford, *Kind and Usual Punishment* (New York: Alfred A. Knopf, 1973); and Ben H. Bagdikian, *The Shame of the Prisons* (New York: Pocket Books, 1972). Miss Mitford, like most egalitarians, seems to agree with the ideal of Eugene V. Debs expressed in the statement, "While there is a soul in prison, I am not free."

57. See Robert A. Diamond and Arlene Alligood, eds., *Crime and the Law* (Washington, D.C.: Congressional Quarterly, 1971), pp. 19-22. Some egalitarians are advocating the "death" penalty "for corporations found guilty of certain crimes or recidivism: their charter would be revoked." Ibid., p. 22. Also useful is Edwin H. Sutherland, *White Collar Crime* (New York: Dryden Press, 1969).

58. The text of the Ford pardon of Nixon reads as follows: "NOW, THEREFORE, I, Gerald R. Ford, President of the United States, pursuant to the pardon power conferred upon me by article II, section 2, of the Constitution, have granted and by these presents do grant a full, free, and absolute pardon unto Richard Nixon for all offenses against the United States which he, Richard Nixon, has committed or may have committed or taken part in during the period from January 20, 1969 through August 9, 1974. In witness whereof, I have hereunto set my hand this eighth day of September in the year of our Lord Nineteen Hundred Seventy-Four, and of the independence of the United States of America the 199th." Quoted in John H. Ferguson and Dean E. McHenry, *The American System of Government,* 13th ed. (New York: McGraw-Hill, 1977).

59. See Clark Mollenhoff, "Commentary: Unequal Justice," *Des Moines Sunday Register,* 26 October 1975, p. 45.

60. The best summary of this complex issue of law and ethics is that contained in Chapter 1, "The Overreach of the Criminal Law," in Norval Morris and Gordon Hawkins, *The Honest Politician's Guide to Crime Control* (Chicago: University of Chicago Press, 1969), pp. 1-28. See also Francis A. Allen, *The Borderland of Criminal Justice* (Chicago: University of Chicago Press, 1964); Troy Duster, *The Legislation of Morality* (New York: Free Press, 1970); and Edwin M. Schur and Hugo A. Bedau, *Victimless Crimes: Two Sides of a Controversy* (Englewood Cliffs, N.J.: Prentice-Hall, 1974). In this fascinating work, a sociologist (Schur) and a philosopher (Bedau) present their different perspectives on the scope and limits of the substantive criminal law. Schur argues that criminalization of certain consensual transactions has adverse social effects far greater than the original harms. Bedau maintains that the phrase "victimless crime" misrepresents the issue, which is more fruitfully analyzed as a matter of privacy and personal freedom from society's moralism.

61. John Stuart Mill, *On Liberty* (Chicago: Gateway Edition, 1955), p. 13. This classic work of political theory was first published in London in 1859.

62. An insightful brief appraisal of the *Model Penal Code* is contained in Morris and Hawkins, *The Honest Politician's Guide*, pp. 140-42.

63. *The Wolfenden Report: Report of the Committee on Homosexual Offenses and Prostitution* (New York: Lancer Books, 1964), p. 52. For a sharp critique of the *Report*, see Patrick Lord Devlin, *The Enforcement of Morals* (London: Oxford University Press, 1965), pp. 12-14.

64. The quotation is from Daniel P. Moynihan. It is included in Morris and Hawkins, *The Honest Politician's Guide*, p. ix.

65. See Leonard Downie, Jr., *Justice Denied: The Case for Reform of the Courts* (Baltimore: Penguin Books, 1972). In this indictment of the U.S. court system, the author maintains that the courts' interpretation of the law continues to give those with economic power numerous privileges not enjoyed by debtors, tenants, or consumers, let alone the minority poor.

66. See Nicholas N. Kittrie, *The Right to be Different* (Baltimore: Penguin Books, 1971). The author, who is Professor of Criminal and Comparative Law at American University, argues convincingly that though the U.S. legal system safeguards fairly well the individual against police excesses, no such protection exists against the state acting as therapist.

5

SOCIOECONOMIC EQUALITY

Judging from the rhetoric of leftist politicians, it would appear that most egalitarians, though delighted with what has been done to advance political and legal equality, remain more than a little pessimistic about the social and economic inequalities that still abound in the United States. In this respect it should be recalled that conservatives and mainstream liberals have traditionally observed U.S. politics and economics through the lenses of the classical pluralistic model, a perspective first described by James Madison in *Federalist* No. 10. They are thus pluralists, and as such they have always insisted that the democratic way of life involves "balancing and counterbalancing among competing groups and because bargaining and compromise are the characteristic political mode, ultimate policy is in the public interest."[1] Not being militant egalitarians, they also maintain that "The system rarely yields unchecked power to leaders and rarely leaves any group of citizens powerless. To this extent, the accent of the system is not so much on power as on consent."[2] For obvious reasons, this pluralistic perspective usually leads to optimistic, if not smug, conclusions about the justice of U.S. democracy and free enterprise capitalism.

Spokesmen for the more militant egalitarian groups dismiss the pluralist model as being a rationalization for an unjust socioeconomic system and a wholly inadequate tool for explaining existential realities. From their vantage point economic, social, and political power in the United States, as well as wealth, are dispersed quite unequally among groups, and the inequalities are cumulative. They are therefore supporters of the "power elite model" of analysis, since it is their view that political and economic power in the United States is concentrated in the hands of a small, relatively unified elite, which acts essentially irresponsibly despite the countervailing efforts of parties, pressure groups, and labor unions.

In the 1950s, Professor C. Wright Mills of Columbia University popularized the power elite model with such statements as the following:[3]

> The power elite is composed of men whose positions enable them to transcend the ordinary environments of ordinary men and women; they are in positions to make decisions having major consequences. . . . For they are in command of the major hierarchies and organizations of modern society. They rule the big corporations. They run the machinery of the state and claim its prerogatives. They direct the military establishment. They occupy the strategic command posts of the social structure, in which are now centered the effective means of the power and the wealth and the celebrity . . . they enjoy.

In a certain sense, it is unimportant that this model, like the pluralist model, fails to provide a completely adequate understanding of the United States and its institutions. The important thing is that the model exists, and that its widely popularized postulates are now believed by thousands of the nation's disadvantaged who, having lost faith in the platitudes of pluralist democracy, seem ready and eager for a radical restructuring of society.

For upper-class whites, the U.S. economic system, like the government, appears relatively benign, open, and genuinely pluralistic in the best sense of that word. But for those demanding greater social and economic equality, the system seems hostile, exclusionary, even monolithic. Certainly neither the U.S. political system nor its economy is wholly neutral, completely open, or responsive to any and all groups seeking whatever outcomes. The U.S. economy, no less than the government, is clearly biased in favor of some things and groups and against other things and groups. This is so for it is in the very nature of political as well as economic organizations to contain value-bias.

As for specific biases, there is some disagreement as to which ones are dominant. However, most people appear to believe that the U.S. system has an upper-class bias and therefore supports values characteristic of capitalism and Anglo-Saxon culture.[4] It is also widely assumed, at least by egalitarians, that just as the U.S. polity comes down in the end to a case of the *ins* versus the *outs,* the nation's economy essentially is a struggle between the *haves* and the *have-nots.* Certain it is that "Those whose interests are favored exercise a hegemony over those whose interests are not, and this relationship is expressed through the network of values, groups, resources, and authoritative positions that make up the system."[5]

Still, though the U.S. economy is indeed somewhat exclusionary, only the most extreme egalitarian would argue that it is totally closed. Changing circumstances as well as governmental policy decisions definitely effect alterations in the economic balance of power. Moreover, though one can scarcely say that the U.S. economy has, without interruption, become progressively more egalitarian over the past two hundred years, it is a demonstrated fact that thousands do rise from rags to righes and that the average worker is *materially* better off than he was a century or two ago.

Radicals are not easily placated by the pluralists' statistics of progress, preferring instead the belief that U.S. democracy "offers half a loaf to many and a whole loaf to very few."[6] And as the radicals' expanded conception of equality continues its challenge to property rights within the liberal ideology, they find themselves confronting four fundamental questions. What are the concrete data about social and economic inequality in the United States today? Which institutions and forces are most responsible for perpetuating current inequalities? What tactics and strategies must be pursued in order to break through the barriers imposed by discriminatory cultural and ideological values and by biased administration of public policy? Finally, how much social and economic equality can the disadvantaged realistically expect without provoking disruptive conflict?

As is the case involving basic data in other areas of life in the United States, the facts about equality and inequality in the economy are bitterly disputed by equality proponents and their critics. Conservatives feel that political democracy and free enterprise capitalism have maximized both equality and liberty, while egalitarians deny that and insist that U.S. society is still class-ridden and besmirched with gross socioeconomic inequalities. Moreover, egalitarians and conservatives not only dispute the realities of economic discrimination, they also disagree as to what role, if any, the federal government should play in investigating and rectifying whatever inequities are found. Predictably, egalitarians would give a much greater role to government in this area than conservatives would. The latter, like Adam Smith, generally argue that any redistribution of economic resources should be accomplished, not by government fiat, but by the *invisible hand* of competition working through the free marketplace.[7]

In the eighteenth century, when Adam Smith was writing, the concepts of equality and democracy were almost entirely *political* ideas, with only a small band of French revolutionaries preaching anything resembling social or economic equality. But once near-universal adult suffrage, the essence of political equality, approached realization in the early twentieth century, the common man and his leaders began agitating for the spread of democratic equality to other spheres, most notably to the sphere of economics. This agitation occurred because the disadvantaged had discovered what the English Puritans and French revolutionaries had discovered before them: that individuals may be *politically* equal without attaining a full realization of their personalities. Furthermore they had become aware of one of the fundamental tenets of Marxian and democratic socialism, which is that economic power is the parent of political power. Today, of course, even conservatives accept that existential premise, albeit less openly than egalitarians do.

Just as the common man learned that political equality, by itself, was not quite as useful as he had anticipated, he likewise discovered that legal equality, so long as it remained essentially formal, was rather unsubstantial. Indeed, it may be said that these two seminal discoveries— that neither political nor legal equality is a sufficient condition of true democracy—have together lain at the base of all egalitarian movements of the present century seeking greater socioeconomic equality.

Those who demand the maximal degree of equality in the economic sphere in the quickest time usually end up as communists or socialists, whereas those who are somewhat more realistic about goals and time are likely to settle for reform liberalism, welfare-statism, or at most a quite moderate version of democratic socialism. But almost all egalitarians, whatever their ideological commitment, appear to recognize—and deplore—the fact that access to the courts is today a function of economic status as political power is a function of money. The Marxians, to be sure, harp most on this democratic "scandal," but even the most moderate liberals perceive it as a significant flaw in democratic systems and another index of the scope of economic inequality.

Although one cannot say apodictically that the achievement of substantial economic equality would have been impossible without the prior realization of political and legal equality, the available evidence suggests that such a hypothesis is plausible. In any event it is clear that lower class citizens, before they were enfranchised and given a measure of equal protection before the law, lacked both the political and judicial clout essential for acquiring a larger share of the general wealth. It must, however, be stressed that the causal relationship here was reciprocal, which is to say that expanding economic equality was both a result and, to some extent, a cause of advances made in the legal and political spheres. The drive for economic equality, in other words, was never entirely dormant while the struggle for legal and political equality occupied center stage of the democratic theater. *There is always more counterpoint than simple progression in history.*

There seems little doubt that of all nineteenth-century democracies, the United States, for all its imperfections, produced the most socioeconomic as well as political equality. There were few really rich people in the country until the latter half of the century. The poor, who were not then jammed together in great cities, could live fairly decently off the land. And, no less important, the natural tensions between the classes and the masses were significantly muted by the easy informality of social life in the United States, which had already become legendary. Almost all foreign visitors commented on that phenomenon.

Although poverty, which is the most visible result of economic inequality, has always existed in the United States as elsewhere, it was not initially the kind of leading public issue here that it was in nineteenth-century England. There the industrial revolution was considerably more advanced; urbanization had proceeded more rapidly there with all its attendant inequities; and English workers, far more class-conscious than their New World counterparts, were quite early forming unions and taking to the streets in confrontation politics well before U.S. workers were comparably politicized. English intellectuals were also ahead of U.S. thinkers in theorizing about the poverty question, as evidenced by the writings of such socioeconomic theorists as Godwin, Malthus, and Ricardo.[8]

The early phases of nineteenth-century industrialism gave birth to a massive problem of pauperism, which all industrial societies had somehow to confront. England, under the aegis of liberal capitalism, confined able-bodied men to the tender mercies of the free market economy; left the fate of most others to self-help, mutual aid, charity, and ad hoc emergency measures; and offered public assistance in the form of poor laws and workhouses only to the irreducible residuum. This attitude of abstention toward the problems of social poverty and pauperism was best encapsulated in the English Poor Law of 1834, "which limited payment of charitable doles to sick and aged paupers and established workhouses where able-bodied paupers were put to work."[9]

In the United States, perhaps because political democracy here was more advanced, authorities used a more eclectic and seemingly more compassionate approach to poverty that combined relief, preventive measures, and mythic propaganda to engineer quiescence. Thus in large cities like New York direct charity, almshouses, and outdoor relief were frequently resorted to, along with such prevention policies as education, religion, temperance, and work training.[10] Meanwhile, in both the urban and rural areas of the country, myths about poverty abounded: that it was mainly booze that kept workers and their families from enjoying a comfortable life; that education would allow the poor to improve their lot; that the lower classes generally were deficient in discipline and self-control; and, most important, that it was the workers' fault, not society's, that they were poor. It should be added that these beliefs have by no means entirely disappeared from U.S. mythology. Their persistence makes fighting poverty all the harder.

The last thing liberals in the United States and England in the early nineteenth century were willing to do was to recognize the real issues behind the blight of poverty. They refused, for example, to admit that a free labor market and an inexhaustible supply of immigrants were bound to keep wages below a decent level. They denied or ignored the fact that business cycles in an unregulated economy would inevitably produce pockets and periods of widespread misery. And least of all were they willing to concede that the comforts of the middle classes, to which most liberals belonged, were in large measure dependent on the inequalities endured by their inferiors.

The nineteenth century's complacent acceptance of poverty as something both natural and basic to the good society was well exemplified by the following observations made by the Scottish pamphleteer Patrick Colquhoun:[11]

> Poverty is therefore a most necessary and indispensable ingredient in society, without which nations and communities could not exist in a state of civilization. It is the lot of man—it is the source of wealth, since without poverty there would be no labour, and without labour there could be no riches, no refinement, no comfort, and no benefit to those who may be possessed of wealth—inasmuch as without a large proportion of poverty surplus labor could never be rendered productive in procuring either the conveniences or luxuries of life.

For most of the nineteenth century, workers in the United States appear to have been somewhat less poverty-stricken than those in Britain, and also rather less embittered. There were probably several reasons for this: the frontier, the abundance of cheap land, the public school movement, the vast size of the country, the diversity of jobs available, and the uplift spirit of Progressivism. In any event, as noted above, U.S. workers became unionized and politicized long after their British brethren, and to this day there is far less radicalism among U.S. than among British workers. Conservatives point to these facts as prima facie evidence of the greater extent of socioeconomic equality in the United States. Egalitarians, on the other hand, deplore them as a tragic case of brainwashing by the ruling elites, which made it necessary for the U.S. government in the 1960s to try finally to come to grips with poverty amid abundance.

As the nineteenth century wore on, both poverty and affluence increased in industrial societies, while the urban poor were assimilated conceptually into the "working class" or "proletariat." The areas of social disorganization expanded, and almost all governments—even those most committed to laissez-faire capitalism—were forced to extend their public systems of relief and display a less negative attitude toward the problem of material poverty.

With the advent of the twentieth century, U.S. workers, like their British and European counterparts, began demanding not symbolic reform but genuine socioeconomic democracy to include at least a minimum standard of life for all citizens and a guaranteed minimum wage. Such unprecedented demands were encouraged by egalitarians and abhorred by economic libertarians, but for almost a century now they have been steadily escalating in scope and volume. A brief appraisal of why this is so is now in order.

Politically, the chief factors promoting U.S. workers' militance were expansion of the franchise to non-propertied adult citizens, formation of labor unions and workers' pressure groups, establishment of the Populist and socialist parties, and the increasing leftward orientation of the Democratic Party. The first and last factors were particularly crucial, for once the workers were enfranchised, the Democrats, as far back as the Jackson Era, perceived that their best hope of electoral success was to snare the bloc vote of the lower classes by offering workers the prospect of socioeconomic legislation to alleviate their depressed condition. That remains the chief electoral strategy of the Democrats, and it seems to have benefited both the Democratic Party and aspiring workers.

Legally, the chief causal factors were federal anti-trust legislation, a growing friendliness on the part of the courts toward union agitation, the Norris-LaGuardia Act of 1932 that made yellow-dog contracts unenforceable in the federal courts, and the Wagner or National Labor Relations Act of 1935 that formally guaranteed the right of workers to organize and bargain collectively through representatives of their own choosing. This Act and the National Labor Relations Board (NLRB) set up to administer its provisions were a tremendous boon to the U.S. labor movement; and by the end of the 1940s, when the somewhat anti-labor Taft-Hartley Act took effect, union membership in the country had almost quadrupled. Not surprisingly, this growth was accompanied by increased economic and political power for unionized workers and by mounting opposition to the unions' egalitarian pressures from conservatives and businessmen, who had long been wedded to economic libertarianism.[12]

Socially, the greatest boost to workers' morale and confidence came from the conversion of the United States from an illfare state with an essentially self-regulating capitalist economy into a welfare state committed to policies of full employment. This conversion occurred under the aegis of the New Deal and was formalized by the passage by Congress in 1935 of the Social Security Act, which laid the foundations for womb-to-tomb security for all U.S. citizens.[13]

As subsequent events would show, the results of this historic act were somewhat ambivalent. for though it eventually improved the lot of the average U.S. worker and made him more ready to stand up for his rights, it also in a sense deradicalized him, for a time at least, by reducing the attractions of communism and other forms of socioeconomic radicalism. Thus, the Social Security Act was a kind of ideological vaccination of the workers, since by inoculating them with a small amount of "communist" welfarism (social security), it permanently immunized them against the live Marxian or socialist virus. Of course, conservatives believed in 1935, and many still believe, that the vaccine was almost as subversive of true freedom as the virus itself.

A final group of factors, basically international in nature, likewise helped to make the poor in the United States somewhat more aggressive in seeking socioeconomic equality. Chief among these were World War II, in which thousands of poor workers put their lives on the line for the American way of life; and, later, the postwar advances of world communism. True, only a very few U.S. workers have ever been seduced by the lures of communism or socialism. Still, the leaders of the working classes have been able to use the communist threat as yet another reason for maximizing economic equality now before those mired in poverty become disillusioned with democratic government. It is the kind of shock therapy that leaders of aspiring groups have used throughout history—and often quite successfully.

Although the New Deal was the first truly major political movement in the United States to discover poverty and its concomitant socioeconomic inequities, it was not until the 1960s that significant efforts were made toward eradicating poverty throughout the land. A number of interacting factors accounted for this belated awareness of widespread poverty within the otherwise "affluent society" of the United States, chief among which were those just described that had the effect of energizing the nation's working class. But at least three others seem to have been crucial: the growing political power of the poor; the cresting of the Black Revolution and kindred liberation movements; and the popularization of the poverty issue by egalitarian writers and the mass media.

One of the earliest postwar egalitarian writers to push the subject of poverty and economic injustice into the public consciousness was John

Stanley. During the mid-1950s, when most people in the United States were euphoric about the future of democracy, Stanley offered a graphic portrait of impoverished rural America, the thirty percent of farmers who produce only three percent of farm sales. In fact, he argued, and quite convincingly, that the rural poor are so culturally different from most members of the U.S. middle class that *foreigner* is scarcely too strong a term to apply to them. He wrote in this regard that[14]

> Rural poverty is lived in isolation, in the imprisonment of broken fences and unpruned fruit trees that bear small, hard, wormy fruit. Rural poverty is as various as the terrain of the country. It is the lot, in God's mysterious justice, of millions of human beings, including the "single-men-barracks" types, the dark-skinned pickers in the "factories-in-the-fields," and the blue-eyed "crackers," some of whom have their huts dug into the sides of the red hills planted with stunted corn, and whose principal passion is a transference of all their resentment and frustration to a hatred of the Negro—a fellow prisoner. . . . Their final humiliation is their removal—in one light it looks like a deliverance—from their wasted properties, rented or mortgaged, to the great institution of the industrial slum or housing project. Thomas Jefferson died a long time ago.

Considerably more important than Stanley as a discoverer of poverty, because he was better know and more influential, was the egalitarian and socialist writer Michael Harrington. Indeed, before Harrington came along, it had been a long time since anyone had put the case for socioeconomic equality with so much learning, practical experience, and passionate conviction. He also played a major role in the recent devaluation of moral poverty and the transformation of the place of poverty in the U.S. value system.

The work on poverty that brought Harrington to the attention of the reading public and made his ideas a force in national politics was *The Other America,* published during the Kennedy Administration.[15] In this and other works, Harrington traced the roots of the poverty problem to the class character of U.S. society and to the commercial logic that pervades governmental decisions. He also stressed, over and over again, that poverty is "a culture, an institution, a way of life,"[16] and that "To be impoverished is to be an internal alien, to grow up in a culture that is radically different from the one that dominates society."[17] Given his empathetic views, it was only natural that Harrington would agree with those social scientists who have always stressed that "In political life, the poor are fatally handicapped by their lack of resources. Most are too ignorant, too young and unsophisticated, too sick, too miserable, or too old to achieve anything like their political potential."[18]

One of the most striking results of the merging in the 1960s of the Black Revolution and the poverty media blitz was the decision of the Kennedy-Johnson Administration to launch a major federal attack on economic inequality. Though many factors were involved in this controversial decision, three seem to have been central: Kennedy's travels; his sympathetic reading of Harrington's *The Other America;*[19] and the Democrats' fear of losing the black vote if they failed to make a dramatic anti-poverty move. Of course, to point this out is not to embrace, uncritically, a simplistic explanation of one of the most complex events in the history of the poverty struggle. It is simply being realistic.

According to numerous authorities, President Kennedy's consciousness of poverty was strongly "sharpened and accentuated by his tour of West Virginia in the primary campaign of 1960," well before the Harrington book was published and called to his attention.[20] And by 1963 he had committed himself to a major attack on poverty; but then he was gunned down in Dallas, leaving the commitment to be taken up by his successor.

President Johnson promptly made the Kennedy commitment his own, saying, "That's my kind of program."[21] He would then go on to demonstrate in a variety of ways his belief that no single problem would so test his Great Society's ability to cope with contemporary realities as the issue of economic inequality, especially urban poverty. He was right.

Johnson's war on poverty really began with his eloquent message to Congress on March 16, 1964, which revealed the Texan's astute manipulation of the public mood of grief and guilt after Kennedy's martyrdom to prod Congress into taking meaningful action against inequality in all its forms. In that famous address, he pointed out that "We are citizens of the richest and most fortunate nation in the history of the world" but one-fifth of our population "have not shared in the abundance which has been granted to most of us, and on whom the gates of opportunity have been closed." We shall therefore commence a "national war on poverty," he promised, "because it is right, because it is wise and because, for the first time in history, it is possible."[22]

The heart of Johnson's message was his proposal that Congress proceed at once to enact the Economic Opportunity Act of 1964, which he suggested would strike at the causes and not just the consequences of poverty. Indeed, almost two-thirds of the message was devoted to detailing specificities of his revolutionary proposal. But, of course, what most people remembered were the unequivocal commitment to a war on poverty and the ringing, almost Biblical rhetoric. Nothing like it had been heard in Washington since the days of F.D.R.

Acting with amazing dispatch considering the innovative nature of the Johnson proposals, Congress followed the chief executive's bidding and passed the Economic Opportunity Act of 1964. It also created the Office of Economic Opportunity (OEO) within the Executive Office of the President as a coordinating command post to distribute federal funds to other agencies and to operate a variety of anti-poverty programs through its own staff. The most important of these were Operation Headstart for disadvantaged preschool children, the Neighborhood Youth Corps for teenage school drop-outs, and the Community Action Programs that were to be administered with maximum feasible participation of the members of groups for whose benefit the act was passed. The Community Action Programs quickly became the most controversial of OEO's activities and the most criticized by conservatives. But despite the controversy that surrounded the Programs, their purpose was clear enough—namely, to avoid the fragmentation and middle-class bias that had characterized most traditional welfare projects and to apply a *curative* strategy to the problem of the poor.[23]

Hoping to gain the liberal community's full backing for his war on poverty, Johnson appointed R. Sargent Shriver, Jr., brother-in-law of President Kennedy, to head the Office of Economic Opportunity and to be the overall director of the anti-poverty crusade. Shriver had earlier headed the experimental overseas Peace Corps, one of the most innovative ventures of the New Frontier, and he became the last member of the Kennedy family to remain in the Johnson Administration. Later he would serve as ambassador to France, and in 1972 would run unsuccessfully for the vice presidency on the same ticket with Senator George McGovern.

One of the unexpected but significant results of the founding of OEO was the degree to which its activities advanced not only economic but also legal equality. This meshing of two key egalitarian objectives stemmed from the vigorous work of the OEO-financed lawyers, who informed disadvantaged people of their legal rights and who, by dint of determined litigation, won important constitutional victories over restrictive legislative and administrative policies. A couple of statistics will suggest the efficacy of the OEO lawyer's work. It has been estimated that before the creation of OEO, less than half of the nation's poor who were eligible for welfare were actually receiving benefits. Within a few years the percentage of welfare recipients had substantially increased, despite high prosperity; and by 1969, the number of persons receiving Aid to Families with Dependent Children had almost doubled over what it had been in the year of OEO's creation.[24] Though there were several reasons for this extraordinary expansion of the welfare system in the years of the Great Society, there can be no gainsaying the crucial part played by OEO lawyers and community organizers.

Another quite unintended result of the Economic Opportunity Act was an escalating series of picketings, sit-ins, and riots that resulted, in part at least, from the long hours spent by OEO lawyers and organizers motivating the poor and encouraging them to pressure state-local and federal bureaucrats. Traditionalists viewed such tactics as revolutionary and freedom-destroying, and they insisted—quite rightly—that Congress had not meant to energize the poor to that degree. But, notwithstanding such criticisms, the pressure politics confirmed that OEO was achieving one of its basic goals: bringing the poor into the system by which government policies affecting them would be determined. The question was whether the poor's maximal participation was creating understanding or confusion.

The war on poverty was by no means confined to the Economic Opportunity Act and the OEO-sponsored Community Action Programs, though they generated most of the acrimony that divided egalitarians and libertarians. It included also a number of other programs that, directly or indirectly, were designed to advance the socioeconomic equality of the nation's poor while carrying out Johnson's conviction that overall planning for socioeconomic justice must of necessity originate in the executive branch.

An integral part of the war on poverty was a succession of Great Society enactments that included the Civil Rights Act of 1964, the Voting Rights Act of 1965, the Civil Rights Open Housing Act of 1968 and, most revolutionary, the health insurance program known as Medicare. The authorization of Medicare in 1965, over the bitter opposition of the American Medical Association, was of direct economic benefit to the aged of all classes, and it represented a major step forward in social legislation because, for the first time in the United States, social insurance programs had been developed to cover a substantial part of the health care costs of senior citizens. Medicare and state-controlled Medicaid programs constituted what might be called *semi-socialized* medicine. But because of the commitment to the myth of free enterprise, the enabling legislation paid maximum deference to private medicine and the insurance industry and ended up being a mass of needless complications. One of the ironies of Medicare, which is largely financed by social security payroll taxes, is that the nation's doctors, who spent a generation fighting the concept when they might better have been seeking new ways to fight disease, found themselves among the primary beneficiaries of the legislation. Indeed, spokesmen for the poor have frequently complained that the law meant far more to the doctors than to poor people.[25]

More than has generally been realized, the Johnson war on poverty, in all its multi-faceted splendor, was less a case of reform liberalism than yet another chapter in the long cyclical history of Populism, the quintessential protest ideology of the United States since at least the days of Jacksonian democracy. As such it rested "on a base of individualism, egalitarianism, and materialism, demanding that the wealth of the nation be distributed more equitably between rich and poor."[26]

Though the war on poverty was indeed moderately populistic, it did not, of course, go as far in pushing economic equality as would left-wing Populism. That doctrine, advocated recently by such men as George McGovern and Fred Harris, proposes substantial redistribution of wealth and fundamental changes in U.S. society. Even further from the Johnson anti-poverty crusade were the proponents of socialism, who believe not only in the redistribution of property, but also in "the creation of a community, and a kind of person, where cooperative effort would be natural and shared rewards assumed."[27] But when all that is said, there is still no denying that the war on poverty was a great leap forward from the palliatives of the New Deal, Fair Deal, and New Frontier, since it stressed rehabilitation far more than relief.

As most observers expected, conservatives treated the war on poverty as though it were little more than a conspiratorial view of economic determinism, which perhaps, in a way it was. Indeed, they suspected it was a first cousin of socialism, which has always viewed "competitive individualism as destructive and inevitably unsatisfying."[28] In addition, well aware of the popular antipathy to socialism in the United States, they lost no opportunity to denounce the anti-poverty crusade as both socialistic, if not communistic, and inimical to the basic freedoms of the U.S. middle class.

Though Samuel Johnson once wrote that "a decent provision for the poor is the best test of civilization,"[29] a thought clearly shared by the Old Testament prophets, modern political conservatives have generally assumed poverty to be the natural condition of the masses and thus ineradicable. Indeed, they feel—and have always felt—that "too much public benevolence fosters indolence and moral flabbiness."[30] During the election of 1964, Barry Goldwater insisted that the war on poverty, which he thought overrated, could only be won "when we *work* our way to wealth."[31] Somewhat later Maurice Stans, reflecting on the "New Economics" of the Kennedy and Johnson Administrations, spoke darkly of "The risk of loss of personal freedoms—a price which most likely would have to be paid for the all-powerful central government that long-range economic planning and controls would bring and high spending would create."[32]

The conservative counterattack on the poverty war reached a soaring crescendo of passion in the 1968 elections, when the right wing succeeded in making welfare a bigger political issue than poverty had been in the early '60s. They did that by harping constantly—and demagogically—on welfare chiselers, radical agitators, and incompetent welfare bureaucrats. Of all the right-wing politicians who chanted the anti-welfare litany, Ronald Reagan unquestionably made the most political capital out of it and even got the California legislature to reduce eligibility. Meanwhile, a recession hit the country, and legislators everywhere came under mounting pressure to tighten their welfare budgets without regard to protests from the poor. Of course, the poor complained about the cutbacks but did not revive the confrontation politics of the mid-1960s. They were apparently too weary to do so.

In retrospect, it now appears that egalitarian leaders in the Great Society years played into the hands of conservative foes of the poverty war by neglecting their natural allies and, all too often, resorting to counterproductive tactics. They relied, in the first place, much too heavily on the bureaucracy and the judiciary, while paying too little attention to the nuts-and-bolts of ward politics, such as registering the unregistered and voting as a bloc on election day. Secondly, their polemical stress on what is *dserved by,* and *owed to* the poor—however morally justified—was obviously more certain to generate a negative legislative reaction than more pragmatic language. Most people in the United States were simply not prepared to embrace the idea that tax-supported welfare is *owed to* or *deserved by* anybody whatever. Thirdly, their advice to the poor to leave menial jobs and seek public assistance was probably not in the best interest of either the poor themselves or the nation at large. The leaders who reportedly offered such advice probably believed that an increase in the welfare rolls would perforce lead to a better system and, at the same time, be good for the recipients. Fourthly, most egalitarian spokesmen in the 1960s appeared to be operating with minimal theoretical baggage, a flaw that became fatal when the innards of the poverty war were exposed to public and legislative scrutiny, and the program's defenders were unable to come up with coherent theories of equitable entitlement to income and minimum provision of public goods. Finally, the anti-poverty crusaders, preferring ideological purity, legalistic rhetoric, and grand public relations gestures, paid little more than lip-service to such groups as the elderly, the rural poor, and labor-oriented liberal politicians, who might have been induced to coalesce with them. Through that neglect, the crusaders revealed an unforgivable ignorance of the U.S. political process and both deceived and ill-served their vast, amorphous constituency.

Egalitarians were both shocked and embittered when, shortly after taking office on January 20, 1969, the Nixon Administration made clear that it had little sympathy with the war on poverty and would dismantle as much of it as possible, most notably OEO, which by then had become "the scene of great confusion."[33] The Nixonians maintained that the Johnson crusade had federalized programs that should have been left to state-local initiative, and in the process created more partisan rancor and intergovernmental squabbling than anything else. They also argued that continuing the war would result only in throwing good dollars after intractable problems.

To wean the public over from the Great Society's problem-solving focus and its soaring idealism, Nixonians constantly stressed the costs of fighting poverty, the burgeoning federal bureaucracy, the mounting welfare rolls, th overselling of the program, the disregard of human nature, the crab-like pace of achievement in poverty eradication, and the appalling quality of Community Action Program (CAP) administration. It was, indeed, hard to find anybody who was enthusiastic about the latter; and as one objective observer has noted, the CAPs "were little more than a number of separate 'component programs' put together in one binder. It was the rare program that developed those linkages among programs that community action was supposed to facilitate."[34] Another respected observer noted that with the advent of the war on poverty, the nation found itself "confronting the uncomfortable possibility that human beings are not very easily changed after all."[35] While objective observers were merely pessimistic about the poverty war, the Nixonians were almost gleeful in their conviction that the war had been a liberal "crash" program that did not amount to a hill of beans in terms of rehabilitating poor people.

Although the war on poverty had become unpopular even before Nixon took over the White House, the task of *bureaucricide* in this case proved rather more difficult than expected. A majority of Congress opposed OEO's outright demise, as did, of course, the nation's influential liberal media. Gradually, however, the Nixon men succeeded in achieving most of their goals. Thus, "The Office of Economic Opportunity was eventually 'reorganized' by the Nixon administration, which transferred its educational and manpower training programs to other departments and then relegated OEO to the status of the 'laboratory agency.' "[36] In the meantime, the Legal Services Corporation was set up as an autonomous agency to carry on the controversial legal-aid activities formerly financed by OEO; the migrant workers' program was shifted to the Department of Labor; and various health projects were transferred to HEW.

Clearly, the war on poverty had been something less than an outstanding success, but the precise reasons for its failures are still a matter of sharp debate. Conservatives believe it was ill conceived, hastily thrown together, never really integrated, and oversold from the start. Liberals, on the other hand, deny that it was a total failure and insist that with a little more zeal and support from its originators, it could have brought about a massive reduction of economic poverty. As for specifics, liberals and egalitarians point to its weak funding, the high turnover in administrative personnel, the lack of cooperation from local political figures, the failure to get at the root causes of poverty, and—perhaps most lethal—the popular identification of the whole endeavor as a "black program."[37] In any event, whatever the reasons, the war on poverty by the early 1970s had been transformed into a war on the poverty-fighters! Of such ironies is the stuff of U.S. politics compounded.

Mr. Nixon did not, however, always come down on the side of middle-class liberties and against the equality claims of the disadvantaged, for in 1969 he became the first president in U.S. history to propose a comprehensive Family Assistance Plan (FAP) or guaranteed annual income "despite opposition or indifference to it from at least half his cabinet."[38] His income maintenance proposals were incorporated into a general Welfare Reform Program, which he presented to Congress as a substitute for the nation's chaotic welfare system. Speaking on national television on August 12, 1969, he sounded almost like an egalitarian when he declared that "The tragedy is not only that it [the welfare system] is bringing states and cities to the brink of financial disaster, but also that it is failing to meet the elementary human, social and financial needs of the poor. It breaks up homes. It often penalizes work. It robs recipients of dignity. And it grows. Benefit levels are grossly unequal."[39]

Mr. Nixon proposed that the bulk of the existing welfare system, with its byzantine bureaucratic procedures, be dismantled and replaced with a federally administrated plan, in accord with which all low-income families with children would be eligible to receive family assistance. The federal government would provide uniform benefits to insure that a family of four received an agreed upon minimum income; and, of course, as earned income increased (beyond $750 per year), federal aid would be reduced. Adult family members would be required to register for work and accept suitable employment when offered. The states meanwhile might supplement federal grants, though they would be under no legal obligation to do so.

In the beginning, despite the suspicions of egalitarians, it appeared that Mr. Nixon was strongly determined to do something about the bad features of existing welfare policies: the "disincentives to work, discouragement of family life, inequalities among the states, and discrimination against the working poor."[40] He waxed considerably more eloquent than usual in his television address when, in defense of his Family Assistance Plan, he argued that[41] for the first time, the government would recognize that it has no less of an obligation to the working poor than to the nonworking poor, and for the first time, benefits would be scaled in such a way that it would always pay to work. With such incentive, most recipients who can work will want to work. This is part of the American character.

The Nixon Family Assistance Plan easily got through the House of Representatives, yet by the end of 1972 the measure was dead. The Senate, as so often happens, proved to be a major stumbling block. The opposition there has been aptly described in the following summary:[42]

Within the Senate Finance Committee liberals flayed the bill as inadequate and inhumane, using as their standard a generous income guarantee which the majority of American voters would surely have rejected. The conservative senators on the committee . . . divested FAP's pretensions to consistent welfare reform. They dissected the process of compromise by which conflicting program features were fused and structural reform frustrated. "Work incentives?" exclaimed Senator Williams "What work incentives?"

The ultimate executioner of the Family Assistance Plan was not the Senate but Nixon himself, for it is clear that after persistent pressure from the anit-equality right wing of his party, the President simply lost interest in the proposal and finally entirely abandoned it. Thus, after his landslide victory of 1972, President Nixon did not even bother to resubmit his proposal to Congress. In retrospect, one is justified in questioning the depth of his commitment to income maintenance, since the program did, after all, represent a federalization of a problem that Republicans traditionally had argued should be left to the states. In any event, the Nixon income maintenance plan was still-born; and within the President's inner circle, only Patrick Moynihan appeared to mourn its demise, and he left the White House staff at the end of 1970.[43] Democratic liberals were not entirely blameless in FAP's demise, for they demanded "a more generous bill and were unwilling to settle for half a loaf when the salesman was Richard Nixon, their longtime enemy."[44] FAP may not have been "the most important social legislation in 30 years,"[45] as Nixon once called it, but it deserved better at the hands of Congress than an ignominious death.

President Nixon's general philosophy of the poverty problem, which fairly closely paralleled that of most economic libertarians, is well illustrated by the following statements from his August 8, 1969, television address:[46]

Poverty will not be defeated by a stroke of a pen signing a check; and it will not be reduced to nothing overnight with slogans or ringing exhortations.

Poverty is not only a state of income. It is also a state of mind, a state of health. Poverty must be conquered without sacrificing the will to work, for if we take the route of the permanent handout, the American character will itself be impoverished.

Nixon's old-fashioned views on economic inequality were to some extent echoed, and buttressed, by the writings of the influential urbanologist, Edward C. Banfield. In a book that was popular during the first Nixon Administration, Banfield quite perceptively pointed out that what has changed in the poverty equation in recent years is not the objective position of the poor but their psychological perception of their deprived status. He wrote in this regard:[47]

The poor today are not "objectively" any more deprived relative to the non-poor than they were a decade ago. Few will doubt, however, that they *feel* more deprived—that they perceive the gap to be wider and that, this being the case, it *is* wider in the sense that matters most. . . . This subjective effect may have more than offset whatever objective reduction occurred in income inequality.

A more liberal, but equally pessimistic, position was taken in 1969 by a prestigious Presidential Commission. Note the following observations from the Commission's final report:[48]

The poor inhabit a different world than the affluent, primarily because they lack money. Often they live an isolated existence in rural and urban pockets of poverty. But most of the poor do not live apart from the larger society in terms of their hopes and aspirations. Through television, magazines, and newspapers, they become aware of what others have. Their aspirations for education and achievement often differ from those of the middle class only in the possibility for realization. . . . The poor are living poorly and are aware of it. They are generally unhappy with their circumstances and would like to be unpoor.

Conservatives, who are apparently willing to accept widespread poverty as the price of economic liberty, strongly aided and abetted Nixon's Thermidorian Reaction against Johnson's poverty war. They, indeed, went further. They implied, in countless speeches and statements, that the freedom-equality paradox in the United States had by the 1960s reached a maximal peril point, and largely because of the Johnson Administration's many-sided assault on economic inequality. A statement by the John Birch Society, put out a short time before the war on poverty got started, illustrates the almost paranoid fears of the far Right about federal efforts to promote socioeconomic justice. The statement reads in part:[49]

> We are opposed to collectivism as a political and economic system, even when it does not have the police-state features of communism. We are opposed to it no matter whether the collectivism be called socialism or the welfare state or the New Deal or the Fair Deal or the New Frontier, or advanced under some other semantic disguise. And we are opposed to it no matter what may be the framework or form of government under which collectivism is imposed. We believe that increasing the size of government, increasing the centralization of government, and increasing the functions of government all act as brakes on material progress and as destroyers of personal freedom.

The Birchers and other right-wingers who argued in this fashion were simply being consistent with their basic ideological belief, which is that liberty should be given lexical and moral priority over competing values in the economic sphere.

It may be true, as somebody once said, that there are doors to the inevitable everywhere. But, of course, the trick is to knock on the right door at the right time. Thus, in the 1960s, egalitarians seemed certain that a whole series of new doors to socioeconomic equality would inevitably open and give further momentum to their cause. But after the war on poverty failed, they had considerable trouble locating the right door.

Eventually they found the right door, and it turned out to be an old one: the door of Social Security. Egalitarians, to be sure, have still not succeeded in recapturing the heady excitement and euphoria that attended the equality crusade in the Kennedy-Johnson years, but when they knocked wisely, if belatedly, on the oldest door in the welfare state, they recovered at least some of their optimism and momentum. So it was that in the election year of 1972 they convinced the Nixon Administration and the Democratic Congress to approve certain amendments to the Social Security system that provided Supplementary Security Income to the aged, blind, and disabled. The new program took effect on January 1, 1974, when the Social Security Administration took over more than a thousand state and local aid programs and mailed supplementary income checks to roughly three million aged, blind, and disabled people, who had previously been the responsibility of state-local welfare departments.

Under the 1972 anti-poverty legislation, "about 5 million to 6 million . . . persons with little or no resources and without any other income will be guaranteed a monthly income of at least $130 for an individual or $195 for a couple."[50]

Another event of 1972 also heartened egalitarians: George McGovern's plan to give $1,000 to everyone and his subsidiary proposal for confiscatory estate taxes. Of course, after McGovern was defeated in the November election, little more was heard of either of these proposals, but the very fact that they were put forward by a major party's presidential candidate brought some cheer to the nation's otherwise gloomy egalitarians.[51]

Some five years later, in 1977, they reacted with mixed emotions when President Carter urged scrapping the existing welfare system and adopting a new program guaranteeing jobs or a decent income for the nation's needy. The Neo-Populist Democrat from Georgia, leaning somewhat in the egalitarian direction, announced a statement of twelve welfare principles that would underpin the new system, which, however, would not be fully implemented until 1981. "Under this system, every family with children and a member able to work should have access to a job," Carter declared.[52] Leaving the details to be worked out by his assistants, Carter indicated in a general way that his proposed one-payment plan would eliminate, among other things, the present Aid to Families with Dependent Children, the controversial food stamp program, and the recently enacted Supplementary Security Income plan. Though, of course, they could not be sure, egalitarians hoped that the new system, if adopted, would be both more egalitarian and more equitable than the existing polymorphic welfare system that has long infuriated just about everybody—recipients no less than working taxpayers.

Initial reactions seemed to suggest that conservatives would not be any more enthusiastic about Carter's wide-ranging welfare reform proposals than they had earlier been about Nixon's FAP. Indeed, since the 1960s, conservatives have become increasingly gloomy about the possibilities of effectively resolving the freedom-equality paradox in the socioeconomic realm. If their casual comments and polemical statements are to be taken at face value, they postulate a kind of freedom-equality asymptote that runs as follow. In a democracy, the development of equality and freedom can be plotted as two curves. One represents the expansion of equality, the other represents its asymptote, the curve of freedom. Both curves are exponential, which is to say that, in the beginning, they both gradually rise and approach one another. Then as political democracy and capitalism mature, their rate of increase rises, pushing their curves up ever more steeply until they reach a sort of vertical explosion. They never quite meet, and there is instead a falling together of the freedom and equality curves. The decline of the former inevitably leads to a decline of the latter, since the fate of the two value concepts is interconnected, and neither can be long advanced in isolation. In other words, the politics involved in the promotion of freedom and equality is definitely *architectonic.*

In the mid-1970s, the most extreme proponents of liberty (after anarchists) and, by logical extension, the most vociferous critics of attempts to advance economic equality by governmental interventionism were not Republicans or mainline conservatives but members of the small Libertarian Party. Libertarians combine conservative laissez-fairism with progressive views of personal behavioralism, as illustrated by the following statements that recently appeared in their Party paper:[53]

> Libertarianism is nothing more nor less than the politics of Liberty. While other parties and groups seek to use the tools of politics to give some groups power over others, to enrich some at the expense of others, or to impose some set of values on those who disagree with those values, Libertarians seek nothing more than Liberty.
>
> In economics, Libertarians advocate the establishment of the purely free market, that is, a market unhampered by government intrusions. We advocate the free, voluntary exchange of goods and services, unhampered by attempts of government power to redistribute income from poor to rich or rich to poor, by attempting to benefit this group at the expense of that, or by attempts to restrict the free exchange of goods and services between human beings. We seek the elimination of wage and price controls of all forms which cause shortages and unemployment, the elimination of import and export quotas, the ending of subsidies, whether to big business or any other interest group. . . . Moved by a passion for justice, by compassion for those oppressed by State power and privilege, we have raised the banner of Liberty.

Although Libertarians and mainline conservatives clearly have a good many things in common, especially their mutual love of the free market, they have at least one fundamental difference. The difference is that while conservatives oppose only welfare for the poor, Libertarians oppose governmental welfare of any kind, whether destined for the rich or the poor. As they are fond of putting it, "We . . . [oppose] those welfare programs which enhance the power and wealth of a privileged minority at the expense of the poor and middle classes—the subsidies to Lockheed, Penn Central, Pan Am, and other big businesses existing in cozy relationships with government power."[54] Egalitarians, it need scarcely be said, warmly applaud their attacks on welfare for the rich and powerful. They do not, however, agree that liberty should always be assigned a higher priority than equality.

Generally speaking, conservatives in the United States look upon socioeconomic equality as a mirage, and they continue to be possessive individualists, arguing that whether people merit their natural and social assets, they possess them legitimately and thus are entitled to what they can earn therefrom in an open, free market. Furthermore, with a singlemindedness worthy of the Ancient Mariner, they never tire of telling horror stories about federal equality programs that allegedly are spinning out of control. Among these is their charge that the budget for federal income maintenance and social insurance programs now exceeds the Pentagon budget, and that does not include the billions that go each year for housing, health, and education. What is more disheartening to the poor is the critics' assertion, largely documented, that the federal social programs designed to mitigate economic inequality are actually helping the middle class more than the poor. Increasingly the phrase *social pork-barrelling* is being used by writers to describe the way that Congress has expanded programs for the disadvantaged into billion-dollar subsidies for the middle class. It would be hard to find a more apt label for that particular species of legislative legerdemain.

In the final analysis, what the conservatives are now doing, besides continuing to stress freedom and rewards based on excellence, is promoting the politics of contracting expectations to counter what egalitarians like to call the revolution of *rising entitlements.* The anti-egalitarian position in this binary conception has been well stated by Caspar W. Weinberger, former director of the Office of Management and Budget and secretary of Health, Education and Welfare in the Nixon and Ford Administrations. He wrote the following in a national news magazine:[55]

> After five and a half years in various posts in Washington, I come away with a deep concern that if the enormous growth of our pervasive Federal government continues, it may take from us our personal freedom at the same time it shatters the foundations of our economic system. . . . Equalizing of income for all is egalitarian tyranny, not equal opportunity.
>
> Equal opportunity means the right to compete equally for the rewards of excellence, not to share in its fruits regardless of personal effort.
>
> Equal opportunity, based on excellence, benefits all. By rewarding excellence, we share in the fruits of genius. The egalitarians miss this point. They would divide the wealth equally, overlooking the crucial

fact that all human progress throughout history owes its origins to the talented and the enterprising. We must keep a system that allows us to use the talents and excellence of all, no matter what their origin. . . .

If we fail to see this as our real agenda, we risk delivering our destinies over to the cold and lifeless grip of a distant egalitarian government whose sole purpose is to ensure an equally mediocre existence for everyone.

Economic individualists such as Weinberger are, to a great extent, simply paraphrasing the libertarian views of the Social Darwinist Herbert Spencer, a leading intellectual of the Victorian Age. It was Spencer who wrote such anti-egalitarian things as[56]

Pervading all nature we may see at work a stern discipline, which is a little cruel that it may be very kind. . . . We must call those spurious philanthropists, who, to prevent present misery, would entail greater misery upon future generations. . . . Law-enforced charity checks the process of adaptation. . . . The process *must* be undergone, and the sufferings *must* be endured. . . . The truth is that, with the existing defects of human nature, many evils can only be thrust out of one place or form into another place or form—often being increased by the change.

Among contemporary Neo-Spencerians, Robert Nozick is one of the wittiest and most provocative, though he has not had Weinberger's public exposure. In the mid-1970s, he published a provocative book that enjoined both moral philosophy and the government to let the free market work its way.[57] His arguments, though controversial, were finely crafted, and what they amounted to was a new justification for the minimal, property-protecting state. The book, however, ignored the disadvantaged who lack market leverage, and seemed to imply that earnings are generally properly won and never arbitrarily denied—a very big assumption.

Egalitarians accuse people like Weinberger and Nozick of polemical overkill and condemn their writings as a classic example of sacrificing equality for the privileged freedoms of a small elite. As one egalitarian journal recently put it, "Despite our democratic creed, we are not a very egalitarian society. Social and class distinctions seem to be hardening, income inequalities rising and the sway of corporate America constantly increasing."[58] Leftists say, moreover, that attacks on welfare and other equality programs "provide a good scapegoat, and simultaneously reinforce the work ethic and add to pressures for people to accept lower and lower wages."[59]

Obviously, there is a certain amount of truth in charges by conservatives that intensified socioeconomic equality programs must lead to greater centralization, obsessive economic preoccupations, and a possible decline in initiative, responsibility, contentment, and respect for authority among the nation's poor. But although egalitarians may concede that, they usually counter by saying that the United States is still mainly a welfare state for the rich, and that despite the social programs initiated since the Great Depression, there are more economically deprived people in the country today than ever before. The inequality equation, they argue, is getting worse because of the Nixon-Ford Administration's insensitivity to the needs of the poor, coupled with a bomb-building, corporate-tax-forgiving policy in other areas of the nation's life. They also frequently point out that as the percentage of elderly people in the U.S. population increases, the demands made on the government's social programs, especially Medicare and Medicaid, will invariably expand rather than diminish.

The simple truth of the matter is that from the egalitarian perspective, the social and economic inequalities persisting in U.S. society are both astonishing and unconscionable. These inequalities, moreover, affect a vast range of individuals and groups, but especially racial and ethnic minorities, fatherless families, the elderly, and the handicapped. Why, it is asked, cannot the government simply give money to the needy instead of such things as food stamps, transportation stamps, clothing vouchers, fuel coupons, and housing allowances, all of which must clear a maze of bureaucratic red tape before they are delivered to recipients? Farmers and businessmen, it is pointed out, are given cash benefits, but apparently the government feels that the poor cannot be trusted with direct allocations of tax monies, save in exceptional cases.

The poor, even more than conservatives, are angry with the massive bureaucratization of poverty and welfare programs, for it is they who must stand in line and deal with the monster on a daily basis, while conservatives merely harangue the voters about something that is far removed from their sheltered existence. Little wonder that egalitarians are thinking more and more about fundamental structural changes in the U.S. security program, which according to one writer,[60]

> is shaped by 21 committees of Congress, 50 state legislatures and 1500 county welfare departments. It started as a log cabin and turned into a skyscraper with the log cabin architecturally incorporated. . . . The difficulties of progress have never been more visible than in the failure to streamline and harmonize the fragmented parts in 40 years.

Why, then, is something not being done to bring about a root-and-branch restructuring of the government's anti-poverty program, since apparently just about everybody opposes the present system? The question is surely a valid one, and the only answer is that there simply are too many institutional and ideological obstacles built into the system to allow for any sort of quick, wholesale transformation. Furthermore, it needs to be emphasized that the nation's poor have generally swallowed the myth that the United States is a wide-open society and, visualizing themselves as capitalists-on-the-make rather than as incipient revolutionaries, they simply have never applied the pressure from below that might have forced those on top to initiate fundamental socioeconomic change. This attitude of *optimistic resignation* on the part of the poor has long been the despair of U.S. radicals, who view it as nothing less than a massive case of *menticide.*

Professor Louis Hartz, following up certain insights of Tocqueville, theorized in the 1950s that the lower classes in the United States have not turned the quest for socioeconomic equality into a violent revolutionary movement because virtually everybody has accepted the liberal values of Locke from the beginning and, without a feudal class to destroy, there never has been an incentive to initiate the kind of fundamental value struggles that have so long characterized European political and economic conflicts.[61] It was therefore perhaps natural that in the United States unionism, one of the key means for promoting economic equality, became not a revolutionary crusade for social justice but *pork chop consensualism,* which settled for minimum wages, maximum hours, social security, and time-and-a-half for overtime instead of genuine socioeconomic equality all along the line. U.S. workers, in other words, have eschewed the lures of utopia and chosen the sybaritic materialism of the welfare state. According to Hartz, that was wholly to have been expected.

Yet another thing that has prevented the radicalization of the quest for equality in the United States is the fact that competition among the nation's disadvantaged groups is often more violent and protracted than that between the dissenters and the system they purport to oppose. There are no doubt several reasons for this anomaly—historical, cultural, racial, to name just three. But unquestionably one of the most important is the scarcity of access to the system, especially via the media, which compels the complainers to out-shout, out-demonstrate, and otherwise outdo one another to attract the attention of politicians and the general public. Thus it is no accident "that in recent years in America blacks, women, students, and others have each claimed to be the 'most oppressed' group in American society, [and] have each tried to characterize themselves as the true 'niggers of the world.' "[62]

On top of the internecine warfare that constantly divides the various segments of the lower classes, there remains the semantic and empirical difficulty of arriving at mutually agreeable criteria of such abstract concepts as *deprived, disadvantaged,* and *poor.* Traditionally, socioeconomic inequality has been construed in narrow pecuniary (usually income) terms and most, though not quite all, of the disadvantaged groups seem to have gone along with that construction. They may, however, have been hurting themselves and their cause by so doing, since a strictly materialistic conception of *deprived* neglects the psychological and political roots of exploitation in relationships conditioned by domination and submission as well as by depersonalization and alienation. Thus, for example, industrial workers might have their wages doubled and be provided with every conceivable benefit that the welfare state is capable of devising, yet still be *deprived* if their conditions of work remain unchanged and if the status of their trades is not psychologically or otherwise raised. Aware of all this, the nation's radicals have long contended that egalitarian reformers are wrong to focus on equalizing income without at the same time giving more thought to the fundamental social problems inherent in the very nature of industrial capitalism—problems that exist regardless of whether incomes are equitable.

Conservatives, fearing a radical destabilization of the precarious democratic balance if socioeconomic egalitarianism gets out of hand, are understandably pleased that the quest for equality has so far emphasized the *material* face of politics characterized by power, command, authority, and sanction. What they most fear now is that this quest may be radicalized by the super-militants, who will begin stressing the ideal face of politics described by legitimacy, equity, obligation, and justice.

If one can take the 1960s as prophetic rather than as a mere digression from national tradition, one can make a plausible case for the argument that the radical movement in the United States has somewhat more strength and support than commonly thought, thus lending credence to conservative fears. It is possible that somewhere between two and three million people participated directly in the anti-poverty, anti-war, and civil rights protests of the 1960s, while millions of others, though remaining on the sidelines, sympathized with the goals if not always the tactics of the protesters, To be sure, most of the protest groups disbanded or became inactive in the 1970s; yet many groups have continued, and new ones have been formed, to fight for radical socioeconomic causes. None of this, of course, portends the early downfall of capitalism, but recent developments at least suggest that the future quest for equality may be more radical than it has been up to this point.

In 1975, former U.S. Senator Fred Harris, campaigning as a Neo-Populist for the Democratic presidential nomination, gave an inkling of the advanced egalitarian position when he stated that "If we take the rich off welfare—stop the direct subsidy and the tax subsidies to the super-rich and the giant corporations—we can get this country back to work."[63] In the same year, John Kenneth Galbraith published a new book that recapitulated a major theme of his past work: that economic inequality is needlessly created through the exercise of unrestrained market power by large industrial corporations. And what is his solution to that problem? A fiscal policy better designed to redistribute income equitably; direct wage and price controls in those sectors of the economy that create an inflationary dynamic of their own; and no controls where market forces are allowed to determine price levels.[64] Two years earlier, to the considerable delight of militant egalitarians, Galbraith argued in a widely discussed book that because socialism is necessary, it can happen—i.e., capitalism will evolve into socialism.[65]

The most eloquent and provocative proponent of a more radical approach to the quest for economic equality is not Galbraith but Michael Harrington who, as indicated earlier, was one of the "discoverers" of massive poverty in the affluent society. During the early 1970s, Harrington, in a series of speeches, articles, and books, stepped up his attacks on capitalism and recent Republican Administrations and berated Democrats and liberals for not showing more of an innovative spirit in confronting the deepening issue of socioeconomic inequality.

According to Harrington, the Nixon-Ford Administration, tacitly abetted by timid moderates, effectively propagated a myth or "Big Lie" about recent attempts to end economic inequality—namely, that government cannot solve social problems by "throwing money" at them. Such a shabby generalization, he believes, revives the "wisdom" of Herbert Hoover and seems on the way to becoming an article of faith for sectarian, free-market ideologues in the Republican Party. Though willing to concede that egalitarian solutions are sometimes new problems in disguise, Harrington insists that the so-called "failures" of the Great Society "occurred not because Washington acted too radically or too prodigiously, but because it acted too timidly, following corporate priorities even as it spoke in populist rhetoric."[66]

Harrington has consistently maintained that Medicare and the Social Security amendments of the 1960s were real successes. He also stresses the little-known fact that though Social Security is the largest single social outlay, it is the least bureaucratic of the federal programs. As for the "failed" programs, he argues that they were always underfunded and were established with minimum structural changes. In regard to the future, he advocates a truly redistributive incomes policy, the end of tax discrimination in favor of the rich, socialization of certain crucial investment decisions (rails and energy, for example), a rejection of the "Big Lie" about the Great Society, and, finally, an end to governmental subservience to corporate priorities.[67] In those goals, most egalitarians concur.

Just about everybody now seems to agree that the democratic welfare state, a unique invention of the twentieth century, represents the most thoroughgoing assault on socioeconomic inequality the world has ever known. A still controversial concept, it "stresses the role of government as the provider and protector of individual security and social good through governmental economic and social programs. This role for government represents a shift from that of a minimal protector of persons and property to that of a positive promoter of human welfare."[68] Although conservatives will no doubt continue to complain that it destroys freedom, vitiates group voluntarism, weakens individual initiative, and encourages fiscal irresponsibility, few openly advocate its total abandonment. Indeed, all governments are today welfare states to a degree, though the industrialized nations can, if they choose, obviously do more to advance socioeconomic equality than can the underdeveloped countries.

Since World War II, it would appear that Britain has placed a higher priority on achieving socioeconomic equality than almost any other country, though the welfare state is by no means uncontroversial even there. Thus British Tories, while willing to go further on the road to equality than U.S. conservatives, view equality in terms of equal opportunity in contradistinction to their socialist opponents who maintain that real equality can be achieved only with extensive redistribution of wealth. In recent years, the British welfare state has encountered enormous problems, for with less and less wealth to redistribute, the policy of leveling up has tended to become a process of leveling down. The country also seems to be increasingly plagued with the petty politics of envy, as are other democracies.

Statistics clearly indicate that in Britain, the United States, and most other democratic countries, the lower classes are now receiving benefits from the welfare state of which they could scarcely have dreamed a century ago. Chief among these benefits are such tangibles as free elementary and secondary education, subsidized housing, family allowances, unemployment insurance, disability payments, retirement pensions, and free or nearly-free medical care. The provision of these benefits, most of which are also available to the non-poor, has unquestionably reduced economic inequality and thereby enhanced the general freedoms of the disadvantaged. Of course, on the negative side, the benefits have necessitated massive bureaucratization and additional taxation, and in some respects they have no doubt reduced the freedom of the affluent upper classes. To egalitarians, that is a small price to pay for advancing equality; to most conservatives, it is an enormous price.

Notwithstanding the general raising of living standards in the postwar Western world, poverty is far from being abolished, and arguments about the socioeconomic policies of welfare states continue to rank among the most bitter debates in democratic countries. Even in the most advanced democracies, property remains highly concentrated in the upper income classes, while in the United States the pattern of income distribution has remained fairly constant since World War II. In the words of one highly-regarded textbook, the United States is still "a sharply stratified society, in which a very few people receive very large proportions of income and wealth, the majority share a relatively modest proportion, and a substantial number receive very little indeed. . . . And the top twenty percent earns more total dollars than the bottom sixty percent, though the latter group includes more than three times as many people!"[69] This, of course, is no surprise to egalitarians, who have long insisted that the maldistribution of national income is one of the few real constants in the U.S. system.[70] There are many reasons for this, but surely one of the most important is the fact that in the area of taxation only the federal income tax makes any real pretense of being progressive. When that is coupled with the fact that government spending benefits primarily the wealthier segments of the population, it becomes clear that the welfare state, more often than not, advances the privileges of the top of the income-and-wealth pyramid at the expense of the poor and disadvantaged.[71]

Among egalitarians, Marxists and radical leftists remain convinced that the socioeconomic realm is that area of democracy where the freedom-equality dilemma is most basic, most deeply rooted, and most subversive of social justice. With scant concern for balance, they ceaselessly relate the horrors of capitalism in apocalyptic prose, as if to crack an epiphany out of them at all costs, and tirelessly inveigh against the malefactors of great wealth. Both they and the more moderate egalitarians are now demanding a change of priorities for the future, which will put the accomplishment of socioeconomic equality near the top of the priorities' list.

Conservatives, perceiving that the achievement of real economic democracy would turn into a dance of death for their privileged ranks, show no sign of reducing their adamant opposition to the fiscal, financial, and general policy proposals of the income-redistributers. Like the radicals of the Left, they agree that the field of income distribution brings the freedom-equality dilemma into its sharpest focus; but they remain firmly attached to the view that more, not less, entrepreneurial freedom is required to produce the kind of economic growth that alone is capable of simultaneously advancing liberty and equality within a democratic context. Few, of course, would say so publicly, yet it is clear that a number of economic libertarians, now as in the past, believe that a substantial reservoir of poor laborers is a psychological necessity if the dirty work of society is to be done and if employed workers are not to become too militant about wages and working conditions.[72]

Finally, acutely aware that the inequality derived from income distribution is as much a sociocultural as economic concern, egalitarians have recently turned their quest for justice into a veritable crusade against three of the most ancient social blights—racism, sexism, and inferior education. Because this three-cornered crusade has become central to the current quest for equality in freedom, it will be the focus of the next three chapters.

NOTES

1. Grahame J.C. Smith, Henry J. Steck, and Gerald Surette, *Our Ecological Crisis: Its Biological, Economic, & Political Dimensions* (New York: Macmillan, 1974), p. 173.
2. Robert Dahl, *Pluralist Democracy in the United States: Conflict and Consent* (Chicago: Rand McNally, 1967), p. 190. John Kenneth Galbraith is probably the leading economic pluralist, and is rather more egalitarian— even socialistic—than most political pluralists. All pluralist theorists are essentially equilibrium theorists. Galbraith's best known work is perhaps *The Affluent Society* (Boston: Houghton Mifflin, 1958).
3. C. Wright Mills, *The Power Elite* (New York: Oxford University Press, 1956), pp. 3-4.
4. See E.E. Schattschneider, *The Semisovereign People* (New York: Holt, Rinehart & Winston, 1960), p. 71.
5. Smith, Steck, and Surette, p. 176.
6. Kenneth M. Dolbeare and Patricia Dolbeare, *American Ideologies: The Competing Political Beliefs of the 1970s,* 3rd ed. (Chicago: Rand McNally, 1978), p. 48.
7. See Adam Smith, *Selections from "The Wealth of Nations"* (Chicago: Henry Regnery, no date). This is a handy abridgement of one of the most famous and lengthy works of economic theory. According to Smith, every individual in his economic endeavors is "led by an invisible hand to promote an end which was no part of his intention. . . . By pursuing his own interest he frequently promotes that of society more effectually than when he really intends to promote it." Though this hymn to selfishness sounds quite conservative, Smith also wrote that "People of the same trade seldom meet together, but the conversation ends in a conspiracy against the public, or in some diversion to raise prices." Quoted in Williard W. Howard and Edwin L. Dale, Jr., *Contemporary Economics* (Lexington, Mass.: D.C. Heath, 1971), p. 56. Egalitarians maintain that in the United States today Smith's "invisible hand" has atrophied.
8. In this regard, see Oswald St. Clair, *A Key to Ricardo* (London: Routledge, 1957).
9. William L. Langer, ed., *An Encyclopedia of World History,* 5th ed. (Boston: Houghton Mifflin, 1972), p. 658. This legislation supplanted the Great Poor Law of 1601 and amendments thereto.
10. See Raymond Mohl, *Poverty in New York: 1783-1825* (New York: Oxford University Press, 1971).
11. Ibid., p. 163. (Quoted)

12. Merle Fainsod, Lincoln Gordon, and Joseph C. Palamountain, Jr., *Government and the American Economy,* 3rd. ed. (New York: W.W. Norton, 1959), pp. 168-96.

13. Ibid., pp. 766-97. The innovative feature of the 1935 Act was its initiation of *insurance* programs, the purpose of which was to eliminate the need for *assistance* programs. Insurance, unlike assistance, does not suggest charity.

14. John Stanley, "Poverty on the Land," *The Commonweal,* 18 November 1955, p. 163.

15. Michael Harrington, *The Other America: Poverty in the United States* (Baltimore: Penguin Books, 1962). This is a rather angry account of what the author regards as the disgraceful condition of the poor in the United States.

16. Ibid., p. 22.

17. Ibid., pp. 23-24.

18. Walter F. Murphy and Michael N. Danielson, *Carr and Bernstein's American Democracy,* 8th ed. (Hinsdale, Ill.: The Dryden Press, 1977), p. 37.

19. Apparently the Harrington book "made a vivid impression on Walter Heller, chairman of the Council of Economic Advisors, who passed it on to President John F. Kennedy," Reo M. Christenson, *Challenge and Decision: Political Issues of Our Time,* 5th ed. (New York: Harper & Row, 1976), p. 73.

20. Ibid.

21. Ibid. (Quoted)

22. Ibid., p. 74.

23. Among critiques of the Community Action concept, perhaps the most discussed was that by the Democratic liberal and now U.S. Senator, Daniel P. Moynihan. According to Moynihan, attempts "to organize poor communities led first to the radicalization of the middle-class persons who began the effort; next to a certain amount of stirring among the poor, but accompanied by heightened radical antagonism *on the part of the poor* if they happened to be black; next to retaliation from the larger white community; whereupon it would emerge that the community action agency, which had talked so much, been so much in the headlines, promised so much in the way of change in the fundamentals of things, was powerless. A creature of a Washington bureaucracy, subject to discontinuation without notice. Finally, much bitterness all around." Daniel P. Moynihan, *Maximum Feasible Misunderstanding: Community Action in the War on Poverty* (New York: Free Press, 1969), pp. 134-35. For a general description of the various programs in the war on poverty, see Joseph A. Kershaw, *Government Against Poverty* (Chicago: Markham, 1970).

24. Frances Fox Piven and Richard A. Cloward, *Regulating the Poor: The Functions of Public Welfare* (New York: Random House, 1971), pp. 350-51. Professors Piven and Cloward maintain that it has always been the function of relief to "regulate labor"; thus, the waxing and waning of relief is actually employed as means of social control. Ibid., pp. 3-4.

25. According to two reliable authorities, "In 1965 the AMA admitted spending over $1.1 million in a vain effort to prevent the passage of Medicare, which it called 'socialized medicine.' The Association could claim some success, however, in restricting the coverage of the act and in having helped delay passage for seventeen years." Murphy and Danielson, p. 144.

26. Dolbeare and Dolbeare, p. 114.

27. Ibid., p. 119.

28. Ibid.
29. Quoted in Christenson, p. 105.
30. Ibid.
31. Barry Goldwater, *Where I Stand* (New York: McGraw-Hill, 1964), p. 110.
32. Maurice H. Stans, "The Other Side of the 'New Economics,'" *U.S. News and World Report,* 13 December 1965, p. 84.
33. Thomas R. Dye, *Power and Society: an introduction to the social sciences* (North Scituate, Mass.: Duxbury Press, 1975), p. 367.
34. Richard M. Pious, "The Phony War on Poverty in the Great Society," *Current History,* November, 1971, p. 272.
35. Amitai Etzioni, "Human Beings Are Not Very Easy to Change After All," *Saturday Review,* 3 June 1972, p. 45.
36. Dye, p. 367.
37. Ibid. Other factors leading to the demise of the war on poverty were Watergate, Vietnam, the energy shortage, and the Nixon Recession. No less important was the fact that "the public was weary of the whole business." Ibid. On this general subject, see also Mark R. Arnold, "The Good War that Might Have Been," *New York Times Magazine,* 29 September, 1974, p. 56; and Sar Levitan, *The Great Society's Poor Law* (Baltimore: Johns Hopkins Press, 1969).
38. James MacGregor Burns, J.W. Peltason, and Thomas E. Cronin, *Government by the People,* 9th ed. (Englewood Cliffs, N.J.: Prentice-Hall, 1975), p. 454.
39. Quoted in Dye, p. 370.
40. Ibid.
41. Ibid. (Quoted)
42. Theodore R. Marmor and Martin Rein, "Reforming the Welfare Mess: The Fate of the Family Assistance Plan, 1969-72," in *Policy and Politics in America,* ed. Allan P. Sindler (Boston: Little, Brown, 1973), p. 235.
43. Daniel P. Moynihan, *The Politics of a Guaranteed Income: The Nixon Administration and the Family Assistance Plan* (New York: Random House, 1973). On the general subject of a guaranteed income, see also U.S., Congress, Subcommittee on Fiscal Policy of the Joint Economic Committee, *Hearings: Income Maintenance Programs,* 90th Cong., 2d sess., Vol. 1, June 1968.
44. Christenson, p. 111.
45. Ibid., p. 110. (Quoted)
46. Richard M. Nixon, *Presidential Documents* (Washington, D.C.: U.S. Government Printing Office, 1969), p. 1112.
47. Edward C. Banfield, *The Unheavenly City* (Boston: Little, Brown, 1970), p. 124.
48. President's Commission on Income Maintenance Programs, *Poverty Amid Plenty* (Washington, D.C.: U.S. Government Printing Office, 1969), p. 21. Also useful and relevant is Theodore Marmor, "On Comparing Income Maintenance Alternatives," *American Political Science Review* 65 (1971): 83-96.
49. Quoted in James A. Burkhart, Samuel Krislov, and Raymond L. Lee, *American Government: The Clash of Issues,* 4th ed. (Englewood Cliffs, N.J.: Prentice-Hall, 1972), p. 55.
50. Wilbur J. Cohen, "Toward the Elimination of Poverty," *Current History,* June 1973, p. 272.

51. A brief but excellent comparison of the McGovern "demogrant" and
     Nixon's FAP is contained in Arthur M. Okun, *Equality and Efficiency: The
     Big Tradeoff* (Washington, D.C.: The Brookings Institution, 1975), pp. 110-
     12.

52. Quoted in William J. Eaton, "Carter Urges One Payment Welfare Plan,"
     Des Moines Register, 3 May 1977, p. 4A.

53. R.A. Childs, Jr., "Introduction to Libertarianism—Raising The Banner of
     Liberty," *Libertarian Party News,* September-October, 1975, p. 3.

54. Ibid.

55. Caspar W. Weinberger, "On Losing Our Freedom," *Newsweek,* 18 August
     1975, p. 11.

56. Quoted in Ebenstein, pp. 650, 651, 660.

57. Robert Nozick, *Anarchy, State and Utopia* (New York: Basic Books, 1974),
     p. 160.

58. "Energy and National Will," *The Nation,* 30 April 1977, p. 514.

59. Dolbeare and Dolbeare, p. 227. One of the best recent theoretical studies of
     the welfare problem, which amply suggests the tensions of tomorrow implicit
     in today's politics, is Nicholas Rescher, *Welfare: The Social Issues in
     Philosophical Perspective* (Pittsburgh: University of Pittsburgh Press,
     1972).

60. TRB, "Alice in Welfareland," *The New Republic,* 4 October 1975, p. 1.

61. See Louis Hartz, *The Liberal Tradition in America* (New York: Harcourt
     Brace and World, 1955). Hartz and numerous other social scientists believe
     that in the United States the so-called Lockean consensus is so complete and
     pervasive that it imposes an unrecognized, almost tyrannical coerciveness
     upon potential deviants, forcing them into conformity with it. As one
     theorist has put it, U.S. "divisions are over how much of the economic pie is
     to be gained by each interest or segment of the population, rather than over
     more fundamental questions of the method of organizing the economy or
     principles by which distribution should be guided." Kenneth M. Dolbeare,
     Directions in American Political Thought (New York: John Wiley & Sons,
     1969), p. 334. In his highly popular book, Hartz concluded that "instead of
     recapturing our past, we have got to transcend it. As for a child who is
     leaving adolescence, there is no going home again for America." Hartz, p.
     32. The issue of *compulsive consensus* is likewise stressed in Daniel Boorstin,
     The Genius of American Politics (Chicago: University of Chicago Press,
     1953). What all this adds up to is that the United States is a land of *repressive
     stability* stemming from an *ideologized quiescence*—at least in the minds of
     some scholars.

62. Benjamin R. Barber, "Justifying Justice: Problems of Psychology,
     Measurement, and Politics in Rawls," *American Political Science Review* 69
     (1975): 671.

63. Quoted in *Des Moines Register,* 2 September 1975, p. 4.

64. See John Kenneth Galbraith, *Money: Whence It Came, Where It Went*
     (Boston: Houghton-Mifflin, 1975).

65. John Kenneth Galbraith, *Economics and the Public Purpose* (Boston:
     Houghton-Mifflin, 1973). Somewhat similar views were expressed in the
     same year in Staughton Lynd and Gar Alperovitz, *Strategy and Program:
     Two Essays Toward a New American Socialism* (Boston: Beacon Press,
     1973).

66. Michael Harrington, "The Big Lie About the Sixties," *The New Republic*, 29 November 1975, p. 15.

67. See Michael Harrington, *Socialism* (New York: Saturday Review Press, 1972).

68. Jack C. Plano and Milton Greenberg, *The American Political Dictionary*, 4th ed. (Hinsdale, Ill.: The Dryden Press, 1976), p. 19.

69. Kenneth M. Dolbeare and Murray J. Edelman, *American Politics: Policies, Power, and Change*, 3rd ed. (Lexington, Mass.: D.C. Heath, 1977), pp. 94-95.

70. See Robert J. Lampman, *The Share of Top Wealth Holders in National Wealth* (Princeton, N.J.: Princeton University Press, 1962), p. 24. See also *Business Week*, 1 April 1972, p. 56.

71. See Gabriel Kolko, *Wealth and Power in America* (New York: Praeger, 1962), p. 34. Also useful is William Proxmire, *Uncle Sam: The Last of the Bigtime Spenders* (New York: Simon and Schuster, 1972).

72. See in this regard, Herbert J. Gans, "The Uses of Poverty: The Poor Pay All," *Social Policy* 2 (1971): 20-31. The best conservative response to such arguments is Milton Friedman, *Capitalism and Freedom* (Chicago: University of Chicago Press, 1962). Friedman states bluntly that when "equality comes sharply into conflict with freedom, one must choose. One cannot be both an egalitarian . . . and a liberal." p. 195. See also Friedrich Hayek, *The Road to Serfdom* (Chicago: University of Chicago Press, 1944).

6

EQUALITY, RACE, AND ETHNICITY

Of all the crusades for social justice in recent times, none has generated more widespread participation, controversy, or passion than the struggle for racial and ethnic equality. That struggle, a continuous thing in most countries since World War II, has been especially conspicuous in the United States. For that reason, and because of the general focus of this study, the story of racial and ethnic relations in the United States will be emphasized throughout this chapter.

Of course, throughout history racial, ethnic, and religious minorities have generally been the people who were most disadvantaged by political, legal, and economic discrimination; and thus the preceding chapters of this book dealt, in part at least, with the racial dimension of the freedom-equality paradox. But whereas Chapters 3, 4, and 5 were concerned with specific substantive areas of democratic public policy, the focus of this chapter will be on the general scope and nature of racial-ethnic inequality and the remedial actions that have been taken, primarily by governments, to remove this barrier to equal opportunity for all.

Virtually everybody but confirmed racists agrees that racism or racial-ethnic prejudice is one of the most blatant forms of inequality. It is also generally recognized that patterns of racial inequality are directly related to practically every social problem that concerns people in contemporary society. This follows from the fact that most of today's social problems clearly arise from the lack of access of minorities with low resources to conventional opportunity structures, whether these be political, economic, legal, or educational. Egalitarian reformers have traditionally attacked patterns of racial inequality on a variety of philosophical and empirical grounds. Yet the simple truth is that in constitutional democracies such patterns are patently unjust in and of themselves, for they so clearly violate the human values that are central to the democratic way of life.

Scholars have variously defined racism as "A belief that differences among people are rooted in ethnic stock"[1]; as "the doctrine that there is a connection between racial and cultural traits"[2]; and, more specifically, as "the dogma that one ethnic group is condemned by Nature to hereditary inferiority and another group is destined to hereditary superiority."[3] Racism has also been regarded as an especially virulent type of ethnocentrism, since it indiscriminately fuses biological groupings with religious sects, linguistic groups, ethnic minorities, and cultural associations. Furthermore, as a distinguished social scientist has recently emphasized, racism[4]

> is quite different from a mere acceptance or scientific and objective study of the fact of race and the fact of the present inequality of human groups. Racism involves the assertion that inequality is absolute and unconditional, i.e. that a race is inherently and by its very nature superior or inferior to others quite independently of the physical conditions of its habitat and of social factors.

Racism is not only one of the most ancient causes of inequality in social relations, but almost every racial or ethnic minority, at some time in its history, has been victimized by the prejudice it generates. Asians have discriminated against caucasians, blacks against whites, Jews against Arabs, Arabs against Jews, and just about everybody against gypsies. But by far the most pervasive form of racism in modern times, and the kind that has produced the most social inequality is white supremacy racism, particularly as practiced in the New World, South Africa, Rhodesia, and parts of Europe.

Although racism can arise in any place where there are distinctive groups of people living in close proximity, it seems to emerge most often in societies that are quite heterogeneous in terms of race, ethnicity, and education levels. (In this regard, Brazil would appear to be an exception.) Moreover, though skin color is only one component of the biological definition of race, it seems to be central to the creation of racist attitudes and behavioral patterns.

It needs to be stressed here that the racial groups which bear the brunt of discriminatory racism are not always *numerical* minorities, as witness the case of South Africa, but they often are. Furthermore there is something one might call *reverse racism,* which arises when formerly deprived races gain political and economic hegemony and then proceed to treat other groups, including their previous superiors, in a discriminatory fashion. This kind of racism seems to be rather common now in the Third World, where yellow, brown, and black peoples, having thrown off the yoke of caucasian colonialism, are today the ruling elites in their respective areas. In the eyes of Third World apologists, this kind of reverse or reactive racism is more understandable and less reprehensible than the virulent type of racism traditionally associated with European imperialism. But, be that as it may, there can be little doubt that *all* forms of racism diminish both social equality and individual freedom. So do all forms of anit-ethnic bias, which is a kind of racism.

There is also little doubt that racism is a moral as well as a sociopolitical problem; and as such, it is, or should be, of intimate concern to all religious institutions. In the modern world, especially in the West, Christianity has been the dominant, and therefore most influential religious organization. Sad to say, Christianity's record on racism has been ambivalent in both theory and practice, but especially in practice.

Although the New Testament nowhere categorically demanded the end of slavery, thereby implicitly legitimating it, the basic doctrines of Christianity have generally been anti-racist. The early Christians were especially egalitarian in outlook, and racism seems to have been all but unknown among them. Thus, for example, it is stated in the Acts of the Apostles that the Apostle Philip on one occasion baptized "an Ethiopian eunuch, a member of the court of Candace, queen of Ethiopia, her chief treasurer,"[5] and it is probable that the early congregations in Alexandria contained substantial numbers of Ethiopians and other dark-skinned peoples.

In modern times, the Portuguese Catholic missions did not, in principle, acknowledge differences between races, and a baptized Christian was allowed to marry another Christian of any race. Spanish missions, on the other hand, introduced the concept of race separation under the term *casticismo* (purity of the Castilian heritage) and sometimes limited intermarriage between Castilian Spanish immigrants to the New World and non-white Christians. The French Catholic missions in Canada, like the Portuguese, generally did not prohibit marriage of whites with Indians and, indeed, even encouraged it. As for Protestant Christianity, the evangelical Calvinist sects of the United States and South Africa maintained a policy of racial segregation against non-caucasians in deference to theological arguments tortuously deduced from the order of the creation and predestination. In light of this fact, it is rather ironic that the majority of North American Indian and black Christian converts became evangelical Protestants—especially Baptists and Methodists—rather than Catholics.[6]

Although almost all Jews are caucasians, Christian countries, until quite recent times, subjected the Jews under their control to a kind of religio-ethnic racism than is generally known today as anti-Semitism. This hostile and sometimes violent antipathy to Jews is one of the oldest forms of racism and has existed to some degree wherever Jews have settled in the Diaspora. The ancient Romans persecuted the Jews on the ground that they lacked patriotism because of their refusal to participate in worship of the emperor. Their Christian successors were angry with the Jews for not accepting Jesus as their long-promised Messiah and for centuries vilified them as "crucifiers of Christ." In the late Middle Ages, European Christians accused the Jews of ritual murder because of the alleged sacrifice of Christian children at Passover, a legend that was revived in the twentieth century and became part of Nazi anti-Semitic doctrine. The Nazis also went back to medieval times for the Jewish yellow badge, which they ultimately compelled all Jews to wear as a means of ready identification. This badge was first made obligatory for Jews by the Twelfth Ecumenical or Fourth Lateran Council, which met in 1215 and marked "the zenith of ecclesiastical life and Papal power."[7] Although the Council dealt with many other matters besides Jewish-Christian relations, it promulgated a number of legal and other types of restrictions that would adversely affect Jews for centuries. Thus, it branded Jews as outcasts with whom there was to be no fraternization or intermarriage; it forbade them to hold public office or employ Christian servants; and it required them to remain in their homes throughout Easter week. Acting in the spirit of the Fourth Lateran Council, several Christian countries subsequently expelled Jews from their territory: England did so in 1290, France in 1394, and Spain in 1492. The slightly more tolerant Germans did not actually banish the Jews but designated them *servi camerae* or serfs of the state.[8] In that capacity they were heavily taxed and subjected to the most menial jobs.

The earliest persecutions and massacres of Jews were largely religious in inspiration; but since the nineteenth century, anti-Jewish discrimination has most often been based on ethnic-nationalistic and racial pride considerations. Once mythic nationalism supplanted religious internationalism as the basic commitment of Europe and most of the modern world, the Jews found themselves particularly vulnerable, for they lacked a national homeland and clung fiercely to religious and cultural traditions that were foreign, and sometimes obnoxious, to their neighbors. Anti-Semitism, of course, reached its tragic culmination in Hitler's nominally-Christian Third Reich, which was responsible for the slaughter of some six million Jews. Since World War II, anti-Semitism as an ethnic-racial problem has been confined largely to the Middle East and Islamic North Africa. This is ironic, since Jews in the Middle Ages fared considerably better in Islamic than in Christian lands.[9]

Spurred on by the Nazis' anti-Semitism and by the colonial powers' white supremacy racism in Asia and Africa, the United Nations has recently taken the lead in fighting all forms of social inequality based on race, religion, or ethnicity. Even before the U.N. was established, the post-World War I peace treaties had contained important provisions designed to afford better protection to minorities. Thus, certain states in eastern and central Europe, along with Iraq, were forced to agree to a series of obligations toward their racial, linguistic, and religio-ethnic minorities. Basically these provided that all groups would be equal before the law and would enjoy similar civil and political rights without distinction as to race, language, or religion. Minority languages were likewise to be tolerated in the courts and educational institutions. Germany, unfortunately, was not among the countries required to accept provisions for the protection of minorities, save for a fifteen-year obligation respecting the population of Upper Silesia.

In a series of statements and proclamations during and after World War II, among which the earliest were the Atlantic Charter of August 14, 1941, and the Allied Powers' Declaration by the United Nations of January 1, 1942, a commitment to basic human rights and social justice, and by implication equality, was made one of the principal peace objectives of the anti-fascist grand alliance. Shortly after World War II, in pursuit of that objective, the victorious powers set up the International Military Tribunal for the Trial of German Major War Criminals indicted for war crimes, crimes against peace, and crimes against humanity, a large part of which were racially or ethnically inspired. The Tribunal, which sat in Nuremberg under the presidency of Britain's Lord Justice Geoffrey Lawrence from November 20, 1945 to October 1, 1946, applied a rather cautious approach to the concept of crimes against humanity by generally confining it to deportations, exterminations, and genocide. But the egalitarian principles on which the Tribunal acted were later endorsed by the General Assembly of the United Nations. In addition, the Tribunal rejected out of hand the Nazis' contention that only a state, and not individuals, can be found guilty of war crimes. Unfortunately for the cause of racial equality, the Tribunal's somewhat novel principles and rulings have not received the universal acceptance their sponsors had predicted and hoped for. At least two of the reasons for this were the novelty of the trial and the paucity of supporting precedents. Libertarian critics of the Nuremberg Tribunal, among whom was the late Senator Robert A. Taft, apparently felt that the court's actions were more threatening to individual freedom than supportive of minority equality, chiefly because they violated the old legal principle, *"Nullum crimen sine lege, nulla poena sine lege."*

The writing of the United Nations Charter at the fifty-nation San Francisco Conference in 1945 significantly advanced the cause of racial and ethnic equality around the world, at least in a symbolic sense. Moreover, under pressure from the smaller countries, the great powers amended the draft Charter to make stronger the organization's "concern for 'fundamental human rights,' 'social progress' and 'better standards of life'—matters of the highest concern to newly independent and dependent countries throughout Asia and Africa."[10] At the same time, the Economic and Social Council was elevated into a major organ of the U.N., and a wholly "new body, the Trusteeship Council, was also added and given responsibilities for supervising governments of dependent people and of advancing their welfare."[11] On the negative side, although the Charter binds member states to respect and observe all human rights, it also includes a "domestic jurisdiction" clause in Article 2, Section 7 which for the most part excludes litigation about those rights from U.N. jurisdiction. The United States, it should be noted, took the lead in inserting that clause into the Charter.[12] In recent years the United Nations, in the spirit of its Charter, has spoken out particularly forcefully against white racism in Rhodesia and South Africa, forced labor in eastern Europe, and discrimination against the Buddhists in Vietnam.

One of the most significant postwar results of Nazi racism was the drafting by the U.N. in 1948 of the Convention on the Prevention and Punishment of the Crime of Genocide. That Convention, closely reflecting the philosophy of the Nuremberg Tribunal, made genocide, whether committed in war or peace, a crime under international law to be punished by the international community. Article II of the Convention defines genocide as[13]

> any of the following acts commited with intent to destroy, in whole or in part, a national, ethnic, racial or religious group as such: (a) Killing members of the group; (b) Causing serious bodily or mental harm to members of the group; (c) Deliberately inflicting on the group conditions of life calculated to bring about its physical destruction in whole or in part; (d) Imposing measures intended to prevent births within the group; (e) Forcibly transferring children of the group to another group.

More important, Article IV explicitly provides that "persons charged with genocide or any of the other acts enumerated . . . shall be tried by a competent tribunal of the state in the territory of which the act was committed, or by such international penal tribunal as may have jurisdiction with respect to those contracting parties which shall have accepted its jurisdiction."[14] In addition, according to Article VII, genocide is not to be considered a political crime for purposes of avoiding extradition.

Although the Genocide Convention went into effect in 1951, no court of international criminal jurisdiction has yet materialized. Moreover, though well over half a hundred nations had become signatories of the Convention by the late 1960s, no remedial action has ever been taken under it. Still, it is important that the international community has defined genocide as a matter of international concern, which means that any contracting state has the right to call upon the U.N. to intervene to prevent or suppress acts of genocide when they occur. Of course, whether the U.N. does in fact intervene against genocide will depend on a number of political and other factors. Regrettably, the United States has not yet seen fit to ratify the Genocide Convention. If the U.S. government did so, it would be in a far stronger moral position to condemn such egregious acts of genocide as Idi Amin's wholesale slaughter of members of the Langi and Acholi tribes in Uganda.

A particularly vital milestone on the road to racial and ethnic equality was achieved in 1946 when the U.N. Human Rights Commission, under the chairmanship of Eleanor Roosevelt, was established. A still more important one was realized two years later, when the Commission completed its magnificent Universal Declaration of Human Rights as a "standard of achievement." This was subsequently ratified by a unanimous vote of the U.N. General Assembly (three Soviet bloc countries, Saudi Arabia, and the Union of South Africa abstained). The Declaration not only contained general definitions of the traditional democratic civil and political liberties, but also emphasized a vast array of economic, social, and cultural rights, such as the right to social security; right to a job; right to education; and right to enjoy the arts and to share in scientific advancement and its benefits.

The declaration was only a statement of lofty principles until several years later when two agreements—one on civil and political rights, the other on economic, social, and cultural rights—were finally negotiated to give the ideals binding force. They became effective in 1976 with the attainment of the requisite number of ratifications. At the Helsinki Conference of 1975, attended by thirty-five nations, the principles of the declaration were supplemented and given new strength by twenty pages in the Final Act that dealt with "Cooperation in Humanitarian and Other Fields." Though the human rights pledges in those pages are somewhat vague and limited, they add yet another building block to the growing international law of equality in freedom.

As in the case of the Genocide Convention, the United States is not yet a party to the Universal Declaration of Human Rights. Its rationale for not signing is that U.S. rights take precedence over such an agreement and that in any case the U.S. practice is above that set forth in the declaration and subsequent treaties. With the United States standing on the sidelines, international enforcement of basic human rights is likely to be as faint-hearted as enforcement of the ban on genocide. Nevertheless, the Human Rights Commission can investigate complaints, and it can also turn the U.N. floodlight on violations. In addition, it might mediate disputes.

U.S. egalitarians took heart when President Carter, in early 1977, broke new ground in a much publicized address before the United Nations by strongly emphasizing his government's moral commitment to worldwide human rights. He promised he would try to make the United States a party to the four basic U.N. human rights agreements: the Genocide Convention; the Treaty for the Elimination of All Forms of Racial Discrimination; the Covenant on Economic, Social and Cultural Rights; and the Covenant on Civil and Political Rights. Furthermore he proposed moving the U.N. Human Rights Commission from Geneva to the New York headquarters in order that the U.S. news media might more effectively spotlight the human rights issue. And finally, he endorsed an old proposal by Costa Rica for a U.N. High Commissioner for Human Rights as a first step toward the creation of stronger international machinery to deal with human rights issues.[15] In his address, Carter seemed to be tacitly acknowledging that as long as the great powers ride political hobby horses instead of showing real impartial concern for human rights, the U.N. Human Rights Commission is not likely to be accorded significant enforcement powers. Though the state of human rights remains dismal over a great part of the world, Carter's own moral commitment to the cause of liberty and equality appears to be deep and genuine. Some reactionaries fear it may be too deep.

Inequities arising from racism have also been vigorously fought by regional organizations in the Western world. Thus, in 1959, the Organization of American States established the Inter-American Commission on Human Rights; and in November of 1969, the Inter-American Specialized Conference on Human Rights adopted an instrument entitled American Convention on Human Rights (also known as the Pact of San José, Costa Rica). This convention, inspired by the sense of urgency generated in the United Nations, set up the Inter-American Court of Human Rights to settle disputes among member states and develop substantive law in the field of individual and group liberties. Acting earlier along similar lines, the European Economic Community countries and several others in Western Europe ratified a strong human rights agreement for themselves that permits individuals who claim their rights have been denied to take the offender to an international court.

These highly publicized trans-national assaults on the various forms of racism are significant in both a symbolic and procedural sense. Symbolically, they have served notice on the world's racists that they are, in effect, international outlaws without a moral, legal, or other warranty to impose their vicious patterns of discrimination upon disadvantaged groups. Procedurally, they establish practical institutional arrangements for dealing, at the international level, with allegations of racist activities. Of course international law, whether dealing with racism or any other subject, has always been difficult to enforce against strong-willed offenders. Still it is useful for a variety of reasons to have the case against racism-inspired inequality solidly based on specific international agreements.

Of the additional dimensions annexed to egalitarianism in the twentieth century, the most important is clearly the concern for the equal status of racial-ethnic minorities. Moreover, as has just been demonstrated, this is no longer a merely local thing but has become a universal phenomenon. The best evidence for that broad conclusion is the establishment of the United Nations, the series of anti-racist conventions drawn up and approved by it, the rising tide of anti-colonialism, the demise of Western European imperialism, and the recent rise to prominence of the equality-sensitive Third World.

Formerly one of the chief breeders of racial inequality, the United States, as will shortly be shown, has done much in the last few years to shake off that albatross. While that was occurring, the attention of the world's egalitarians has gradually shifted to the racist policies of Rhodesia and the Union of South Africa, particularly the latter. It was in 1948, when Truman was moving against segregation in the United States, that South Africa formalized an official policy of white supremacy racism known as *apartheid* or separate development.[16] In crude political terms, the policy is designed to insure the continuous domination of the country's four million whites over nineteen million non-whites through strict physical separation of the races, especially in housing and public accommodations. In 1959, the apartheid policy was extended to include the eventual setting up of eight reserves or *Bantustans* as homogeneous homelands for the natives. Though the white South African government justifies apartheid in terms of separate development and peaceful coexistence of the races, it is apparent that the country is now actually a police state in which all citizens, whites as well as non-whites, have had to surrender fundamental rights of free speech and protest in order to survive as functioning members of the social system.

The post-World War II attempts to shore up the patterns of racial inequality in South Africa are diametrically opposed to the egalitarian black independence movements that have been sweeping other parts of Africa and Asia in recent years. Not surprisingly, the black freedom fighters of sub-Sahara Africa have attacked South Africa's apartheid policy in every possible forum, and particularly in the United Nations. At the same time they have bitterly assailed Rhodesia's white racism and have threatened to wage full-scale guerrilla war to liberate the blacks of both countries. As the result of such efforts, dents have been made in the walls of segregation, all of which has led black leaders to proclaim that the cracked columns of Africa's white racist structures are cautionary signs of the fragility and mutability of nominal freedom without equality. Some go further and maintain that next to the Nazi policy of genocide against Jews, the South African apartheid policy represents the most extreme form of racism practiced in any modern society. Rhodesia, they say, is not far behind.

Even within South Africa itself, courageous equality fighters have openly assailed the government's racist policies, and many have suffered severe deprivations for so doing. Included among the outspoken domestic critics have been famous authors, the National Union of South African Students, the South African Institute of Race Relations, the Women's Defense of the Constitutional League (the Black Sash), and certain Christian churches, excluding the Dutch Reformed Church. On occasion, there have even been riots by natives against the severe restrictions under which they are forced to live. A few of these have resulted in heavy losses of life, such as the 1976 disturbances in the African township of Soweto, which started when 10,000 school children protested the use of Afrikaans as a medium of instruction in Bantu shcools.[17]

The South African natives alone can never overthrow the tyrannical apartheid system, nor can the U.N. as it is presently structured. The best hope for ending the blight of racism on the African continent would appear to lie in an increase of diplomatic and economic pressure on the white racist governments by the United States and the independent black states. In any event, the revolution of color is now in full swing in Africa, and the black governments in the middle of the continent are sponsoring a growing number of secret training camps for freedom fighters, who may one day succeed in liberating the southern natives from their white oppressors. For their part, Rhodesian and South African whites maintain that not every transformation is a reformation, and most of them appear to believe that a switch to black rule would simply substitute black racism for white racism. Perhaps so, but at least the number of those disadvantaged by racism would have been substantially reduced merely because of the demographic arithmetic of Rhodesia and South Africa. Another possible outcome might couple an increase in equality with a decrease in freedom for both races, as has happened recently in Uganda and Angola.

It is certainly true, as Morris B. Abram, former U.S. representative to the U.N. Commission on Human Rights, has said, that "The world's colored races have become increasingly aware of their numerical majority and increasingly bitter at their continued status of social, economic and political inferiority."[18] That in fact was foreseen back in 1903 by W.E.B. DuBois, who predicted that the main issue of the twentieth century would be "the problem of the color line—the relation of the darker to the lighter races of men in Asia and Africa."[19] Economic deprivation is the most obvious consequence of racial inequality. But in the long run, psychological retardation may turn out to have been the most damaging. Be that as it may, it is now apparent that race war will one day erupt if the non-white peoples of the world are not soon granted full racial equality in freedom. That is the minimal demand of the new revolutionists of color.

In the United States, white supremacy racism, with its attendant discriminations against racial and ethnic minorities, has always lain just beneath the surface, as though to mock the noble dreams of the nation's founders. Genocide was practiced against the native Indians until the twentieth century, and as early as 1619 black captives from the west coast of Africa were brought over as indentured servants and, later, as slaves. The story of the U.S.-African slave trade, which has been told endless times, is one of the most tragic episodes in all of U.S. history; and, indeed, the patterns of behavior it spawned have become a curse that still bedevils almost every facet of U.S. democracy and culture. In the nineteenth century, racism in the United States likewise adversely affected the destinies of Chicanos, Asians, and white ethnic immigrants from southern and eastern Europe. Though not as strong or virulent as in the past, racism remains deeply embedded in U.S. culture and thus continues to obstruct the minorities' quest for equality in freedom.

Some time ago, *The Economist* of London proclaimed "It is in the United States that the racial problem is likely to be solved first. Likely to be solved, or finally and fatally to explode our planet."[20] True or not, it is a fact that serious efforts to solve the U.S. racial problem began back in the early nineteenth century and reached a crescendo of remedial action in the 1860s. Thus, on January 1, 1863, Lincoln's Emancipation Proclamation was issued, declaring free all slaves in the secessionist southern states and opening the U.S. Army and Navy to black volunteers. The consequences of this presidential order were more significant than is sometimes realized. For, among other things, it took from the Confederacy its potential source of slave soldiers, led to the enlistment of nearly 180,000 ex-slaves in the

Union Army, and, most important of all, helped to identify the Union cause with the egalitarian crusade against slavery. The fact that Lincoln, to a certain extent, was pressured into acting by northern abolitionists in no way diminished the timely importance of what seems, in retrospect, to have been a fit and necessary war measure. In any event, it mightily advanced the cause of racial equality, while in the process it inevitably reduced the freedom of white slaveholders.

Following the end of the Civil War, Congress and the states approved three amendments to the U.S. Constitution, which extended the racial equality concept of Lincoln's Emancipation Proclamation. As indicated in Chapter 3, the Thirteenth Amendment (1865) constitutionalized and universalized what Lincoln had earlier done by executive order; the Fourteenth (1868) granted citizenship to the freedmen and guaranteed them due process and equal protection of the laws; and the Fifteenth (1870) extended the suffrage to black adult male citizens. The Fourteenth Amendment, as noted in Chapter 4, has been especially helpful to the nation's blacks, since it gave them for the first time full legal equality with whites. In a very real sense, the Reconstruction Amendments were "the victory terms dictated by the North to the South";[21] and Congress, quite wisely, required the southern states to ratify the Fourteenth Amendment before federal troops were withdrawn and the states restored to full participation in the government.

For a brief time during Reconstruction, blacks in the South were almost equal to whites. However, after the Yankee troops were withdrawn from the southern states, the old white supremacists returned to power; and within a few years they had devised a surrogate form of slavery known as segregation, which anticipated South Africa's apartheid system. The laws that established the patterns and etiquette of racial segregation were called *Jim Crow* laws.[22] These, to the dismay of egalitarians, were validated by the U.S. Supreme Court in the famous *Plessy* case of 1896.[23]

With the end of Reconstruction, the freedmen learned what a number of other racial and ethnic groups have learned throughout U.S. history: namely, that much of what passes for egalitarian reform in the United States is mere symbolism, designed to placate aspiring groups with public policies that have more form than substance, more glitter than problem-solving efficacy. Symbolism, to be sure, has been enormously significant in the long struggle of oppressed races for equality with their masters. Yet one needs to make a clear distinction between tactical ideological symbolism and governmental policy symbolism. The former brings cohesion and unity into an egalitarian movement; the latter, in effect, brainwashes the disadvantaged by reducing them to quiescence when they need to be militant. This is simply another way of saying that for the racial and ethnic minorities of the world, revolutionary symbolism is more helpful than counterrevolutionary symbolism. Revolutionary violence is another matter.

A decisive landmark in the history of U.S. blacks was the founding in 1905 at Buffalo, New York, of the Niagara Movement, "the first Negro protest organization" in the present century.[24] The founders were a group of 29 black intellectuals, headed by W.E.B. DuBois, who was a Harvard Ph.D. and professor at Atlanta University. In essence, the Niagara Movement was a repudiation of the accommodation strategy of Booker T. Washington, proclaimed in his Atlanta Compromise address of 1895, and it symbolized the growing radicalization of young blacks angry at the spread of Jim Crow laws. Its egalitarian ideology was summarized in these famous words of DuBois:[25]

> We want full manhood suffrage and we want it now. . . .
> We want the Constitution of the country enforced. . . .
> We want our children educated . . . We are men!
> We will be treated as men. And we shall win!

In 1909, on the hundredth anniversary of Lincoln's birth, the Niagara Movement merged with a group of sympathetic whites that included Jane Addams, John Dewey, William Dean Howells, and Lincoln Steffens to form the National Association for the Advancement of Colored People (NAACP). Egalitarian in every sense of that word, the NAACP began at once a crusade to better the lot of blacks through litigation, legislation, and education. For a long time only the first and last tactics were effective, and until recently the organization represented almost exclusively middle-class blacks. Still, within a few years of its founding, the NAACP had become a powerful national lobby and an incessant propagandist for racial equality. The group's propaganda efforts were centered in *Crisis* magazine, the first editor of which was the brilliant Dr. DuBois. They became increasingly effective as their pressures on ruling elites intensified, and as their revelations of white injustices to blacks became for the first time nationally known and deplored. This was especially true of their compilation and dissemination of lynching statistics.

Since 1939, the spearhead of the NAACP's anti-racism activities has been the highly regarded Legal Defense and Education Fund. This wing of the NAACP, composed mainly of lawyers, has been extraordinarily successful in advancing constitutional rights for blacks. At the same time it has shown other racial and ethnic groups how to use the technique of lobbying-through-litigation to pressure the establishment into expanding the scope of racial equality.

In the spring of 1954, the long years of patient NAACP litigation paid off handsomely when the U.S. Supreme Court, in the historic *Brown* case, overturned its 1896 *Plessy* holding and invalidated racially-segregated schools as violative of the equal protection clause of the Fourteenth Amendment.[26] Approximately a year later, the Court decreed that southern school boards must proceed *with all deliberate speed* to desegregate the public schools under their control.[27]

Notwithstanding the generation of litigation that ensued, the two *Brown* decisions were towering monuments to the quest for racial equality in freedom, and their impact was felt throughout the world. Technically, the decisions affected only a few southern and midwestern black students and their schools. But, what was more important, they[28]

> constituted a fundamental value revolution in . . . [U.S.] jurisprudence. Up until May 17, 1954, the moral authority of the "supreme law of the land" lay with the segregationists rather than with their opponents. . . . After "Black Monday," however, attempts to prop up the Jim Crow system would be devoid of a legal or moral sanction and, if state action were involved, they would also be unconstitutional.

The Warren Court's new interpretation of the Fourteenth Amendment not only mightily helped to advance equity in the criminal justice field, as Chapter 4 has already made plain, but also generally broadened the whole philosophy of racial and ethnic equality. This was so because it was the Fourteenth Amendment, along with the commerce regulation clause of Article 1 of the U.S. Constitution, that formed the Court's main legitimating base for that extraordinary sequence of federal laws that, in the 1950s and 1960s, finally extirpated Jim Crow racism from nearly every area of public life.

The demise of Jim Crow was most dramatic and most violently-resisted in the field of public education. But no less important were the judicial and legislative mandates to end racism in public accommodations, employment, housing, and voting (here the Fifteenth Amendment was crucial).[29]

Few aspects of the U.S. struggle for racial equality are more interesting than the unprecendented extent to which racial minorities have been assisted, not through a redistributive tax system or by state-local initiatives but by judicial reformulations of legal and constitutional doctrines.[30] There are obvious advantages in such an approach to egalitarian reform: it can be done quicker and more incisively than by alternative means; it produces a dramatic impact on public opinion; and, initially at least, it involves somewhat smaller dangers of political conflict. But as the earlier chapters of this study have suggested, there are serious drawbacks to the use of this approach in a majoritarian democracy, not the least of which is that the non-elective judiciary, shielded from the winds of politics, may be out of touch with the dominant public opinion. In any event, in the United States both the legislative and judicial agencies of government *can* and *do* initiate reform. And for this dual approach to policy reform—a peculiarity of the U.S. constitutional system—few people have more cause to be grateful than the racial and ethnic minorities that in recent years have been its chief beneficiaries.

Though legal-constitutional racism is now dead as a dodo in the United States, and though there has been a substantial reduction of institutional racism in both the public and private sectors, a dismaying residue of de facto racism persists in a wide variety of processes and agencies. This residue is all the more intolerable to egalitarians precisely because it is utterly without legal, moral, or constitutional sanction.

Take, for example, the military, which was one of the first public institutions to launch a vigorous assault on racial inequality. That assault resulted from President Truman's Executive Order 9981, which decreed an end to racial discrimination in the military and equality of treatment and opportunity in the future for all service personnel.[31] Interestingly, that historic equality order was promulgated almost six years before the first *Brown* decision and in the same year that the Supreme Court, in a widely-publicized case,[32] held that court orders enforcing private restrictive covenants based on race and color are unconstitutional because they violate the equal protection clause of the Fourteenth Amendment. The Order also followed by about a year publication of *To Secure These Rights,* a hard-hitting report by Truman's Committee on Civil Rights that condemned all forms of racial inequality.

Following Executive Order 9981, the armed forces made unusually rapid progress in integrating most military units—so much so that by the mid-1960s it was generally agreed that the military was the most thoroughly egalitarian institution in U.S. society. But then, in the late 1960s and early 1970s, a recrudescence of military racism surfaced in the form of race riots on navy ships, racial violence at domestic and foreign bases, aggressive off-duty segregation of whites and non-whites, and mounting complaints from black servicemen of harassment and unequal treatment by white superiors.

To deal with this extra-legal racism and the kinds of inequality it allegedly was spawning, the Department of Defense established in 1971 the Defense Race Relations Institute (DRRI), the main purpose of which was to develop course materials and train course instructors for a comprehensive services-wide program of race-relations teaching. At last report virtually every member of the armed services was taking or had taken the DRRI course, which deals, among other things, with the dynamics of racial prejudice, the highlights of minority-group history, and the nature of intra-service race-inspired incidents. The historical teaching data appear to be especially wide-ranging and helpful, as it deals not only with the black experience but also with the heritage of Chicanos, Puerto Ricans, Indians, Asians, and others. It seems probable that[33]

> No organization has ever tried to teach race relations on such a scale. A thousand instructors are trained each year, and they fan out to all the services. In addition . . . , nearly every major military installation has a human-relations council, which deals with race problems, among others.

Two final points are worth noting in this regard: blacks are given every opportunity to become race-relations instructors, and officers are now rated on how well they handle race relations in their outfits.

The armed forces have not yet proved that deeply ingrained racial attitudes can be altered through a positive teaching program, though they seem to be making progress. The best evidence of that is the fact that blacks and other minorities, despite the persistence of some racial inequality in the military, are enlisting in record numbers. Indeed, if that were not the case, the draft would long since have been reinstated.

In the private sector, one area in which the legacy of racism continues to be an obstinate bar to full equality is that of industry's hiring and firing policies. This is so notwithstanding the accomplishments of the welfare state in reducing economic inequality both here and abroad, accomplishments that were described in detail in Chapter 5.

Traditionally, save perhaps in the most menial jobs, non-whites have been the last to be hired by private industry and the first to be fired when, as in recessions, companies have to trim their employee rolls. This tradition has given rise to the familiar *last hired, first fired* litany that has recently become a symbol of the racial minorities' struggle against economic racism.

As is well known, it has long been a basic principle of organizational behavior, both in and out of private industry, that seniority (time on the job) shall be the basic determinant of the order of employee firing. In practice, this means that those who have worked longest and have accumulated the most seniority in a given firm will normally be the last to be dismissed. Many, perhaps most, labor-management contracts specify that seniority will be the main determinant of the order of layoffs. This principle, for obvious reasons, is particularly dear to the hearts of old-time unionists.

On the surface, the seniority principle seems eminently fair and, indeed, would be if it were not for the cold, hard facts of historical racism. But given the nation's three hundred years of white racism and the fact of recurring recessions, it is obvious that a slavish addiction to this principle will almost invariably result in greater hardships for non-whites than for whites, at least in the sensitive area of layoff policy.

In seeking ways to resolve this complex race-inspired problem, one must commence with the contractual obligations of seniority in the firing field and the relevant federal statutes dealing with hiring and firing in the private sector. As just noted, it is a fundamental fact of U.S. labor-management relations that a significant number of labor contracts are solidly grounded on the seniority principle. Yet it must also be emphasized that private contracts, if they are to be valid, must not violate public law. With that in mind, what is the basic federal legislation in this area?

As far as egalitarians are concerned, the decisive federal law affecting hiring and firing is the Civil Rights Act of 1964. Title VII of that act, as amended, makes it an unfair employment practice for any interstate-commerce employer—commercial, trade union, or governmental—to discriminate economically in any way against persons because of race, color, religion, sex, national origin, or age for those between forty and sixty-five. Any employer that affects interstate commerce and has fifteen or more workers is subject to the law's provisions. In addition, both business employers and trade unions are obligated to keep detailed hiring and firing records and to take affirmative action to bring about non-discriminatory hirings and firings. Supplementing and strengthening the 1964 Act are the Equal Pay Act of 1963, the Equal Employment Opportunities Act of 1972, and various presidential orders requiring contractors and sub-contractors of the federal government to implement affirmative action hiring programs or face loss of federal funds.[34]

The Equal Employment Opportunity Commission (EEOC), which consists of five members appointed by the president and approved by the Senate, has the chief responsibility for bringing about compliance with Title VII. EEOC works closely with state officials and makes use of conciliation machinery whenever possible. If, however, conciliation does not work, EEOC, since 1972, has been authorized to seek court orders directing employers or trade unions to end discriminatory conduct. Hearings, of course, are held on all complaints; but if the commission perceives a willful and persistent pattern of defiance, it may ask for an accelerated hearing before a three-judge federal court, from which direct appeals to the U.S. Supreme Court are possible.

For some time now EEOC has been contending, along with anti-racist egalitarians, that seniority lists cannot be used at layoff time when they clearly frustrate minority-employment goals. But the rest of the government, at least during the Nixon-Ford Administration, supported the view that employers and unions do not violate the law when workers are laid off on the basis of seniority. To the dismay of anti-racists, the Justice Department went along with that view.

In recent years, blacks and other minority-group workers have filed numerous past-discrimination suits in the lower courts, and have frequently won retroactive seniority over whites and, in some cases, millions of dollars in back pay. But since the U.S. Supreme Court maintains that retroactive seniority must be granted to workers *only if they can prove job bias,* and since that is hard to do, it is probable that long-established seniority systems will not henceforth be the whipping boys for job-bias activists that they have been in the recent past. New seniority systems benefiting minorities, that have been negotiated in the last few years between companies and unions, may well be challenged by white unionists when they come up for renegotiation.

The expanding involvement of the federal government in the struggle for racial equality is by no means limited to the activities of EEOC. The Community Relations Service, now located in the Department of Justice, was established by the Civil Rights Act of 1964 (Title X) and is at least as active as EEOC in promoting racial justice. The CRS[35]

> not only aids in resolving disputes and difficulties as they erupt, but also helps communities to achieve the kind of progress which will enable them to avoid racial upheavals. Its goal is to help bring about rapid and orderly progress toward securing a life of justice, equal opportunity, and human dignity for all American citizens.

As for implementing its broad egalitarian mandate, the CRS, among other things, helps communities defuse situations of racial tensions and conflicts, provides experts to give an independent perspective upon which disputants can mutually depend for an objective judgment, arranges professional mediation of racial controversies, and works at all times as closely as possible with appropriate state and local public and private agencies so as to maximize the peaceful resolution of community conflicts.

Of equal importance in the struggle against racism is the under-appreciated United States Commission on Civil Rights, which was created by the Civil Rights Act of 1957, the first major piece of civil rights legislation since Reconstruction. The Commission[36]

> investigates complaints alleging that citizens are being deprived of their right to vote by reason of their race, color, religion, sex, or

national origin, or, in the case of Federal elections, by fraudulent practices. It appraises the laws and policies of the Federal Government with respect to denials of equal protection of the laws under the Constitution, and collects and studies information concerning legal developments constituting the same. The Commission serves as a national clearinghouse for civil rights information, and in turn submits reports of its activities, findings, and recommendations to the President and Congress.

Though it got off to a rather slow start, the commission has since acquired a solid reputation for the excellence of its reports and has come to be recognized as a valuable gadfly within the federal bureaucracy. The commission's resources of staff and research funds have always been severely limited; yet despite that drawback, it has been responsible for four major achievements in the field of race relations. Thus, its detailed research reports provided the first hard data about the precise scope and nature of racial inequality in the United States. Its public hearings contributed greatly to the emergence of a civil rights consensus in the 1960s. Its empirical findings about discrimination helped to energize congress into legislating against various forms of racial inequality. And through relentless pressure and publicity, it has kept the spotlight on public officials who prefer *benign neglect* to *affirmative action* in the general area of minority rights. Precisely because the commission has shown such a devotion to the goal of full racial equality, egalitarians were bitterly disappointed when the Nixon Administration, in late 1972, forced the resignation of the Director, Reverend Theodore M. Hesburgh. Since his departure, Father Hesburgh has continued to crusade for human rights by lecturing and writing, while the commission, following in his footsteps, remains the most respected voice of racial justice within the federal establishment. That was especially true during the latter years of the Nixon Administration when, according to a Commission report, "Federal civil rights enforcement . . . [moved] at a snail's pace."[37]

During the Nixon-Ford years, the commission was particularly critical of the foot-dragging in civil rights matters by the U.S. Department of Agriculture, then headed by Secretary Earl Butz, although it is doubtful if its passivity was much more conspicuous there than elsewhere in Washington. As one means of dealing with this problem, the commission recommended that the Office of Management and Budget (OMB) be given responsibility for directing and coordinating efforts to end racial-ethnic discrimination in all federally-funded programs, a suggestion seconded by most egalitarians. In addition, the Commission got to the root of the discrimination problem when it wrote in its 1973 report that[38]

> The enforcement failure [of the early 1970s] was the result, to a large extent, of placing the responsibility for ensuring racial and ethnic justice upon a massive Federal bureaucracy which for years had been an integral part of a discriminatory system. . . . Moreover, since nonenforcement was an accepted mode of behavior, any official who sought to enforce civil rights laws with the same zeal applied to other statutes ran the risk of being branded as an activist, a visionary, or a troublemaker.

Although blacks are the most numerous and most vocal of the minorities struggling for racial equality with whites, they are by no means alone. Right behind them are Chicanos, concentrated now in five southwestern states, who are making massive efforts to unite *la Raza* into a more effective political force.[39] Marching with them are Puerto Ricans and other Spanish-speaking citizens, who are also busy refining their power-seeking tactics, most notably in the *barrios* of Miami, Newark, New York, and Chicago. Then, of course, there are the Indians, numbering now close to a million and for the first time in their history becoming articulate crusaders for equal rights in such urban centers as San Francisco, Oklahoma City, Minneapolis, Phoenix, and Chicago.[40] The contemporary circumstances of Indians are particularly dreary, perhaps the worst of all minorities in the United States. As has been pointed out,[41]

> The average annual income per Indian *family* is about $1,500 per year; unemployment is very high, reaching ten times the national average in some areas. U.S. Census reports show that about 60 percent of families living on Indian reservations were below the poverty line in 1973. . . . The average educational level for all federally-educated Indians is under five years, and dropout rates are twice the national average in both federal and local schools.

In the case of Indians, the original Americans, the racial-ethnic equality issue is complicated by a distinctive world-view that stands in sharp contrast to the values and mores of the dominant white society. Because of that, it is not just a question of assuring Indian individuals equal rights in every field with mainstream whites. It is also a question of granting equal rights and status to Indian *communities* within the general confines of U.S. pluralism. Radical Indian egalitarians, along with their Chicano counterparts, are now insisting on a multi-minority cultural pluralism in which every minority will remain distinctive and have status and legitimacy equal to that of white society. Traditionally most minority groups, inspired by the melting pot concept, have accepted the inevitability of the disintegration of community interests in favor of individual ones.[42]

But Indian leaders, or most of them, now reject that anti-communitarian pessimism and insist on the recognition of autonomous community rights even as individual rights are institutionalized. This stand obviously raises anew the classic question of the roles of individuals and groups in democratic society, but so far the U.S. government has avoided facing up to the question by simply denying to Indian tribes and Chicanos the political and cultural autonomy that treaty law supposedly guaranteed to them. For more than a century now, collective, tribal interests have been suppressed in favor of a "pragmatic" concept of arbitrary, individual interest, though even there the government's record has been more promise than performance.[43] The Bill of Rights, for instance, has often passed Indians by.

Blacks, Indians, Chicanos, Puerto Ricans, and all other racial-ethnic minorities have at last awakened to the fact that politics is a case of "Who Gets What, When, How"[44]; and having belatedly grasped that axiom of political science, they are now playing the game of politics morning, noon, and night in order to finally achieve the goal of equality in freedom. As ruling elites here and abroad should know by now, "There is no stopping place between the granting of a few rights and full citizenship. . . . No Americans have asked for more than this—or settled long for less."[45]

It should not, however, be thought that there exists today a universal consensus for maximizing the government's role in the quest for racial-ethnic equality. For though nearly all U.S. citizens agree, in theory, with the abstract doctrine of equal rights for all races and ethnic groups, the country has always been, and remains, fiercely divided about how best to implement that doctrine through public policy.

The groups most adamantly opposed to the federalization of this particular equality issue are conservative libertarians and southern white supremacists. Though divided on many things, these two loosely-defined forces are united in their opposition to most of the anti-racist civil rights legislation and court decisions of recent years, including especially the affirmative action and equal opportunity administrative programs derived from the 1964 Civil Rights Act. Philosophically, both groups contend that the federalization of the struggle for racial equality is destroying significant amounts of personal freedom and once again bringing to the fore democracy's freedom-equality paradox, just as earlier happened when the government was promoting political, legal, and economic equality for the disadvantaged.

How, one may wonder, can pushing racial equality diminish anybody's freedom? And precisely whose freedom is being threatened by improvements in the status of blacks, Chicanos, and Indians?

Conservatives, who deny that they are racists, maintain that the current quest for racial equality imperils freedom in at least three ways: by unduly increasing the government's control over the internal affairs of business, labor, and educational organizations; by saddling employers with soaring personnel management costs; and by penalizing established elites in order to render compensatory justice to disadvantaged racial and ethnic minorities.

As for specific groups that allegedly have experienced diminished freedoms, conservatives mention WASPS, Jews, middle class people of all races, and lower class white ethnics. In this regard, critics maintain that two groups, Jews and WASPS, have especially been deprived of basic professional freedoms because of affirmative action programs that give precedence in hiring to racial minorities. In addition, they believe that middle-class businessmen are being drowned in a sea of bureaucratic red tape as they try to cope with the massive number of reports that must be filed under the various equal opportunity programs. They maintain also that lower class whites, who usually are unable to attend private schools, have lost their freedom of choice in the matter of schools because of forced busing, while the various racial minorities are petted and pampered with public funds. To what purpose? they ask.

More fundamentally, conservative libertarians complain that the growing federalization of the quest for racial equality unconstitutionally deprives white people—especially white ethnics—of the freedom to limit their associations to members of their own race, if they so choose. Some even argue, with a certain plausibility, that the whole spectrum of postwar racial equality programs has eroded the freedom of white people to lead a decent, secure life in the nation's cities, and has thereby been a major cause of the white flight to the suburbs. Finally, they protest that the increased construction of low-income, racially-integrated public housing in white suburban areas is destroying the white race's freedom to build and maintain their own *ethnic turfs* at the same time that black and other minority enclaves are *de facto* segregated by the omnipresent threat of crime and violence against outside intruders. This, they say, is a double standard of treatment that is both immoral and undemocratic.

Among the political proponents of this conservative libertarian view, none is more articulate than North Carolina's Republican Senator Jesse Helms, who in 1977 introduced a bill to halt excess regulation of private institutions under racial equality programs. Helms is particularly concerned with discrimination against white males in the education field as well as the costs of affirmative action programs in all areas of the private sector. Since he is a Republican, his bill will likely fail.

A more philosophical attack on massive state interventionism to correct racial, ethnic, and economic wrongs has been made by Murray Rothbard, who in the early 1970s wrote a controversial book espousing what William

F. Buckley,[46] Milton Friedman, Barry Goldwater, Friedrich Hayek, and other conservative libertarians have long advocated: a return to free market "anarchism." Clearly placing the value of freedom above that of coerced racial equality, Rothbard emphasizes anew the old Lockean rights to life, liberty, property, and defense, and insists that the free market remains the most efficient and decentralized device for the rational allocation of resources. His assumption that laissez-faire will in the long run be better for everybody, including racial and ethnic minorities, is an obvious throwback to eighteenth-century state-of-nature theorizing. Moreover, like Social Darwinists in the last century, Rothbard sees the modern egalitarian welfare state as actually a device for plunder that tries to play Robin Hood. Earlier, Marx and Engels saw the modern state as the tool of the bourgeoisie; in Rothbard's right-wing view, it is the tool of the proletariat! True to his conservative proclivities, Rothbard likewise deplores the racial egalitarians' effort to separate property rights from human rights and insists that secure property rights are an absolutely essential condition for the exercise of every species of human rights. In the final analysis, Rothbard rejects democratic and egalitarian utilitarianism for an old-fashioned natural law absolutism. Although his work is more a manifesto than a political theory treatise, it has the virtue of dramatizing in a somewhat novel way the perennial problems involved in the freedom-equality paradox.[47]

Naturally, anti-racist egalitarians totally reject the argument of people like Helms and Rothbard that speedy progress toward racial equality in all areas of society is somehow incompatible with the maintenance of personal liberty for whites and middle class people. It is their view that racial equality, far from diminishing freedom, enhances just about everybody's liberty in some regard, even though governmental coercion may have to be increased in order to break down established patterns of institutional racism. They particularly resent the charge that the pursuit of racial equality has ruined U.S. cities and lessened the freedom of urbanites. Because the United States is a racist society, they argue, there is a tendency to attribute all or most of the problems of our cities to the presence there of large clusters of racial minorities, whereas the truth is that whites have not been fleeing to the suburbs because of blacks or government equality programs but because of soaring city taxes, crime, poor urban schools, inadequate transportation, and declining job opportunities. It may, of course, be a fact that both egalitarians and their critics are partially right in this controversy, for the white flight is almost certainly not the result of a single factor. Few significant social changes ever are.

One of the extraordinary things about the U.S. minorities' problem is that though blacks, Chicanos, and Indians were fiercely damaged by white racism over the centuries, they have still managed to wage a continuous and increasingly successful fight against it. That is true partly because they will not let the ruling elites forget that traditional racial attitudes have conduced to a broad range of interlocked inequalities that persist through all the winds of change. Socially, white racism has led to housing ghettoization and to limited upward mobility among minorities. Economically, it has led to mass unemployment, the most menial of jobs, and frequent firings. Politically, it earlier entailed disenfranchisement and still involves serious obstacles to advancing in politics and government. Psychologically, it has diminished the self-esteem of minorities, reduced their motivation for achievement, and, occasionally, turned deprived individuals into fanatical zealots who prefer violence to the slow incrementalism of the democratic process. Of course, all of these things are changing, but not nearly fast enough for militant egalitarians.

The spiraling crusade for racial equality has dramatized better than anything else could the fact that the United States remains the country of the most extravagant hopes and the most profound disappointments. It has also served to emphasize the extent to which racial and ethnic consciousness has been escalating in the United States since the Camelot days of the Kennedy Administration. And yet, while approving all this, racial militants are deeply chagrined that there has not been a concomitant development of *class* consciousness, which they feel would double the effectiveness of their crusade. It certainly is a fact that class consciousness has not kept pace with assertions of racial and ethnic pride, and there are at least six reasons for this: the relative affluence of U.S. society; the existence of substantial upward mobility in the U.S. system; the expansion of a large middle class; general acceptance of the U.S. class structure and its legitimacy; cross-cutting allegiances to churches, unions, professional groups, and various voluntary organizations that interfere with class solidarity; and the absence of a tradition of class-struggle politics in U.S. history.[48]

Today's radical racial egalitarians would like to see a revival of the Populist experiment of the 1890s in which minorities and have-not whites would coalesce on the basis of their economic class interests and form a new political majority in the South and in the large cities of the North. The radicals eschew the coalitional strategy of middle class moderates that plays down economic division along class lines, and insist that all political issues in the future must be defined in economic rather than social status terms. Furthermore they maintain, as do all Marxian theorists, that class tensions must be *emphasized,* not played down. For until class politics replaces race politics, and until Marx replaces Jefferson and Dr. King in the strategic planning of all minorities, the deprived racial groups will continue to get only crumbs from the nation's bulging table. Some racial radicals, of course, even advocate violent revolution or total minority separatism, though such tactics are rarely openly espoused.[49] In any event, it is now apparent that the concept of total assimilation via the melting pot is rapidly being replaced, in the thinking of minority militants, by the concept of autonomous *acculturation,* symbolized not by a homogenizing pot but by a tossed spring salad bowl in which the polychromatic ingredients retain their distinctive tastes and identities while at the same time contributing to a succulent whole that is greater than the sum of its parts. This is but another way of saying that the new racial egalitarians are stressing the *Pluribus* more than the *Unum* in the nation's motto.[50] Nationalistic libertarians decry that emphasis as divisive.

For more than two centuries, white supremacy racism was a mythology used to explain and justify the maldistribution of power and material rewards in U.S. society. For a time it probably helped to reduce tensions between the nation's racial and ethnic groups by explaining and justifying differences in their lifestyles and socioeconomic well-being. But in the racially ecumenical world of the 1970s, the mythology and its symbolic iconography have been thoroughly deflated; and if the status strivings of ascending racial minorities are blocked in the future, radical direct action and possibly violence will almost certainly ensue. The non-whites of the United States how have a dream—the dream of getting ahead and making it in an open democratic society—and they are in no mood to see that dream, so movingly articulated by Dr. King, turn into a nightmare. It therefore seems safe to predict that with white libertarians becoming ever more formalistic about their freedom, which they call the "first principle" of constitutional government, and with black and other minority egalitarians demanding a firmer *instrumental* approach to social justice, there is scant likelihood that quiet repose will be the destiny of U.S. law or politics in the foreseeable future.

NOTES

1. Plano and Greenberg, p. 78.
2. W.A. Lessa, "Racism," in *A Dictionary of the Social Sciences,* eds. Julius Gould and William L. Kolb (New York: The Free Press, 1964), p. 571.
3. Ruth Benedict, *Race, Science and Politics* (New York: Viking Press, 1943), p. 98.
4. J. Comas, "Racial Myths," in *The Race Question in Modern Science* (Paris: Unesco and Sidgwick & Jackson, 1956), pp. 52-3.
5. Acts 8:26-40.
6. On this general subject, see Brian Bunting, *The Rise of the South African Reich* (New York: Smith, 1965); E. Franklin Frazier, *Race and Culture*

Contacts in the Modern World (Boston: Beacon Press, 1965); and A. Grenfell Price, *White Settlers and Native Peoples: An Historical Study of Racial Contacts Between English-speaking Whites and Aboriginal Peoples in the United States, Canada, Australia and New Zealand* (New York: Cambridge University Press, 1950).

7. Sister Mary Loyola Vath, *Visualized Church History* (New York: Oxford Book Company, 1954), p. 128.

8. Three good general studies of anti-Semitism are Charles Y. Glock and Rodney Stark, *Christian Beliefs and Anti-Semitism* (New York: Harper & Row, 1966); Jacob R. Marcus, *The Jew in the Medieval World: A Source Book, 315-1791* (New York: Meridian, 1938); and Hugo Valentin, *Anti-Semitism Historically and Critically Examined* (New York: Viking Press, 1936).

9. Arabs, who themselves are Semitic caucasians like Jews, argue that they are not hostile to Jews or Judaism but only to *Zionism,* a Jewish nationalist and political movement which spearheaded the creation of the state of Israel in Palestine. In 1975, the Arabs, supported by communist and Third World countries, induced the General Assembly of the United Nations to issue a declaration formally denouncing Zionism as a form of racism. The United States and several European countries vehemently protested the action, but to no avail. As one reason why they do not hate Jews, Arabs like to point out that both they and the Jews are children of Abraham: the Arabs the offspring of his son Ishmael, the Jews of his son Isaac.

10. Cecil V. Crabb, Jr., *American Foreign Policy in the Nuclear Age,* 2nd ed. (New York: Harper & Row, 1965), p. 397.

11. Ibid.

12. The literature on the United Nations is copious. Official publications include the *Yearbook of the United Nations, United Nations Bulletin* (issued bi-weekly), and the *Annual Report of the Secretary-General on the Work of the Organization.* Useful general studies are Inis L. Claude, *Swords Into Plowshares,* 3rd ed. (New York: Random House, 1964); Ernst B. Haas, *Beyond the Nation-state: Functionalism and International Organization* (Stanford, Calif.: Stanford University Press, 1964); and Ruth B. Russell and Jeannette E. Muther, *A History of the United Nations Charter* (Washington: Brookings Institution, 1958).

13. William W. Bishop, ed., *International Law Cases and Materials,* 2nd ed. (Boston: Little, Brown, 1962), p. 476.

14. Ibid.

15. A useful source of national and international developments in the human rights field is *The United Nations Yearbook on Human Rights,* which has appeared annually since 1946. In addition, two journal articles on the subject are particularly valuable: E. Schwelb, "International Conventions on Human Rights," *International Comparative Law Quarterly* 9 (1960): 654-70; and M.S. McDougal and G. Bebr, "Human Rights in the United Nations," *American Journal of International Law* 58 (1964): 603-41.

16. The word apartheid in Afrikaans means "apartness." Although after World War II there were tentative moves toward a less rigid social philosophy in the country, these were aborted by the 1948 electoral victory of D.F. Malan and his Afrikaaner National Party. The Nationalists fought the election pure and simply on the "race issue" under the new slogan of apartheid, and in no time

at all that had become the dominant myth of the state and government. In essence what apartheid does is to create four rigid color-castes (white Europeans, Asians, Africans, and Coloreds) that in theory are "separate but equal," though certainly not in practice. The obvious, if not always stated, objective of the caste system is to insure the indefinite maintenance of white supremacy. That objective so infuriated the other member nations of the British Commonwealth that South Africa felt compelled to withdraw from the Commonwealth in 1961.

17. Among the best analyses of South Africa's racial caste system are those found in Ellen Hellmann, ed., *Handbook on Race Relations in South Africa* (London: Oxford University Press, 1949); Leo Kuper, *An African Bourgeoisie: Race, Class, and Politics in South Africa* (New Haven: Yale University Press, 1965); and Pierre L. Van Den Berghe, *South Africa: A Study in Conflict* (Middletown, Conn.: Wesleyan University Press, 1965).

18. Quoted in William P. Lineberry, ed., *Great Decisions 1970* (New York: Foreign Policy Association, 1970), p. 45.

19. W.E.B. DuBois, *The Souls of Black Folk* (Chicago: A.C. McClurg & Co., 1903), p. 2.

20. Quoted in Lineberry, p. 38.

21. J.W. Peltason, *Corwin & Peltason's Understanding the Constitution,* 7th ed. (Hinsdale, Ill.: Dryden Press, 1976), p. 184.

22. The popular nickname of segregation laws was apparently derived from the name of a minstrel routine—the *Jump Jim Crow*—"performed beginning in 1828 by its author, Thomas Dartmouth (Daddy) Rice, and by many imitators, including Joseph Jefferson." *Encyclopaedia Britannica: Micropaedia,* 15th ed., s.v. "Jim Crow Laws."

23. *Plessy* v. *Ferguson,* 163 U.S. 537 (1896). Technically, this case dealt only with *Jim Crow* public transportation laws. But the Court, through dictum, in effect legitimated the entire *Jim Crow* legal structure, which provided "separate but equal" public facilities for blacks and whites. In practice, the facilities were separate all right but rarely, if ever, equal.

24. Harry A. Ploski and Roscoe C. Brown, Jr., eds., *The Negro Almanac* (New York: Bellwether Publishing Co., 1967), p. 166.

25. Ibid.

26. Four state actions were consolidated under one citation: *Brown* v. *Board of Education of Topeka; Briggs* v. *Elliott; Davis* v. *County School Board of Prince Edward County;* and *Gebhart* v. *Belton,* 347 U.S. 483 (1954).

27. *Brown* v. *Board of Education,* 349 U.S. 294 (1955). For the origins of the *all deliberate speed* formula, see Alwin Thaler, "With All Deliberate Speed," *Tennessee Law Review* 27 (1960): 510-17.

28. Francis M. Wilhoit, *The Politics of Massive Resistance* (New York: George Braziller, 1973), pp. 23-24.

29. Ibid., pp. 201-30.

30. On this general subject, see William G. Andrews, *Coordinate Magistrates: Constitutional Law by Congress and President* (New York: Van Nostrand, Reinhold, 1969); Samuel Krislov, *The Supreme Court in the Political Process* (New York: Macmillan, 1965); and G. Theodore Mitau, *Decade of Decision: The Supreme Court and the Constitutional Revolution, 1954-1964* (New York: Scribner's, 1967).

31. The first part of President Truman's Order read as follows:

WHEREAS it is essential that there be maintained in the armed services of the United States the highest standards of democracy, with equality of treatment and opportunity for all those who serve in our country's defense: . . .

1.   It is hereby declared to be the policy of the President that there shall be equality of treatment and opportunity for all persons in the armed services without regard to race, color, religion or national origin. This policy shall be put into effect as rapidly as possible, having due regard to the time required to effectuate any necessary change without impairing efficiency. . . . (Ploski and Brown, p. 106.)

32.   *Shelley* v. *Kraemer,* 334 U.S. 1 (1948).
33.   The quotation is from the sociologist Charles Moskos, Jr., in Bruce Bliven, Jr., "A Reporter At Large: All-Volunteer—II," *The New Yorker,* 1 December 1975, p. 141.
34.   For a useful discussion of this broad topic, see Richard P. Nathan, *Jobs and Civil Rights: The Role of the Federal Government in Promoting Equal Opportunity and Employment and Training* (Washington, D.C.: Brookings Institution, 1969).
35.   General Services Administration, *United States Government Manual, 1973/74* (Washington, D.C.: Government Printing Office, 1973), p. 292.
36.   Ibid., p. 414.
37.   United States Commission on Civil Rights, *Federal Civil Rights Enforcement Effort—A Reassessment* (Washington, D.C.: Government Printing Office, 1973), p. 11. For an excellent appraisal of the Commission's background and philosophy, see Theodore M. Hesburgh, "The Commission on Civil Rights—and Human Rights," *The Review of Politics* 34 (1972): 291-305. Father Hesburgh has for some time been President of Notre Dame, which at its 1977 commencement awarded an honorary degree to President Carter, in part because of his crusade for human rights.
38.   United States Commission on Civil Rights, p. 11.
39.   These books are useful introductions to the Chicano movement: William Madsden, *The Mexican-Americans of South Texas* (New York: Holt, Rinehart, and Winston, 1964); Joan W. Moore, *Mexican-Americans* (Englewood Cliffs, N.J.: Prentice-Hall, 1970); Armando Rendon, *Chicano Manifesto* (New York: Macmillan, 1971); and Stan Steiner, *La Raza: The Mexican Americans* (New York: Harper & Row, 1970).
40.   The emergence of Indians as equality seekers is described in John Collier, *The Indians of the Americas* (New York: Norton, 1947); Vine Deloria, Jr., *Custer Died for Your Sins: An Indian Manifesto* (New York: Macmillan, 1970); and Stan Steiner, *The New Indians* (New York: Harper & Row, 1968).
41.   Dolbeare and Edelman, p. 137.
42.   That attitude underpins the argumentation in Theodore W. Taylor, *The States and Their Indian Citizens* (Washington, D.C.: U.S. Department of the Interior, Bureau of Indian Affairs, 1972).
43.   See Vine Deloria, Jr., *Behind the Trail of Broken Treaties* (New York: Delta, 1974). Deloria thinks there is a pressing need to "clarify the status of Indian tribes and eliminate the inconsistencies that are presently found in the federal relationship with Indians." p. 159.

44. See Harold D. Lasswell, *Politics: Who Gets What, When, How* (New York: McGraw-Hill, 1936).

45. Burns, Peltason, and Cronin, p. 212.

46. For a stinging critique of egalitarian liberalism, see William F. Buckley, *Up from Liberalism* (New York: Honor Books, 1959). Buckley has long been one of the most perceptive of contemporary conservative writers.

47. See Murray Rothbard, *For A New Liberty* (New York: Macmillan, 1973).

48. See Dye, p. 82.

49. One of the most interesting approaches to class-based politics is that contained in Chandler Davidson, *Biracial Politics: Conflict and Coalition in the Metropolitan South* (Baton Rouge, La.: Louisiana State University Press, 1972). Davidson bluntly proposes "a biracial coalition . . . with economic goals radical enough to mobilize large sectors of the less affluent of both races." p. 220.

50. In this regard, see Wilhoit, pp. 281-83. Also useful is L. Paul Metzger, "American Sociology and Black Assimilation: Conflicting Perspectives," *American Journal of Sociology* 76 (1971): 627-47. Among recent books dealing with racial equality, two are especially recommended: Edward Peeks, *The Long Struggle for Black Power* (New York: Charles Scribner's Sons, 1971); and June Sochen, ed., *The Black Man and the American Dream: Negro Aspirations in America, 1900-1930* (Chicago: Quadrangle Books, 1971).

7

SEXUAL EQUALITY

Related to, and almost as passionate as the quest for racial-ethnic equality has been the twentieth-century quest for sexual equality, spearheaded primarily by militant feminists and secondarily by so-called sexual "deviates." Few campaigns for equality have been so derided by the general public as that waged by females, and for the simple reason that "Of all the minority groupings in . . . [U.S.] society women evoke the most amusement and the least apparent anxiety. The battle of the sexes, after all, is a historical fixture—a source of numberless jokes, farces, and ironical comments."[1]

Conservatives, in fact, question whether women should actually be viewed as a *disadvantaged minority* along with blacks and other racial groups, since it is known that they comprise more than fifty percent of the nation's population and, in certain ways, are favored above men. But quite apart from numbers, women definitely are a *status* minority, and as such have been the victims of some of the grossest kinds of inequality. As one expert has well observed, "The revelant political data are not whether objective standards of deprivation exist, but whether subjective ones do... . [Thus] women as a grouping *can* be considered to be deprived if their economic and social-status opportunity structures are compared with those of men."[2]

Female inequality is, indeed, one of the oldest forms of discrimination, going back to the dawn of civilization, if not earlier. Under early Roman law, for example, a husband could execute his wife, and a father his daughter, for adultery. In England, even after the promulgation of Magna Carta, a woman could not legally accuse a man of murder and, of course, was rarely directly involved in politics or government. In eighteenth-century France, at the height of the Age of Reason, the otherwise enlightened *philosophes* generally envisaged the liberation of only the masculine half of humanity and seemed to regard women as created to please men.

In seeking a historical perspective on what is now called sexism, one discovers that the extent of equality enjoyed by women varied from place to place, although virtually everywhere they were the victims of some forms of political, governmental, and economic discrimination. In ancient Babylonia and in Egypt, for instance, women enjoyed substantial independence and a fairly high status. This was best exemplified by the Code of Hammurabi, which granted married women considerable financial and personal freedom, most notably in the provision that the bride-price, required of the bridegroom, should remain the property of the female. That provision, however, assumed that the wife was "a careful mistress" and "without reproach."[3] In addition, the Code provided that "Women could trade on their own account, independent of their husbands, and could be judges, elders, witnesses, and scribes."[4]

The position of women in ancient Egypt appears to have been even higher. Among other things, "They owned property, worked in many sectors of the economy, took part in public life, and mixed freely with men."[5] Some scholars believe that women were the dominant sex in Egypt, an assumption that may be partly confirmed by the unusual number of queens and female deities the country had. This alleged reversal of roles may also have been what Herodotus had in mind when he wrote that the Egyptians "in most of their manners and customs, exactly reverse the common practice of mankind."[6]

Rather more typical of ancient realities was the status of women among the early Jews. Although it is a matter of controversy, it appears that Judaism originally held women in somewhat low esteem. At least in the synagogues, women were expected to keep silent, and in Jewish divorce practices, they were practically at men's disposal. In addition, women were effectively excluded from politics and government as well as from religious leadership positions. It is true that the Jews had a matrilineal kinship system that involved tracing descent through the female line, yet it did not follow that women, in consequence of that fact, wielded great power. Ancient Israel, in other words, was not a matriarchy.[7]

Christianity, which grew out of Judaism, in no sense brought a revolutionary social change in the status of women, although their status was to some degree altered. Thus, Jesus forbade divorce and thereby improved the marital position of women. In terms of worship procedure, Christian women definitely moved forward from the lowly position of their Jewish counterparts who, during the synagogue worship service, were separated from the men by an opaque lattice. It would also appear from Paul's epistle to the Romans that early Christian women sometimes served as prophets and used their charismatic gifts within their congregations.[8] Moreover, it is now well established that in the early days of the Church women were martyrs as well as men, though they were not allowed to be priests. Finally it is important to recall that Christians from the first insisted upon strict monogamy, and that strengthened the married woman's position in the family and society.

Notwithstanding these improvements in the status of women, it is a historical fact that the Christian Church, perhaps even more than Judaism, thought of women as temptresses and sirens and as generally inferior to men. Thus, Paul wrote to the Corinthian Church that "a man . . . is the image of God and reflects his glory; while woman is the reflection of man's glory."[9] On another occasion, Peter enjoined married women to "be submissive to your husbands. . . . You must not adopt the external attractions of arranging the hair and wearing jewelry and dress; yours must be the inner beauty of character, the imperishable attraction of a quiet and gentle spirit, which has great value in the sight of God."[10]

Considering the prestigious position in the early Church of the Apostle Paul, it is not surprising that his espousal of something close to Christian sexism became authoritative Christian doctrine. He believed that[11]

> Women were all tainted with the sin of Eve and therefore needed discipline. . . . Woman was dangerous to men. . . . It was woman who had brought sin into the world. Marriage although never explicitly condemned was placed third and lowest in the scale of Christian purity. . . . Thus the view of woman as a thing both inferior and evil found expression very early in the history of the Church and while not accepted . . . by all groups did find expression . . . in the idea of the subjection of women.

During the Middle Ages, women had a particularly rough time because so many European men were involved in wars, blood feuds, and crusades or else were celibates locked away in monasteries. The Church did provide at least one means through which *unmarried* women might lead a dignified existence by allowing those who were interested to spend their lives in nunneries. Of course, only a limited number of women found such a life acceptable. Perhaps the greatest risk of all to the pre-modern woman was the risk of being burned as a witch. That was no small concern, since it is generally believed that as many as 100,000 women were victims of medieval and Renaissance-Reformation witch-hunts which rarely bothered men.[12]

Somewhat countering the Pauline conception of the inferior status of women was a late medieval theory that asserted their superiority in certain realms. This theory was manifested in the cult of the Virgin and in the related pedestalization of ladies through the ideal of chivalry, which reached its peak of popularity in the twelfth and thirteenth centuries. Of course, chivalry, like asceticism was practiced by only a select group, and yet it reveals the inconsistent ideas held about women, suggesting simultaneously their superiority and inferiority. In this connection it should be pointed out that both the early Christian and late medieval doctrines of femininity conduced to the Western world's double standard of sexual morality by severely limiting the interpersonal conduct of women and by saddling them with ethical restrictions that were not binding on men.

In ancient Greece, the fountainhead of democracy, the status of women was generally even lower than their status among Jews and Christians. Indeed, Greek women for a time were little more than childbearing slaves; and even in Periclean Athens, they were usually secluded in their homes, denied the right to get an education, and regarded by their husbands as chattel. Only in autocratic Sparta did Greek women enjoy near-equality with men, as there they participated freely in education, sports, and public affairs. It is also true that in Greek drama, women showed considerable independence of spirit and dignity, as did the *hetaerai* or courtesans. One might even say that Pericles' mistress Aspasia founded the first women's rights movement.

During the Renaissance and Reformation, the position of Western women improved, though not spectacularly. More of them became educated, especially after the invention of printing; several became mistresses of high Church officials, such as Vannozza Catanei, who served in that capacity for Pope Alexander VI; some, like Lucrezia Borgia, achieved considerable political power; and a few even became professors at Italian and Spanish universities. Protestantism liberated women from the seclusion of nunneries, but under the impact of Puritanism and Calvinism the position of women in certain respects declined.

The woman's status in the modern world did not significantly change until the latter part of the eighteenth century, and particularly after the equality-centered French Revolution. Around 1790, the French revolutionary philosopher Condorcet penned an essay on "The Admission of Women to Full Citizenship," which may very well have been the first explicit treatment of that subject. Some two years later, Mary

Wollstonecraft was issuing her historic feminist manifesto, entitled *Vindication of the Rights of Woman.* An obvious child of the French Revolution, the *Vindication* had little immediate effect on the status of women, but its long-term influence has been substantial.

In the New World, women in the United States suffered about as much from the virus of sexism as did their European sisters. This resulted in part from the dominance of English common law, which granted few rights to women, and in part from the influence of the Puritan religion, which in its New England form assigned the dominant position in society to men. Prior to the American Revolution, women were sometimes actually fined and imprisoned for speaking in public, and well into the twentieth century they were being arrested for trying to vote.

As English common law and Protestant Puritanism continued their domination of U.S. culture, the old sexual double standard that rationalized the inferior status of women gradually became institutionalized via the criminal law. Colonial authorities, for example, viewed copulation between a married man and a single woman as an act of fornication, while such an offense committed by a married woman was the capital crime of adultery.[13] Furthermore, though both men and women were subject to prosecution under colonial bastardy statutes, "Far more women than men were prosecuted."[14] Even more discriminatory was the fact that in seventeenth-century Virginia a free white woman who had a child by a black man was liable to a five-year period of servitude, though there were "no special provisions against a white man fathering a child on a Negro."[15]

Under English common law, as interpreted by the eighteenth-century oracle Blackstone, a female became virtually a legal non-person when she got married. This old "fusion" doctrine, generally rejected by U.S. courts today, was based on the assumption "that husband and wife in the eyes of the law are one and the same person."[16] In common law this marital state was known as *coverture.* Among other implications of this was the rule that a wife could not testify against her husband in criminal cases, no matter how serious the crime. Jeremy Bentham, who had little but contempt for the common law, denouced this rule as securing "to every man, one safe and unquestionable and ever ready accomplice for every imaginable crime."[17] In addition, it had the effect of giving "the husband complete freedom to torment and punish his wife as long as he took care to do so only when no one else was present."[18] Because of that effect, the rule was eventually altered to permit the wife to testify against her husband when he was accused of committing a serious crime against her person, such as assault or rape.[19]

Reduced to its simplest terms, the doctrine of *coverture* fused husband and wife into one legal entity—and the one was the husband. Not only that, but the dead hand of the common law also gave the husband complete control of his wife's property and the products of her labors. This extreme form of familial inequality was not actually changed until the nineteenth century when states began adopting Married Women's Property Acts. Mississippi, not usually a leader in equality matters, appears to have been the first state to move in this direction by enacting a law in 1839 to permit married women to deal with their property as single women. Progress came slowly and grudgingly in this regard, and the laws themselves were not uniform, differing as they did from state to state in the degree to which they modified common law property relations. Even today the laws of most states still retain remnants of the *coverture* philosophy, and thus married women do not always get the full rights to which they are morally and otherwise entitled.

The "sexist" treatment of women in the United States extended far beyond the confines of criminal and property law. Indeed, it was institutionalized, like slavery, by the Constitution itself. This was accomplished by that part of Article 1, Section 2 that allows state governments to determine voting prerequisites for both state and federal elections. Since almost all state voting laws in 1787, and for more than a hundred years later, disenfranchised women, the Founding Fathers thus legitimated female inequality in the most fundamental aspect of the political system. It would not, of course, be correct to say that they invented sexism, but it is clear that they made *political* sexism respectable by permitting states to continue to deprive females of the vital suffrage right. It is one of the ironies of U.S. history that the Constitution, as finally amended, granted full citizenship rights to *male* ex-slaves long before it did the same for free white females.

As was the case with blacks, U.S. women in the nineteenth century gradually experienced irreversible changes in their status throughout both the private and public sectors. There were three factors that mainly accounted for these changes: the industrial revolution, the democratic revolution, and the women's rights movement. By the end of the last century, women had begun to vote in certain states, they had acquired somewhat more legal rights, and with the invention of the telephone and typewriter, they began to make up a substantial percentage of business white-collar jobs. In addition, they were "liberated" from the drudgery of housework by being welcomed into the new factories. However, in light of the appalling conditions under which they had to work in mills and factories, it can hardly be said that their transfer from the home to the ranks of the urban proletariat was a genuine liberation.

Perhaps the most significant advance for U.S. women in the nineteenth century occurred in the field of education where, for the first time, middle-class females began to get some of the opportunities that formerly had been granted solely to males. Special women's colleges were established as early as the 1830s; and in the 1860s, a number of universities started admitting women on a coeducational basis. Around 1900, the proportion of colleges that had become coeducational had risen to approximately 70 percent. As increasing numbers of women were graduated from college, the professions opened up to them, but ever so slowly. Elementary teaching, where the pay was extremely low, was the first profession to welcome them with open arms. The older, more prestigious professions, such as law, medicine, and theology, admitted only a token number of females into their ranks until well into the present century.

A historic date in the women's crusade for full equality with men was 1848, for it was in July of that year that the first convention of record concerned with the rights of women convened at Seneca Falls in the state of New York. The prime movers of the convention were three female abolitionists, Elizabeth Cady Stanton, Ann Green Philips, and Lucretia Mott, who had been among the first to perceive the role similarities between blacks and white women. The convention was in session for two days and at its end issued a *Declaration of Sentiment,* which followed the style of the Declaration of Independence and proposed 11 reform resolutions to end traditional discriminations against women. That year, incidentally, also saw the granting to women of property rights roughly equal to those of men in New York and the establishment in Boston of the nation's first medical school for women.[20]

In the initial stages of the new women's rights movement, the reformers, led by such militants as Susan B. Anthony, emphasized their exploitation and "enslavement" by males and vehemently denounced the depersonalization of women in both the family and society at large. One of the more outspoken feminists, Elizabeth Oakes Smith, proclaimed in the 1850s that "We aim at nothing less than an entire subversion of the present order of society."[21] Interestingly, both the rhetoric and the tactics of the early feminists resembled those of the black militants of the ante bellum ear, which shows to what extent women were consciously using the struggle for black freedom to clarify and deepen their understanding of the unequal status of women in U.S. society. Of course, the abolitionist movement was not the only thing contributing to an awareness of their own deprivations. Their increasing educational opportunity and the greater economic freedom that entailed enabled them to interact and communicate with one another far more freely and openly than had been possible up to that time.

In the late nineteenth century, both the black and female militants changed tactics: they muted the radical aspects of their movements and made the attainment of political and voting equality their main strategic goals. The quest for female suffrage thereafter became especially intense in the United States and Great Britain, and often resulted in the wholesale arrest of determined "suffragettes," especially on election day. Yet as things turned out, several countries gave women the vote before the Untied States and Britain got around to doing so. Thus, New Zealand became the first country to grant full suffrage to all women in 1893, and a few years later a dozen northern and eastern European countries had followed suit: Finland (1906); Norway (1913); Denmark and Iceland (1915); the Netherlands and Russia (1917); Austria, Czechoslovakia, Poland, and Sweden (1918); Germany and Luxemburg (1919).

In the United States, women first achieved voting equality in certain western states, starting with Wyoming in 1890. By 1920, a total of 15 states and Alaska had granted them full suffrage; 14 states had given them presidential suffrage; and two additional states had extended them the right of participating in primaries. A great deal of the opposition to women's suffrage came from certain business groups, most notably the liquor industry that feared women would vote as a bloc for the strict regulation or prohibition of alcoholic beverages. Today most of their arguments for the continued disenfranchisement of females sound both demeaning and ludicrous.

Although there were many reasons for the ultimate enfranchisement of all U.S. female adults, not least of which was their own relentless pressure after the 1840s, most experts would probably place World War I near the top of causal agents. For it was in that war that women first came out of the closet, so to speak; and the vital contributions they made to victory provided a major impetus to their enfranchisement both in the United States and Britain, and in other countries as well. A similar progress toward voting equality occurred after World War II, when women were enfranchised in France, Italy, Japan, and in most South American countries. In communist regimes, women have always been theoretically equal to men, in voting and in all other areas. Only in Arab lands is female suffrage still today subject to substantial qualifications.

In the United States, the national enfranchisement of women was finally effected by the Nineteenth Amendment, which was approved by Congress on June 4, 1919, and ratified by the requisite number of states in 1920. In November of that year, women in *all* states participated in their first national election and, like men, cast their votes overwhelmingly for Harding and Coolidge over Cox and Roosevelt. Contrary to the fears of certain businessmen and the expectations of the more idealistic suffragettes, enfranchisement of females has not materially altered the basic structure or patterns of U.S. politics.

The Nineteenth Amendment provides that[22]

> The right of citizens of the United States to vote shall not be denied
> or abridged by the United States or by any State on account of sex.
> Congress shall have power to enforce this article by appropriate
> legislation.

It is now a basic premise of militant feminism that the year 1920 was a
decisive turning point in woman's identity in the Unted States. For not
only did women get the vote in 1920, that was also the year that ushered in
the decade of the flapper, the most enduring symbol of the emancipated
woman. Reflecting the optimism about their future that infected U.S.
women after the Nineteenth Amendment was approved, the flapper
emerged as an extremely ebullient symbol: single, free, worldly,
independent, confident—and quite unlike the girl who had married Dear
Old Dad.

Nevertheless, though the post-World War I era dramatically altered the
image of the U.S. woman, the Twenties and Thirties did not greatly
advance the practical well-being of females. Furthermore, the years of the
flapper and the Great Depression did little to mute the pyrotechnics of
anti-feminism that historically had characterized U.S. sexist politics and
literature. In regard to politics, women did gradually increase their interest
in public affairs after getting the vote, yet made little headway in gaining
high elective or appointive offices at any level of government. As for
literature, it was supremely ironic that the decade that saw the appearance
of the liberated flapper saw also the hardening of male chauvinist literature
via the emergence of the *bitch* as a basic character stereotype in the novels
of such sexist authors as Lewis, Hemingway, Fitzgerald, and Anderson.
The *bitch,* indeed, became so ubiquitous in U.S. literature that it seemed
every author was afraid of Virginia Woolf and instinctively equated the
liberated woman with the trollop. Unfortunately, the kind of sexist
literature that treats women as mere sex partners and breeders is still very
much in evidence—even on today's best-seller lists.

Here it needs to be stressed that the Nineteenth Amendment, however
meritorious, did not in any sense affect state laws dealing with ownership
of property or employment. Militant feminists, therefore, began agitating
in the 1920s for an equal rights amendment that would forever end all
forms of sexual inequality wherever they existed under cover of law. The
ERA, as that amendment came to be called, initially made little headway;
and, indeed, it was not until a full half century after its first introduction
that Congress, on March 22, 1972, finally passed it and sent it to the states

for ratification. By 1977, thirty-five states had given their approval, but unless three more ratify it, it will be dead.

The proposed Twenty-seventh Amendment states that

> Equality of rights under the law shall not be denied or abridged by the United States or by any state on account of sex.
>
> The Congress shall have power to enforce, by appropriate legislation, the provisions of this article.
>
> This amendment shall take effect two years after date of ratification.

The main opposition to ERA's enactment came from southern conservatives and Catholics. Moreover, though the overwhelming majority of state legislators who rejected it were men, the National Commission on the Observance of International Women's Year reported in 1977 that fully one half of U.S. women opposed the amendment or were "indifferent to the issue."[23] It may well be, as the commission believes, that women who support this change are the wave of the future, but it is dismaying to realize that so many U.S. women do not want the kind of role change symbolized by the ERA. As for proponents of the ERA, they argue that while it is possible that a majority of women, for some time to come, will continue to seek fulfillment in marriage and child-rearing instead of in outside employment, it is essential that this be a free choice and not an oppressive cultural requirement, as is now the case.[24]

In the 1970s, Phyllis Schlafly and other vehement opponents of the ERA propagated a number of myths about the amendment that need to be laid to rest. First of all, it is not true that ERA's adoption would require husbands to pay social security taxes twice, once on their own income, and again on the value of their wives' services at home. Some changes in the Social Security laws would be required, but that would probably be in the direction of permitting couples to share their family earnings, as they now file tax returns. Second, it is simply false to say that with ERA's ratification, a husband no longer would have to support his wife, while she would be obliged to provide half the family income. If one of the couple was a wage-earner and the other worked at home, then of course the wage-earner, irrespective of sex, would be required to support the other spouse. Third, the ERA is by no stretch of the imagination an anti-male measure. It simply makes clear that women and men have equal legal standing and that individuals should be treated as individuals. Furthermore, the word woman nowhere appears in the amendment. Fourth, it is foolish to suggest that once the ERA becomes law, there could not be separate bathrooms for men and women nor separate living quarters in prisons. The truth of the matter is that sex classifications based on physical or functional differences would continue to be legal. Fifth, there is no obligation under the ERA for Congress to assign all female draftees to combat duty in wartime. True, women would be subject to any future draft; but as in the past, all kinds of *rational* distinctions among service personnel would be permissible. Finally, it is absolute nonsense to say that upon ERA's ratification, states would be forced to legitimate homosexual marriages. By most traditional legal definitions, a marriage is the union of a man and a woman. Though the ERA does indeed give males and females equal rights, it does not in the slightest change those definitions.

Female activists have been complaining for a long time that the federal courts have not been nearly so attentive to their equality claims as to those of blacks, and until recently at least they were right. In fact, it was not until 1971 that the U.S. Supreme Court first nullified a law on the ground that it discriminated against women and thereby violated the equal protection clause of the Fourteenth Amendment.[25] Before that, "state laws excluding or restricting women's participation on juries had been sustained, as well as many laws purporting to provide special protection for women."[26]

In an interesting women's rights case decided in 1973, the Supreme Court invalidated a federal statute that allowed a serviceman automatically to claim his wife as his dependent but permitted a servicewoman to claim her husband as a dependent only if he was actually dependent on her for more than half of his support. Justice Brennan, speaking for three other justices, declared that sex, like race, was a suspect classification, and that the practical effect of sex discrimination is to "put women, not on a pedestal, but in a cage."[27] While fully agreeing with the holding in this case, militant feminists were keenly disappointed that a majority of the Court did not seize the opportunity to declare once and for all that sex-based classifications in state and federal law are suspect. Justice Powell rationalized the Supreme Court's reluctance to do that by observing that "If the people want to make such classifications improper, they have an opportunity to do so through their elected representatives."[28]

In two controversial 1974 cases, the Supreme Court moved somewhat away from the idea that sex classifications are suspect and are thus to be considered presumptively unconstitutional. In one of these, a Florida law granting a $500 yearly exemption from the state property tax to widows but not to widowers was upheld;[29] in the other, California's disability system for private employers was sustained, though it excludes from benefit coverage medical costs growing out of normal pregnancy.[30] Thus, it appeared, in 1974, that the Supreme Court was marking time until the states would decide whether to accept or reject the proposed ERA. In the meantime, the justices were cautiously moving in the direction of requiring a more severe constitutional test for laws that created gender-based classifications, but without making sex as suspect a classification as race.

The ambivalence of the Supreme Court in the field of women's rights was well illustrated by two 1975 cases. In the first of these the Court, over the bitter dissent of four justices, validated a regulation permitting male naval officers only nine years in which to be promoted or be discharged but allowing 13 years for women.[31] In the second, the Court unanimously overturned a section of the Social Security laws that gave widows of covered employees more benefits than widowers.[32] It was also in 1975 that the Court struck down a law providing that males are entitled to child support from their father until they are twenty-one but females only until they are eighteen;[33] and held that states may not impose rules for jury service on women that differ from those used for men.[34] Finally, in the 1976-77 term, the justices declared unconstitutional an Oklahoma law that allowed women to buy beer at eighteen but required men to be twenty-one because, they said, it "invidiously discriminates" by sex.[35]

By the late 1970s, it was clear that the Court was finally applying a new and stricter standard when adjudicating sex cases. The new standard was stricter than the old *rational basis* test but weaker than the *strict scrutiny* test used for race cases. To satisfy the rational basis test, a law simply must be reasonably related to a legitimate state interest. But laws classifying people by race are "inherently suspect" and must therefore be struck down unless strict scrutiny shows them to be based on a "compelling state interest." The division among the justices in regard to gender classifications is a compelling argument against those who oppose the ERA on the ground that it is unnecessary. It now appears that without adoption of the amendment, a majority of the Court will not apply the strict scrutiny test to sex discrimination cases. Logically, there would seem to be little more reason for the law to differentiate among people on sexual than on racial grounds.

During the 1960s, progress toward female equality was actually more significant in U.S. legislative bodies and executive agencies than in state or federal courts. As has been repeatedly emphasized throughout this study, that situation is usually preferable in majoritarian democracies.

Among the laws passed by Congress in the last two decades to equalize the status of U.S. women, the most consequential were the Equal Pay Act of 1963; Title VII of the Civil Rights Act of 1964; the Civil Rights Commission Act; the Equal Employment Opportunity Act of 1972; Title IX of the Education Amendments of 1972; and the Equal Credit Opportunity Act of 1974. Each of these acts became controversial, as they pitted egalitarians against libertarians, and none would have been necessary had not Congress become convinced that discrimination against women had taken on the dimensions of a national scandal.

The Civil Rights Act of 1964 was beyond question the single most important milestone in the quest for female equality since the adoption of the Nineteenth Amendment. It was, however, only a backhanded deference to the women's rights movement, since it was intended primarily to assure equal rights for *black* U.S. citizens. The language forbidding both sexual and racial discrimination was actually proposed by southern conservatives who wished to vent their anger against northern liberals. In fact, many of the bill's original proponents opposed the ban on sex discrimination because they viewed it as a divisive tactical ploy by southerners to defeat the entire measure. The bill's ultimate passage was the result of support by a strange coalition of northern liberals and southern conservatives.

For several years the act's ban on sex discrimination was more or less inoperative as the federal government devoted most of its equality-pushing efforts to upgrading the status of blacks. Things changed, however, when the Department of Health, Education, and Welfare announced in 1971 that in future it would require all colleges and universities supported by federal funds to file *affirmative action* programs for ending sex discrimination in their hiring and promotion policies. Should any institution refuse to comply, the penalty would be withdrawal of all federal support—a serious threat, since by the 1970s federal funds were accounting for more than half the budgetary resources of some educational institutions. To prove that it meant business, HEW dispatched examiners to a number of campuses to scrutinize compliance plans and check on their implementation. When Columbia University failed to file a satisfactory plan, its federal funds were cut off for five months or so. Eventually, Columbia complied and the federal funds were restored.

Nearly all federal bureaucratic agencies, along with their state counterparts, have lately stepped up their efforts to push female equality in their areas of responsibility. The service academies have even begun to accept females over the bitter objections of old-fashioned conservatives. Aside from HEW, the federal agency that has probably been most active in the field of women's rights is the Office of Federal Contract Compliance (OFCC). Located in the Department of Labor, the OFCC[36]

is responsible for establishing policies and goals and providing leadership and coordination of the Government's program to achieve nondiscrimination in employment by Government contractors and subcontractors and in federally assisted construction programs; coordinating with the Equal Employment Opportunity Commission and the Department of Justice matters relating to title VII of the Civil Rights Act of 1964 and maintaining liaison with other agencies having civil rights and equal employment opportunity activities.

Two other federal agencies merit mention here. One is the Department of Labor's Women's Bureau, which is responsible for devising policies to "promote the welfare of wage earning women, improve their working conditions, increase their efficiency, advance their opportunities for professional employment, and investigate and report on all matters pertinent to the welfare of women in industry."[37] The other is the Interdepartmental Committee on the Status of Women, which was set up by executive order in the 1960s "to maintain a continuing review and evaluation of the progress of Federal departments and agencies in advancing the status of women."[38] Neither of these agencies, essential though they are, has ever quite lived up to their sponsors' hopes.

Of all the groups struggling in the 1960s and 1970s for egalitarian goals, the militant feminists still have the most difficult task proving that they are indeed oppressed and should be taken seriously. Rectifying that required a number of interrelated tactics: saturation propaganda, nationwide organization, and a willingness to indulge in coalition-building, the *sine qua non* for getting clout in the pluralistic U.S. political process. Women who had long been subjectively aware of their deprivations had for years suffered in silence as they yearned for free and fully human lives. Then, when the decade of liberation dawned at the end of the Eisenhower Administration, thousands of them became swept up in the egalitarian ferment of the time and in quick order proved themselves amazingly adept at using the access points in the U.S. system to push their claims of equality. Today it is clear that the new feminist politicking is more than simply a series of power struggles to determine who gets what, when, where, and how. It is that all right, but it is also a basic value revolution that seeks to transform current attitudes toward women while radically altering the nation's public policy priorities. That is precisely why conservatives fear it.

The catalytic agent that got the new women's movement into orbit was the publication in the early 1960s of Betty Friedan's *The Feminine Mystique*.[39] A ringing manifesto of female grievances and aspirations, this forceful and immensely popular work brilliantly exposed the dimensions of female inequality and the demeaning consequences of a male-dominated society. Interestingly, the book appeared two years after President Kennedy issued Executive Order 10980, which set up the President's Commission on the Status of Women, and in the same year that this commission released its report. As militant as the Friedan book, the commission report was based on two crucial assumptions: that "anything peculiarly feminine is a handicap" and that women "were in many respects second-class citizens."[40]

The Friedan book and the report of the President's Commission were soon followed by a veritable flood of feminist works, most of which were couched in the militant liberation rhetoric of the 1960s.[41] Even more important, they provided the impetus for the establishment of a number of new feminist groups, including the National Organization for Women (NOW), the Women's Equity Action League, the Women's National Abortion Action Coalition, and the National Women's Political Caucus. Nearly all the leaders and activists of these organizations were middle to upper-middle-class, and none of them really succeeded in reaching anything like the entire aggregate of U.S. women. But they spoke for more and more women.

Of the groups spearheading the new women's rights movement, the most significant was NOW, which in quite a short time became the world's largest feminist group. Organized in 1966 after the Third National Conference of Governors' Commissions on the Status of Women, NOW and its twenty-eight founding men and women promptly launched a civil rights crusade for women that was soon rivaling, if not surpassing, the civil rights movements earlier established by blacks and various ethnic minorities. They ceaselessly pressured for legislative reform; picketed numerous all-male establishments; boycotted goods that were marketed by sexist advertising; and waged a concerted campaign to change the sexual *Zeitgeist* in the United States. Though from the beginning the militant feminists of NOW were derided as hags, lesbians, and family-wreckers, they persevered and by the early 1970s had almost single-handedly altered both the spirit and the values of U.S. culture and politics. They won back pay settlements from sexist corporations in the courts; they got a few state legislatures to liberalize abortion laws; they induced Congress to pass the Equal Credit Opportunity Act; they persuaded newspapers to quit segregating their help-wanted sections; they desegregated all-male bars; and, perhaps most important, they were instrumental in getting a ban on sex discrimination added to Executive order 11246 that prohibits discrimination by federal contractors.

There can be little doubt that for much of the 1960s and 1970s *NOW was the cutting edge of social change in the United States.* Yet despite its very real achievements, U.S. women continue to be disadvantaged in a wide variety of ways. The earnings gap between male and female workers appears to be widening. Enforcement work by EEOC has been spotty, and its back pay awards have been fairly low. The Equal Credit Act has not been fully enforced because of lack of staff. And pregnant working women are still generally shut out from disability benefits. But even more disheartening, from the feminist perspective, is the fact that the ERA has deeply divided the nation's women, and its ratification seems to be in deep trouble.

In addition to its external problems, NOW has had a number of internal difficulties that in recent years severely limited its effectiveness. In the mid-1970s its membership rolls dipped disastrously and its budget was drastically pared because of reduced contributions. Even worse, there was a deep power struggle within the organization in 1975 that resulted in the formation of two ideologically diverse factions, one moderate in approach, the other quite radical. Fortunately, for the cause of women's rights, the two warring factions disbanded in 1976, and in the following year the organization appeared to have surmounted its internal troubles as it entered a new era of renewed dedication and intra-group harmony.

In regard to operational strategy, NOW apparently believes its reform "legislation will be achieved in much the same way that legislation of any other kind is achieved: by lobbying, by gaining the attention of the media, and by attempting to win over public opinion. No restructuring of society, remolding of women, or reconstruction of family or sexual life is required."[42] This commitment to traditional ways of doing things has been well expressed by Betty Friedan, one of the founders of NOW and its leading moderate:[43]

> [The modern woman] must learn to compete . . . not as a woman, but as a human being. Not until a great many women move out of the fringes into the mainstream will society itself provide the arrangements for their new life plan. But every girl who manages to stick it out through law school or medical school, who finishes her M.A. or Ph.D. and goes on to use it, helps others to move on. . . .
>
> When enough women make life plans geared to their real abilities, and speak out for maternity leaves or even maternity sabbaticals, professionally run nurseries, and the other changes in the rules that may be necessary, they will not have to sacrifice the right to honorable competition and contribution any more than they will have to sacrifice marriage and motherhood.

There are, to be sure, other voices of the new woman than Betty Friedan and NOW, and many of these are proclaiming what has come to be known as *radical feminism*. The radical feminists, often cruelly caricatured in the media, see "sexism as the principal basis of societal organization, a kind of class system of two classes—the male oppressors and the female oppressed."[44] Some even go so far as to propose a philosophy of history that supplants Marxian economic determinism with a kind of *sexual determinism*.[45]

Among the radical feminists, some are socialist or Marxian in orientation while others are not. But whatever their ideological bent, they are one and all determined to effect a truly radical reconstruction of U.S. society and government. The Marxian proponents of female equality refuse to concentrate their efforts solely on women's liberation, arguing that there are many other kinds of capitalistic oppression besides the sexual. Quite logically, they insist on putting economics above sex as the chief agent of inequality; and unlike the more pragmatic radicals and moderates, they stress the role of ideology in shaping peoples' attitudes and behavior, and especially in legitimizing the position of women as housewives. Angela Davis is a leading exponent of this viewpoint.

The non-socialist radicals charge that the socialists fail "to act in terms of an understanding of feminist consciousness and feminist needs and goals."[46] They point out, moreover, that sexism predated capitalism and continues to exist even in socialist countries where capitalism has been abolished. This anomaly leads them to charge that socialists have a rhetorical but not a genuine, reality-centered understanding of women's consciousness. Finally, they assert that socialists have "no real sense of the need to make politics intensely personal, to connect sexuality and the family with the problem and process of change."[47]

The majority of recent feminist works, at least in the West, have not been written from either a socialist or Marxian perspective. Still many have been, and among these are some of the most intellectually sophisticated examples of feminist protest. Several names come to mind in this regard, but Simone de Beauvoir, the friend of Sartre, and Sheila Rowbotham have perhaps produced the strongest statements of the new socialist women's liberation position. Even those activists who deny that woman's independence and equality can come only with socialism find the works of de Beauvoir and Rowbotham immensely stimulating.[48] So apparently do enlightened males.

As U.S. women expand their demands for sexual equality and freedom, one of the most perplexing ideological and practical problems they have had to confront has been deciding what position to take toward female homosexuals. Virtually all female egalitarians believe that lesbianism should be decriminalized and that lesbians should have the same basic social and legal rights as non-lesbians. Yet the women's rights movement in recent years has split sharply on the extent to which lesbian issues should be highlighted and on the degree to which women should link their own struggle to the equality crusades of such groups as Gay Liberation. Generally speaking, the moderates, led by Betty Friedan, would soft-pedal the lesbian issue as a tactical ploy, while the radicals would put increasing emphasis on it. The gay-straight split, implicit in the women's movement from the beginning, did not become a serious problem until the early

1970s, and many believe it was the single most important cause of the recent deceleration of the movement's forward momentum. That seems to be the view of Friedan, among others. It is decidedly not the view of Kate Millet or Gloria Steinem.

In addition to continued popular opposition, the homosexuals' quest for sexual equality suffered a tactical setback in early 1976 when the Vatican issued a strong statement that homosexuals, though deserving of compassion, are definitely sinners. That was followed in the United States by a declaration of the National Council of Catholic Bishops that homosexual conduct is totally contrary to Judeo-Christian morality.[49] The National Council and the Vatican were indirectly responding to pressure from Dignity, an organization founded in 1968 in Los Angeles to promote the acceptance of homosexuals in the Catholic Church. Dignity's approach has generally been educational and low-key, though some of its leaders did denounce the Vatican statement. More important, the increasing militance of Dignity demonstrates that radical homosexuals, whether male or female, Protestant or Catholic, are now intent on getting nothing less than full recognition of homosexuality as an alternative life style.

That has not yet come, but they have already achieved a large measure of success. U.S. psychiatrists have dropped homosexuality from their list of mental disorders. The U.S. Civil Service Commission has held that homosexuals may not be fired merely because of their sexual persuasion. Numerous corporations have issued statements promising equal opportunities for homosexuals. And eighteen states have decriminalized homosexual acts between consenting adults in private, while others no longer vigorously enforce their sodomy statutes. In addition, almost half a hundred cities and counties, following the example of San Francisco, have enacted gay rights' ordinances.

On the negative side, U.S. courts continue to be unsympathetic to homosexual rights, as does the military; and in 1977, a conservative backlash against gay rights arose, resulting in the overwhelming defeat of a Miami gay rights' ordinance. The backlash is forcefully led by the singer and Baptist laywoman Anita Bryant, and it will almost certainly slow down the campaign for homosexual equality if not set it back several years. U.S. conservatives apparently want both gays and women to return to their closets—a desire not likely to be fulfilled.

While the somewhat splintered feminist movement continues to denounce the inequalities to which women have been subjected through the ages, conservative males are now raising the spectre of declining freedom as a consequence of women's gains. Specifically, they are saying that the radical feminists are dramatizing anew democracy's eternal paradox, with alarming results for middle-class males.

Male critics of militant feminism—or male chauvinist pigs as the radicals label them—have been maintaining for some time that if female equality is carried beyond a certain point, it will unfairly abridge the liberties of men and thereby harm society at large. Whether they have ever read him or not, they obviously agree with Calhoun, who wrote in his famous *Disquisition on Government* that[50]

> It is, indeed, this inequality of condition between the front and rear ranks, in the march of progress, which gives so strong an impulse to the former to maintain their position, and to the latter to press forward into their files. This gives to progress its greatest impulse. To . . . push forward the rear into line with the front, by the interposition of the government, would put an end to the impulse, and effectually arrest the march of progress.

The feminists' critics may not want to arrest the march of progress; but like the late Sigmund Freud, they constantly shake their heads and ask in despair, *What do women want?* From the dominant male vantage point, women don't have it bad at all. They gain a firm identity from their husband and children. They have a near-monopoly on elementary school teaching and white-collar clerical jobs. When young and pretty, they are universally admired as ornaments. And when married, they have a life-time provider and need never work outside the home.

At the present time, what male critics object to most about the sexual revolution are those affirmative action programs in business, government, and education that require *compensatory* hiring of females when new positions are created or vacancies in old ones arise. To the critics, such coerced rectification of past abuses is but another form of inequality; and since they insist it is purchased at the price of somebody else's freedom, they consider it neither just nor democratic. As a male journalist recently put it, "there is an unseemly clamoring for 'rights' abroad in the land these days, and affirmative-action programs have played a part in contributing to this."[51] Indeed, they have.

In early 1976, no less an authority than Pope Paul VI echoed the critics' objections when he declared that "The equalizing of rights must not degenerate into an egalitarian and impersonal leveling." Egalitarianism, he continued, is "blindly pushed forward by our materialistic society and . . . thereby runs the risk of either virilizing women or of depersonalizing them. In both cases it does violence to women's deepest qualities." The Pope did, however, side with the feminists when he said that men should "take their part in bringing up and educating children to a greater degree."[52]

Conservative males are also worried by the activities of such groups as the Women's Legal Defense Fund that are suing to open up the legal and other professions to more women. Thus conservative male lawyers, who have traditionally dominated the U.S. legal profession, were understandably shocked when the prestigious law firm of Rogers & Wells (the senior partner is former Secretary of State Williams Rogers) recently lost a lawsuit brought by feminists and was ordered to institute a quota system in future hiring within the firm.[53]

According to a news report about the lawsuit,[54]

> The formula is based on the number of women in the graduating classes of the twelve law schools (among them: Yale, Harvard, the University of Virginia) at which the firm does almost all its interviewing. This year women make up 21.3% of those classes; as a result, at least 25.56% (120% times 21.3%) of all the job offers Rogers & Wells makes will be to women. A similar formula will apply to summer hiring. But the agreement also made it clear that people hired under the quota would be every bit as qualified as those outside it.

As expected, the Women's Legal Defense Fund hailed the Rogers & Wells decision as a big victory for female equality, while their male critics pejoratively dubbed it the 120 percent solution.

Three branches of the feminist movement are especially anathema to anti-feminist men: the Marxian branch that seeks to replace capitalism with socialism; the Platonic unisexual branch that insists that men and women are virtually identical in all respects; and the newly-emergent female separatists, among whom lesbians are prominent, who maintain that women can attain political, economic, and social equality only through voluntary separation from men. This last group, interestingly, first came to prominence in the late 1960s when black leaders like Carmichael and Hamilton had begun to preach a similar version of voluntary separatism for blacks.[55] The feminists' critics insist that the radical wings of the women's rights movement, if victorious, would inevitably diminish both the freedom and equality of women as well as men, and eventually would destroy the Judeo-Christian scaffolding that undergirds Western civilization. Obviously, the feminists totally reject such a gloomy view—or at least the militants do—even though the Holy Father seems to share it.

To the extent that it was economic, the original women's rights movement was centered almost exclusively on trying to break into more white-collar and professional positions. In the 1970s that began to change, as militant feminists started a campaign for a greater share of blue-collar jobs, which traditionally have been union-controlled. As could have been predicted, this greatly disturbed male union leaders, who had always assumed, like their followers, that women were neither interested in, nor qualified for blue-collar work. To an extent, the record of working women in World War II had ended the illusion that "men only" jobs were as exclusively a masculine domain as had been thought, and so in the 1970s the militant feminists decided it was time to permanently revive the old wartime egalitarianism of plant and factory.

The women's success in this controversial area has already been substantial. Indeed, according to former Assistant Secretary of Labor William Kolberg, women are now engaged in "practically every type of occupation that was once the private domain of men." Today, therefore, "Whether it's subway construction, bridge building, boilermaking, bulldozing, truck driving or running big newspaper presses—all tough and dirty or dangerous jobs—the women are at it."[56]

Government statistics generally seem to bear out Kolberg's assertions. Thus, it was revealed that at the end of 1975, women held roughly 18 percent or 5.5 million of the 28.2 million blue-collar jobs in the nation, a substantial increase over the 14.9 percent of such jobs held by women in 1960. Government figures also recently showed a 74 percent increase in a single year in the number of women apprentices in 50 occupational groupings, virtually all of which were formerly the exclusive province of men. In light of these data, it is hard to refute Kolberg's conclusion that though "there are not enough women in all blue-collar occupations to permit anyone to say that sex discrimination is a thing of the past, . . . there is no question that opportunities for women are broadening in all fields, professional as well as blue-collar."[57]

Yet despite the very real gains that women have recently made in business and industry, they still often trail European women in economic rights. They have greater problems with male-dominated unions. They have more trouble establishing legal rights to equal pay and equal opportunity. And, unlike their European counterparts, U.S. women generally do not have free family planning clinics, paid pregnancy leave, nor across-the-board child benefit plans. Of course, the status of European women differs from country to country, and perhaps only Scandinavian women are significantly ahead of their U.S. sisters. Yet it remains a source of understandable irritation to feminists that U.S. society and the U.S. economy should trail any area of the world in the matter of freedom and equality.[58]

Although the AFL-CIO has vigorously supported the ERA and has welcomed legislation mandating equal pay for equal work, none of the organization's executive council seats is held by a woman, at least not as of 1977. That may not, however, be true for much longer, as the new president of NOW, Eleanor Smeal, has publicly committed herself to seek a NOW-labor coalition that will increase the number of women in union executive jobs and at the same time provide a united front to push for such issues as a higher minimum wage and disability insurance for housewives.[59] If it turns out that NOW and the AFL-CIO do, indeed, form a political alliance, their clout in both the economy and the public sector will be tremendously increased. As Gloria Steinem has aptly put it, "Whether women have to start their own unions, democratize the existing ones, or both, women workers need unionism—and vice versa."[60]

The most dramatic recent victory of the women's rights movement was not economic but judicial. That occurred in 1973 when the U.S. Supreme Court used substantive due process to invalidate restrictive abortion statutes in forty-six states, and in the process severely limited the power of state legislatures to regulate the surgical procedures involved in abortions. Specifically, the Court resolved two issues in its abortion decision. It held that the term *person* as used in the Fourteenth Amendment does *not* include the unborn. And, more important, it held that the constitutional right of privacy includes a woman's decision on abortion. It is true that the Constitution does not expressly recognize a right of privacy. But as Justice Blackmun noted in his majority opinion, the Court has long recognized a constitutional right of privacy based primarily upon the Ninth and Fourteenth Amendments. Finally, the Court held that during the first trimester of pregnancy, the decision whether or not to abort a fetus is up to the woman involved and her doctor. During the last six months, the state may regulate abortion standards in the interest of health protection, though only during the final trimester may it forbid abortion, save where necessary to protect the life or health of the mother.[61]

As anticipated, militant feminists, who had hitherto had little success in persuading state legislatures to alter their strict abortion laws, hailed the Court's decision as evidence of the power of the women's movement and of a shift in U.S. social attitudes. They likewise viewed it, quite understandably, as a milestone in the women's struggle for equality.

Equally predictably, the nation's conservatives, male and female, denounced the abortion decision as immoral, constitutionally unsound, and subversive of fundamental freedoms. Basically, the critics argued that four kinds of freedom were effectively eroded by the Court's holding. These included the freedom of the fetus to enjoy a full pregnancy, the freedom of society to establish binding moral values, the freedom of state legislators to adopt social policies without interference from the federal government, and the freedom of fathers to participate in abortion decisions. The more extreme among the critics castigated the decision as judicial legitimation of the most heinous kind of murder—*feticide*. Many of the critics banded together in "Right-to-Life" groups to overturn the abortion decision by lititgation, new legislation, or a constitutional amendment. Although the activities of such groups caused grave concern among feminists, there was no indication in the late 1970s that the Supreme Court was prepared to reverse its approval of abortion.

It is doubtful that most feminists favor abortion-on-demand as an instrument of population control, and there is no evidence that they favor the abolition of motherhood. But feminists have long believed that state regulation of pregnancies, save to protect the mother's health, violated their right of privacy and their fundamental right to make decisions directly affecting their own body. In addition, they appeared to resent the fact that abortion reform measures were consistently voted down by legislative bodies that were overwhelmingly male.

Regarding the specific egalitarian implications of the abortion decision, feminists stressed that middle-class women had always been able to secure abortions with little difficulty, and that now lower-class women would also enjoy that right. For a time that was true, as Medicaid began paying for roughly one-third of all abortions. But then in 1977, the Supreme Court shocked feminists by holding in effect that a woman has a right to a non-therapeutic abortion *only if she can pay for it.* Since President Carter and a majority of Congress appear to share that view, it is no longer clear that the Court's original abortion decision was a significant gain in economic as well as sexual equality.

Notwithstanding the important judicial and economic advances made by women in recent years, the militants among them, like militant blacks, remain dissatisfied because their achievements are still far below their aspirations. The revolution of rising expectations, quite obviously, has affected women no less than racial and ethnic minorities.

Feminists never tire of publicizing the mountainous data that confirm the continued second-class status of women. Here, for example, there has never been a female president, vice president, secretary of state, secretary of defense, or U.S. Supreme Court justice, though women in Asia and Europe have frequently held comparable positions. Moreover, there have been only a handful of U.S. governors, state legislators, congressmen, and senators who were women. And in the private sector of the economy, "Women are only seven percent of doctors, three percent of lawyers, and one percent of engineers. More depressing is evidence that the situation has been getting worse."[62] All of these statistics and others that might be adduced are probative of a point made by the women's rights movement: sex roles involve power relations, and traditional sexual roles in U.S. culture are used to rationalize differential and unequal treatment, status, and power of men and women.

Although militant feminists seemed to prefer Carter to Ford in the presidential election of 1976, they have recently been critical of the new president's record in hiring women. There are only two women in the Carter cabinet: Commerce Secretary Juanita Kreps and Secretary of Housing and Urban Development Patricia Roberts Harris, who is black. In the White House itself, only one woman ranks among the top presidential assistants. The National Women's Political Caucus, founded in 1971 to encourage the election and appointment of more women to public office, seems particularly unhappy that Carter's appointments record in the White House has not matched his pro-feminist rhetoric during the 1976 campaign.[64]

The Carter appointment that has perhaps most pleased feminists was the naming of Eleanor Holmes Norton to be chairwoman of the Equal Employment Opportunities Commission. For some time now, militant feminists along with militant blacks have been attacking the EEOC as a bumbling bureaucratic nonentity, devoid of will, enlightened direction, or capacity to clear its backlog of unsettled complaints, all of which was complicated by the Ford Administration's minimal support for the agency. Present evidence seems to suggest that President Carter intends to breathe new life into the EEOC; and if that is true, Eleanor Holmes Norton may well be the best possible selection for accomplishing that goal.[65] In any event, she appears to be a resolute pro-feminist, and is also black. Incidentally, a few years ago the U.S. Civil Rights Commission recommended the formation of a single agency, a National Employment Rights Board, to handle the problem of employment discrimination, whether based on sex or race. Most women's rights organizations appear to support that recommendation, while conservatives oppose it.

What worries feminists today far more than the ambivalent record of the Carter Administration is the rising wave of demagoguery among right-wingers, focusing largely, but not entirely on defeat of the ERA.[66] From their perspective, the ERA's opponents are using almost the same arguments that male chauvinists used in the early nineteenth century to defeat Married Women's Property Acts. Some women are now suggesting, with a touch of humor, that full equality between the sexes will not be an accomplished fact until the female dummy moves ahead in the world as fast as the male dummy. That, they say, will be a better litmus test of sexual equality than the fate of the ERA, vital though that is.

As feminists, and to a lesser degree homosexuals, consolidate and intensify their quest for full sexual equality in freedom, conservative males show no signs of relenting in defense of their vested interests. They are unwilling to admit that women are treated as unequally as their leaders claim, and they do not believe that the activities of militant feminists are a legitimate extension of U.S. pluralist politics, which has always been based on the assumption that power is, and ought to be dispersed among peaceful, pragmatic competitive groups. What more and more conservatives seem to be fearing is that radical feminists will come to disdain the traditional weapons of bargaining and negotiation and thus reject incremental change in favor of revolutionary innovations. Of course, Marxian feminists have always advocated that, though the great majority of U.S. feminists have not.

Be that as it may, social change in a complicated pluralist system such as that of the United States can rarely ever be accomplished overnight. But so long as the nation's resources are limited, conservative anti-feminists are logical in thinking that if women gain a larger and more equal portion of society's resources, others may receive proportionately less. The task of the feminists is to convince the more moderate and influential males that women are indeed a deprived minority, who are functionally akin to disadvantaged racial-ethnic groups, and as such they need *transitional* assistance if they are ever to become full first-class citizens. They also need to convince the nation's male power elites, from the Supreme Court down to the county courthouse, that the concomitant of genuine female equality need be neither female chauvinism nor substantial male inequality. Even granted that national resources are finite, it is wrong to believe that equality is a zero-sum game in which gains and losses neatly counterbalance each other.

Conservatives were as elated as women and blacks were dismayed when it was announced in June, 1977, that the U.S. Supreme Court, ruling in a Texas case, had held that a seniority system was not necessarily illegal even if its effect was to favor white males over others in bidding for promotions or in securing protection from layoffs. As for discrimination that occurred prior to passage of the 1964 Civil Rights Act, Justice Stewart, speaking for the Court majority, held that "no person may be given retroactive seniority to a date earlier than the effective date of the act ... [for it was not the intent of Congress to] destroy or water down the vested seniority rights of employees simply because their employer had engaged in discrimination prior to the passage of the act."[67]

Although Justices Marshall and Brennan, reflecting the view of black and feminist egalitarians, called the decision "devastating,"[68] white male unionists clearly were happy with what the majority had wrought. Indeed, it was promptly suggested that one of the effects of the Court's holding would be "to prompt a flood of 'reverse discrimination' suits by white males claiming that they were held back so that women and blacks could catch up."[69] That, of course, remains a possibility; but at the present time it does not appear to be an immediate threat to either sexual or racial equality.

No governmental agency, whether judicial, legislative, or administrative, can abruptly halt socioeconomic discrimination against women by fiat, nor can it assure every woman a lucrative job and a college degree. Yet, notwithstanding this basic fact of political life, government can and must create conditions favorable to the elimination of sexual inequalities where they exist. It can also insure that women have equal, and perhaps for a time preferential, opportunities of gaining an education, entering all professions, and working and living wherever they wish. Though the tenacity of sexism remains a fearsome thing in spite of the best efforts of government, it is unlikely in the long run to be able to withstand the inexorable force of the onrushing egalitarian revolution.[70]

When all is said and done, it may well be that Karl Marx spoke the definitive word on sexual equality when he observed that[71]

> Anyone who knows anything of history knows that great social changes are impossible without the feminine ferment. Social progress can be measured exactly by the social position of the fair sex (the ugly ones included).

NOTES

1. S.J. Makielski, Jr., *Beleaguered Minorities: Cultural Politics in America* (San Francisco: W.H. Freeman and Co., 1973), p. 86.
2. Ibid., p. 87.
3. Crane Brinton, John B. Christopher, and Robert Lee Wolff, *A History of Civilization,* vol. 1, *Prehistory to 1715* (New York: Prentice-Hall, 1955), p. 35.
4. *Encyclopaedia Britannica: Macropaedia,* 15th ed., s.v. "Women, Status of."
5. Ibid.
6. Ibid. (Quoted)
7. In this regard, it is interesting to note that in 1970 an Israeli court refused to grant Israeli nationality to children whose father was an Israeli citizen but whose mother was not Jewish.
8. Rom. 16:1-27.
9. 1 Cor. 11:7. The next two verses read: "For man was not made from woman, but woman from man, and man was not created for woman, but woman was for man."
10. 1 Pet. 3:1-4.
11. Vergilius Ferm, ed., *Encyclopedia of Religion* (Paterson, N.J.: Littlefield, Adams & Co., 1959), p. 829.
12. A good study of this madness is Robert D. Anderson, "Witchcraft and Sex," *Sexual Behavior,* September 1972, pp. 8-14.
13. See John Demos, *A Little Commonwealth: Family Life in Plymouth Colony* (New York: Oxford University Press, 1970), p. 97. Also relevant is Keith W. Thomas, "The Double Standard," *Journal of the History of Ideas* 20 (1959): 195-216.

14. David H. Flaherty, "Law and the Enforcement of Morals in Early America," *Perspectives in American History* 5 (1971): 226. It should be noted that most colonial bastardy prosecutions were not accompanied by presentment for fornication or adultery, though obviously one of those crimes must have been involved where bastardy resulted.
15. Ibid., p. 240.
16. W.I.T., Jr., "Notes: Competency of One Spouse to Testify Against The Other in Criminal Cases Where The Testimony Does Not Relate to Confidential Communications: Modern Trend," *Virginia Law Review* 38 (1952): 359.
17. Ibid., p. 360.
18. Ibid., p. 361. (Quoted)
19. See 13 *Peters* 209 (U.S. 1839) and *Bassett* v. *United States*, 137 U.S. 496 (1890).
20. Gorton Carruth, ed., *The Encyclopedia of American Facts and Dates*, 2nd ed. (New York: Thomas Y. Crowell, 1959), pp. 221, 225.
21. Makielski, p. 89.
22. Because upper-class women vote in far greater numbers than lower-class ones do, "it may be that the Nineteenth Amendment introduced a slight political advantage for the values represented by the 'upper classes.' " Peltason, p. 210.
23. *Des Moines Register*, 16 May 1977, p. 10A.
24. A surprising 1976 poll revealed "that while 59% of adult males supported the ERA, only 55% of the women favored it." *Time*, 25 April 1977, p. 89.
25. *Reed* v. *Reed*, 404 U.S. 71 (1971).
26. Peltason, p. 196.
27. *Frontiero* v. *Richardson*, 411 U.S. 677 (1973).
28. Ibid.
29. *Kahn* v. *Shevin*, 416 U.S. 351 (1974).
30. *Gedulding* v. *Aiello*, 417 U.S. 484 (1974).
31. *Schlesinger* v. *Ballard*, 419 U.S. 498 (1975).
32. *Weinberger* v. *Wiesenfeld*, 420 U.S. 636 (1975).
33. *Stanton* v. *Stanton*, 421 U.S. 7 (1975).
34. *Taylor* v. *Louisiana*, 419 U.S. 522 (1975).
35. *Des Moines Register*, 25 January 1977, p. 10.
36. General Services Administration, *United States Government Manual 1975-1976* (Washington, D.C.: Government Printing Office, 1975), p. 342.
37. Ibid.
38. Ibid., p. 640.
39. Betty Friedan, *The Feminine Mystique* (New York: Norton, 1963).
40. Makielski, pp. 90-1.
41. See especially Kirsten Amundsen, *The Silenced Majority: Women and American Democracy* (Englewood Cliffs, N.J.: Prentice-Hall, 1971); Caroline Bird, *Born Female: The High Cost of Keeping Women Down* (New York: David McKay, 1968); Aileen Kraditor, *Up From the Pedestal* (Chicago: Quadrangle Books, 1968); Margaret Mead and Frances Bagley Kaplan, *American Women: The Report of the President's Commission on the Status of Women* (New York: Scribner's, 1965); Kate Millet, *Sexual Politics* (Garden City, N.Y.: Doubleday, 1970); and Robin Morgan, ed., *Sisterhood is Powerful* (New York: Vintage, 1970). A work of the 1950s is also valuable: Eleanor Flexnor, *Century of Struggle: The Woman's Rights*

Movement (Cambridge, Mass.: Harvard University Press, 1959). A magazine article of considerable insight is Alice Rossi, "Women: The Terms of Liberation," *Dissent,* November/December 1970, pp. 531-41.

42. Dolbeare and Dolbeare, p. 181.
43. Friedan, p. 326.
44. Dolbeare and Dolbeare, p. 181.
45. See Shulamith Firestone, *The Dialectic of Sex: The Case for Feminist Revolution* (New York: Morrow, 1970).
46. Dolbeare and Dolbeare, p. 184.
47. Ibid., p. 185.
48. See Simone de Beauvoir, *The Second Sex* (New York: Bantam Books, 1961); and Sheila Rowbotham, *Woman's Consciousness, Man's World* (Baltimore: Penguin Books, 1973). A useful scholarly study of women's liberation that puts considerable stress on economic issues is Barbara Sinclair Deckard, *The Women's Movement: Political, Socioeconomic, and Psychological Issues* (New York: Harper & Row, 1975). This original text combines sophisticated analysis with considerable descriptive material in examining the past and present social, economic, and political status of women. All viewpoints prevalent within the women's movement are discussed and appraised.
49. Challenging the statement of the National Council of Catholic Bishops was a controversial 322-page sex report, published in 1977 and commissioned by the board of the Catholic Theological Society of America. The report, written by a committee of two priests, one nun, and two laymen, shows the growing strength in Catholic ranks of those who reject official Church teachings about sex. Among other things, the report concludes that much pornography is neuter to most adults; that sterilization is a legitimate form of birth control; that widowed and divorced people cannot be expected to live as though they were nonsexual beings; and that priests should recommend stable friendships for homosexuals rather than sexual abstinence. See Father Anthony Kosnik, ed., *Human Sexuality: New Directions in American Catholic Thought* (New York: Paulist Press, 1977).
50. Quoted in Larry I. Peterman and Louis F. Weschler, *American Political Thought: Readings* (New York: Appleton-Century-Crofts, 1972), p. 156.
51. Tom Bethell, "Anti-Discrimination Run Amuck," *Newsweek,* 17 January 1977, p. 11. In 1977 Mr. Bethell was Washington editor of *Harper's* and a contributing editor of *The Washington Monthly.*
52. Quoted in *Des Moines Sunday Register,* 1 February 1976, p. 1.
53. *Time,* 1 March 1976, p. 41.
54. Ibid.
55. See Stokely Carmichael and Charles V. Hamilton, *Black Power: The Politics of Liberation in America* (New York: Vintage, 1967).
56. *Des Moines Register,* 1 March 1976, p. 10.
57. Ibid.
58. A good analysis of this subject is Shari Steiner, *The Female Factor, A Report on Women in Western Europe* (New York: G.P. Putnam's, 1977). Three excellent studies of the economic activities of U.S. women are Juanita M. Kreps, *Women and the American Economy: A Look to the 1980s* (Englewood Cliffs, N.J.: Prentice-Hall, 1976); National Commission on the Observance of International Women's Year, *"To Form a More Perfect Union . . .": Justice for American Women* (Washington, D.C.: Government Printing Office, 1976); and Smithsonian Institution, *Workers and Allies:*

Female Participation in the American Trade Union Movement, 1824-1976 (Washington, D.C.: Government Printing Office, 1975).

59. Smeal became president of NOW in 1977 and immediately gave signs of becoming a most active executive. A Pittsburgh housewife who is now in her late thirties, she has a master's degree in political science from the University of Florida and is a veteran organizer of NOW chapters. It will be surprising if NOW, under her direction, does not wage a strong offensive on all economic issues affecting women.

60. *Des Moines Register,* 6 May 1977, p. 12A. Steinem also pointed out that though there are about four million female union members in the United States, only about 10 percent of women overall are working under union contracts. This is a major reason for the vast male-female pay differential in the U.S. private sector.

61. *Roe* v. *Wade,* 410 U.S. 113 (1973). On the same day, the Court overturned Georgia's anti-abortion law because it set unreasonable conditions for abortions, especially in matters of state residence and hospital accreditation. See *Doe* v. *Bolton,* 410 U.S. 179 (1973).

62. Sohner, p. 151.

63. See Dye, p. 39.

64. In June, 1977, Freddie Wechsler, a spokeswoman for the NWPC, publicly criticized Carter by stating that "expectations for the number of women in decision-making roles have not been met by actual appointments." *Des Moines Tribune,* 10 June 1977, p. 12.

65. The handling of job discrimination by the EEOC is a central concern of William B. Gould, *Black Workers in White Unions: Job Discrimination in the United States* (Ithaca, N.Y.: Cornell University Press, 1977).

66. Right-wing demagoguery was perhaps decisive in the 1976 New York and New Jersey elections in which proposals to adopt *state* equal rights amendments were defeated, though both states had voted in 1972 to ratify the *federal* ERA. See *Time,* 17 November 1975, p. 65.

67. *Time,* 13 June 1977, p. 60. (Quoted)

68. Ibid.

69. Ibid.

70. Among recent contributions to the literature of sexual equality, the following are especially recommended: Lucia H. Bequaert, *Single Women: Alone and Together* (Boston: Beacon, 1976); William H. Chafe, *Women and Equality: Changing Patterns in American Culture* (New York: Oxford, 1977); Jean Baker Miller, *Toward a New Psychology of Women* (Boston: Beacon, 1976); Juanita H. Williams, *Psychology of Women: Behavior in a Biosocial Context* (New York: Norton, 1977); and Gayle Graham Yates, *What Women Want: The Ideas of the Movement* (Cambridge, Mass.: Harvard University Press, 1975).

71. Quoted in *Des Moines Sunday Register,* 12 June 1977, p. 3B.

8.

THE QUEST FOR EQUAL
EDUCATIONAL OPPORTUNITY

If there is one thing that all disadvantaged minorities agree upon today, it is that the attainment of equal educational opportunity is absolutely essential to their quest for first-class citizenship. Indeed, some minority leaders look upon educational equality as even more immediately crucial than social, economic, or political equality since they believe, rightly or wrongly, that the inevitable concomitant of equality in the nation's schools will be increased opportunities in every area of life. Such leaders appear to view education as a kind of circuit breaker that in the course of time will permanently interrupt the vicious cycle of poverty and discrimination that has long entrapped the disadvantaged. One might even say that until recently, nearly all minority spokesmen revealed a faith in the rehabilitative power of education that bordered on the utopian.

Such a faith is understandable given the fact that in the modern world, education, though not a panacea, has emerged as a magic key that unlocks innumerable doors of opportunity. Defined as the development of mental powers and character through systematic instruction in schools and other institutions, education is by any criteria one of the principal sources of power and authority—on a par, in that regard, with money, religion, and military force. Ironically, education traditionally has been both a pro- and anti-equality force, depending on its scope and nature in a given place and time. It has been an anti-equality force when conservative in content and confined to a small elite; it has been egalitarian in thrust when liberal in content and extensive in scope.

Most scholars would probably agree that "The term education can be applied to primitive cultures only in the sense of enculturation, which is the process of cultural transmission."[1] In that sense the education of primitive peoples was quite egalitarian, for it entailed participatory learning throughout society and involved all members of the community about equally. Primitive education or socialization was probably a good deal more complex than is generally thought today, since in addition to instruction in practical subjects such as hunting and fishing, it involved citizenship-training, character-building, and initiation into "a whole set of cultural values, tribal religion, myths, philosophy, history, rituals, and other knowledge."[2] Although hierarchical distinctions existed within all primitive societies, the kinds of educational inequality characteristic of modern communities were simply unknown in their primitive counterparts.

The history of education in the modern sense is usually dated from about 3000 B.C., when what we call *civilization* is thought to have commenced in the Middle East. As all agree, the basis of education in Mesopotamia and Egypt was the art of writing, without which formal education as we know it would not have been possible. With writing, education became a more organized, systematic process than it had hitherto been among primitive peoples, and initially it appears to have been under the tight control of priests.

Egyptians were among the first people to develop formal schools, which at first were divided into schools for scribes and schools for priest trainees. Both types of schools were apparently rigidly structured and were, of course, restricted to a minuscule portion of the population. The schools in Mesopotamia were similar to those in Egypt and were equally elitist. Among other ancient peoples, early schools also flourished in China, India, and in those parts of the New World controlled by the Mayas, Aztecs, and Incas.

In ancient Israel, as in most other pre-industrial societies, education was originally familial, and in that sense egalitarian. The mother instructed the girls, while the father instructed the sons, and for centuries the Hebrew teacher's role was expressed in terms of parenthood. After taking over Palestine, the Jews borrowed a writing system from the Phoenicians and proceeded to set up specialized professional schools that were primarily for the education of scribes and priests. Then, following the downfall of Israel in 722-21 B.C., Jewish education became almost entirely religious in orientation, reflecting the fact that schools were now physically located in synagogues. As one scholar has well observed, "This religiously-based education was to become one of the most important factors enabling Judaism to survive the national catastrophes of A.D. 70 and 135, involving the capture and subsequent destruction of Jerusalem. . . . From this evolved the respect with which the teacher was and is surrounded in Jewish communities."[3] Though the Jews would tenaciously cling to Hebrew as their only language for worship and for study of the Law, only a handful in any generation became truly educated in the full sense of the word. Modern Israel seems even more education-obsessed than ancient Israel.

More influential in the Western world than Egyptian or Hebraic educational practices were those of the early Greeks, particularly the institutions originated by Sparta and Athens. Sparta, in fact, may have been the first society to initiate full-scale coeducational instruction and to establish schools that were precursors of the U.S. military R.O.T.C. programs. The Spartans, though militaristic to the core, established public schools in which both sexes had equal opportunity, and in which civic training went hand in hand with training for war. True, girls were not trained in the full military arts, and deformed children were pitilessly eliminated; yet the beginnings of the modern democratic public school system can be discerned, however dimly, in the Spartan educational establishment from the fifth century B.C. on. For most of their history the Spartans' "puritanical education, proceeding in a climate of austerity, had as its sole norm the interests of the state, erected into a supreme category; the Spartan was trained under a strict discipline to obey blindly the orders of his superiors."[4] Sparta, not surprisingly, became the mightiest military power in the Greek world, and it may well be that her great victories in the Peloponnesian War were won on the playing fields of her public schools.

Athens was far more democratic than Sparta in most ways, yet the city did not have a tax-supported public school system nor did it give particular emphasis to military training. Like its governmental framework, Athenian education was both more permissive and more voluntaristic than Sparta's, even to the point of allowing egregious discrimination against women. Such schools as existed in Athens were entirely private and centered around a few great teachers such as Socrates and the Sophists. Like modern democratic schools, they sought to produce the *kalos kathagos* (wise and good man) with a curriculum that was moral, humanistic, and liberal-arts oriented. Physical education was likewise stressed, though there was probably not the harmony between the intellectual and non-academic sides of education that classicists sometimes suggest. Discipline appears to have been strict and even-handed in all Greek schools, though not as strict at Athens as at Sparta.

Today it is generally conceded that the Greeks invented what we call higher education. The pioneers in this field were the itinerant Sophists,

Socrates' school of rhetoric, Plato's Academy, and Aristotle's Lyceum. Both the Platonic and Aristotelian programs of education were inegalitarian in that they discriminated against women, the poor, and non-citizens. This, of course, is hardly surprising, since nearly all Greek intellectuals held serious misgivings about democracy and equality. Nevertheless, they believed deeply in the power of knowledge to form human character and promote justice. And in the *Republic,* one of the pioneer treatises on educational theory, Plato advocated an extremely egalitarian system of education for all young people, male and female, through the late teens. To be sure, the social system of the *Republic* was extremely authoritarian, and graduate education was reserved for an intellectual elite who had proved their mental superiority by doing well in a series of tests. But up to that point at least, virtually every youth, in Plato's ideal schools, was to be guaranteed full equality of opportunity whatever his class background. There was to be, in other words, social mobility in Plato's educational system.

During the Hellenistic Age, the educational patterns established in classical Greece were expanded, and the state exerted far more legislative control over the schools than had been the case in Athens. The scope of education was considerably expanded; and though most students were males from the aristocratic and urban bourgeois classes, girls were allowed a modest place in the system as, occasionally, were slaves. As greater attention was paid to the education of the common people, the Hellenistic school became "well integrated with society, participating in community rites and ceremonies and welcoming parents and citizens to its functions."[5] The schools were still basically run as private enterprises, but even without state subsidies they managed to become far more comprehensive. This was especially true in athletics, since such sports as gymnastic, track, field, and hockey assumed an especially prominent place in Hellenistic schools. Indeed, as athletic sports gradually replaced the more intellectual activities of the Hellenic period, there emerged something closely akin to modern sports professionalism. Intellectually, this development no doubt represented a decline. Yet in terms of the numbers of people and classes involved, it actually signalled an advance in educational equality.

The Roman system of education, like that of the Jews, was family-centered, and thus the role of the mother as lifelong teacher was enormously influential. Of course, after a certain age, usually around seven, the father assumed responsibility for the education of his sons by teaching him his letters, manly excercises, the use of weapons, and the principles of moral and social conduct. Boys would also accompany their fathers to important ceremonies and social occasions, and even at times to senate. Around the age of sixteen, the boy assumed the *toga virilis,* after which he might be attached to a notable citizen for political experience.

Following a few years of that, there was a period of compulsory military training. Such a system of training upper-class males was obviously quite aristocratic, and in many ways it rather closely resembled the Spartan educational process.

Of all the ancient peoples in the West, the Romans had the most sophisticated system of primary and secondary education. In the teaching of the seven liberal arts the Romans pretty much followed Greek precedents, particularly in the teaching of poetry, grammar, and rhetoric. However, in one important branch of higher education—that of legal training—the Romans made a number of significant innovations for which there were no equivalents at all in Hellenistic education. Law, indeed, became the focal point of Roman higher education as philosophy and mathematics had been in Athens, though the number of law students in Rome must greatly have exceeded the number of advanced philosophy students in Athens. The United States has followed Rome in its obsession with law.

Although Roman education was perhaps only slightly more egalitarian than the system Athens had devised, it included a number of innovations that would influence modern education. The Roman law schools became a model for subsequent professional schools. The growing measure of state aid to education became a basic principle of modern democracy. And the establishment of schools in the most distant parts of the Roman Empire brought educational opportunities to a vastly greater number of people than had been served by Hellenic or Hellenistic schools. Finally, the world is deeply in the debt of Roman educators for having perfected the Greek methods of instruction and for having handed on intact the essence of Greek culture.

The durable character of classical Greco-Roman education was demonstrated by the fact that the Christians, instead of emulating Hebraic schools that were based alomst entirely on the Holy Scriptures, chose to make full use of existing pagan schools. A few early Christian fathers, led by Tertullian and St. Basil the Great of Caesarea, argued that the Church had no use for Athens; but generally speaking, Christians were impressed with the quality of classical schools and, in the course of time, wholly assimilated and took over classical education. Today it is impossible to say with certainty whether the first Christian schools also became more egalitarian; but since many of the early Christians came from the lower classes, their schools probably did advance the cause of educational equality. In any event, there is no question of the existential synthesis of Christianity and classical education. Indeed, after the fall of the Roman Empire in the West, the Church, through its monastic and other schools, kept alive the cultural tradition that Rome had received from the Hellenistic world. This benefited the lower as well as the upper classes.

Throughout the Middle Ages, the Church had a stranglehold on education, and for most of the time the emphases of general education were religious and military. Most teaching took place in churches, monasteries, or cathedrals, and was largely directed toward male children of the aristocracy. Females and children of the lower classes normally received only such education as was acquired by attending church services and listening to sermons.

The late twelfth century in Europe witnessed one of the most significant innovations in all of medieval education: the establishment of universities, the original purpose of which was to extend the range of the cathedral and monastic schools. Of course, only a handful of young people ever attended the early European universities, and in that sense they were extremely elitist—rather like the higher schools of abstract learning sketched by Plato in his *Republic*. Yet for all that, there were several egalitarian aspects of the new universities. Their governance, for example, was quite democratic with the student guilds having more power to influence institutional policy than was permitted in the modern world until the 1960s. Furthermore, students enjoyed the right to strike as well as the right to discontinue lectures, while both students and teachers enjoyed special immunities protecting them against unjust arrests and assuring them the freedom to live their lives in security. It should also be emphasized that it was the universities, over the next few hundred years, that would prove to be the chief seedbed for those radical doctrines and philosophies in which the concept of equality emerged as the central component of Christian and democratic justice.[6]

The Renaissance and Reformation made four lasting contributions to egalitarian education: the invention of printing from movable type, the secularization of higher education, the expansion of elementary education in the vernacular languages, and the encouragement of a new natural science that proceeded from empirical rather than Biblical premises. The first of these was probably the most crucial, for it underpinned the other three and made possible the popularization of the Western heritage in all European languages to a degree hitherto impossible. Indeed, without the assistance of the printing press, it is hard to believe that the "heresies" of Luther and Calvin would ever have conquered half of Europe. The printing press, to be sure, is neutral and can aid authoritarianism as easily as equality, yet its services in the cause of the latter have never been in doubt.

Education in the seventeenth century, though still primarily an elitist process, was advanced by the then utopian ideas of a number of philosophers and pedagogical reformers. Among these were Tommaso Campanella, author of *La Città del Sole;* Sir Francis Bacon, author of *New*

Atlantis; and such pedagogical realists as Wolfgang Ratke and John Amos Comenius, who maintained that some form of universal education is the key to world improvement in all areas of life.[7] Most educational progressives of the seventeenth century believed that knowledge is to be gained by experience with real problems; that things must be studied through experiment and induction; that the mother language of each country should be the language of school instruction; that compulsion should be minimized; and that teaching should take due account of the limits and possibilities of human nature. Virtually all of these beliefs eventually would become the conventional wisdom, though in post-Reformation Europe their impact on the real world was quite limited because of a failure to get a commitment from the ruling elites to institute them on a broad basis. The rulers of that time had other things to worry about, such as the Thirty Years' War.

Popular education made important progress in the eighteenth century for a variety of reasons, not least of which were John Locke's theory of knowledge and the pro-education ideas of men like Babeuf, Condorcet, and Jefferson. Even more than their seventeenth-century forebears, the Enlightenment philosophers were *educational determinists* since they held that the road to universal, continuous progress went straight through the school. Granted, tax-supported school systems for all students scarcely existed anywhere in the Age of Reason; yet their legitimating rationale was clearly established by the century's end. The theme of that rationale was boldly stated by Babeuf when he wrote that "Since all have the same needs and the same faculties, let there be one education for all, one food for all."[8]

John Locke was to eithteenth-century pedagogy what John Dewey would be to that of the twentieth century. A thoroughgoing empiricist and vigorous opponent of the hair-splitting logic of the Scholastics, Locke insisted that knowledge of the world around us can be gained solely through sense perception coupled with rational reflection upon sensible data. Locke also denied the existence of innate ideas, categories, and moral principles, insisting instead that the mind of everybody at birth is in effect a blank slate. From these Lockean premises, two important implications stood out: that real knowledge is quite limited, and that human nature can be molded in almost any direction by the power of educational and experiential nurture. The latter of these, it should be noted, entailed an extremely egalitarian conception of the power of professional educators. All of these ideas were an integral part of Locke's epistemology, which was most clearly set forth in his *Essay Concerning Human Understanding* and *Thoughts Concerning Education.*[9] In light of his subsequent influence, it is not an exaggeration to say that Locke was the founder both of British empiricism and of modern democratic education, two related if distinct phenomena.

Thanks in part to the ideas of Locke, the eighteenth century was the first epoch of Western civilization in which the school system actually became an ordered concern of the nation. A number of reformers began advocating compulsory schooling for all young people, and for the first time the state evinced a serious interest in the training of teachers. Universal public education was still more than a century away, but the number of schools in 1800 was an enormous advance over the number of schools that existed in 1700, four years before the death of Locke.

In the latter half of the eighteenth century Locke's theory of knowledge was rivaled in pedagogical influence by the educational ideas of France's Jean-Jacques Rousseau. Besides being the first serious student of egalitarian thought, Rousseau was one of the founders of progressive, child-centered education, such as John Dewey would be associated with in the twentieth century.

Rousseau's innovative theory of education was expounded in his 1762 work, *Émile ou de l'education,* which has long been regarded as a pedagogical classic.[10] In *Émile,* which is also a treatise on man, Rousseau reproached his predecessors for ignoring the fact that children are not adults and for trying to socialize the young prematurely. "Childhood," he wrote, "has its own ways of seeing, thinking, and feeling; nothing is more foolish than to try to replace them with ours."[11] Though his ideas were speculative rather than experimental, "Rousseau is probably the first to have linked the science of education to the scientific understanding of the child, and for this reason he is rightfully recognized today as the precursor and even the founder of child psychology."[12]

Like modern equality-minded educators, Rousseau believed strongly that children must learn through experience as well as through words, and that schools should be less authoritarian and more supportive of individual student needs. Moreover, by emphasizing the advisory above the indoctrinationist role of teachers, Rousseau was freeing the child from the compulsion of having to act as a small grown-up adult. Even more important from the egalitarian perspective was the fact that Rousseau proposed extended training for girls as well as for boys, though he believed that female education should be more vocational and family-centered than that provided for males.

The nineteenth century, building on the foundations laid in the Age of Reason, came to view education as a kind of alchemic force designed to exorcise the chaos of experience. The great statesmen of the day were particularly eloquent in their praise of popular education. In the 1830's, Daniel Webster averred that "On the diffusion of education among the people rest the preservation and perpetuation of our free institutions." Even earlier, in his first public speech, Abraham Lincoln had pronounced education "the most important subject which we, as a people, can be engaged in." After the Civil War, James A. Garfield, in a letter accepting the Republican Party's nomination for president, extended Lincoln's views when he wrote that without popular education "neither freedom nor justice can be permanently maintained."[13]

In the century between Waterloo and World War I, free public schooling gradually came to be recognized as an integral part of egalitarian democracy and of enlightened nationalism. Many theorists and statesmen were responsible for this recognition, not the least of whom was the Swiss reformer Johann Heinrich Pestalozzi, who worked in the tradition of Rousseau. Pestalozzi became a champion of the underprivileged early in life, and among his vital contributions to democratic education these were outstanding: his insistence on combining love with abstract reason; his philanthropic efforts on behalf of the poor; his demonstration that pedagogy is both art and science; his creation of a lofty professional ethos for teachers; and his initiation of a new child-centered methodology for elementary education. Pestalozzi's influence was strongest in Germany, but it eventually extended to all of the Western world, including the United States, where William Maclure of Philadelphia introduced and popularized his ideas. Today, of course, Pestalozzi's ideas sound commonplace, but "they were revolutionary in his day, when rote learning and iron discipline ruled the classroom."[14]

The decisive niniteenth-century developments in the field of pedagogy were the strong commitment of all Western governments to the ideal of state-supported public education; the enactment of compulsory elementary school laws; the establishment of special colleges for women; the creation of scholarships for poor students; the development of practical studies that helped especially the disadvantaged; the first attempts to educate the mentally retarded; the founding of U.S. land-grant colleges after passage of the Morrill Act in 1862;[15] the opening of the first high school in Boston in 1821 (the English Classical School); the emergence of the first racially-integrated schools; the appearance of graduate schools at a few leading universities; the spread of the kindergarten movement; the statutory creation of state boards of education, beginning in Massachusetts in 1837; the founding of the prestigious *American Journal of Education;* and numerous innovations of the great Horace Mann, who once announced that "A human being is not, in any proper sense, a human being till he is educated."[16] That, in fact, became a key leitmotif of the century's *Zeitgeist.*

In the twentieth century, as egalitarian democracy and nationalism became increasingly dominant, the state-supported public school system became a universal, expanding institution. Moreover, the spread of socialism after World War I significantly deepened the Western world's commitment to education, and made that commitment far more egalitarian than it had hitherto been. Partly under the influence of socialist ideals, the twentieth century gave birth to the first serious attempts to eradicate illiteracy everywhere in the civilized world. Those attempts have not yet succeeded, but they have made striking headway, in the East no less than in the West, as evidenced by the astonishing growth in the number of children enrolled in public or private schools.

Throughout much of the last century, the emergent U.S. school system focused on the so-called *common school,* which was supported by public funds (usually derived from property taxes) and open to every child. It was a secular institution with often no more than one or two rooms, and was under the supervision of a local school board that was usually elective. The *McGuffey Readers,* strongly didactic in tone, were the core of the limited curriculum, and the school term rarely lasted more than six months. The average student was lucky to get through the second or third grade, although urban children fared better since the cities had generally superior schools at all levels of instruction.

By World War I, the typical U.S. citizen was finishing grammar school. By the 1920s he was completing a year or two of high school. And by 1970, the median period of education completed in the United States was 12.1, with more than fifty-two percent of persons twenty-five years old and older having completed four years of high school or more.[17] If present trends continue, it is quite likely that by the 1990's the average adult will have completed at least one or two years of collegiate education.

Although it would be false to say that all twentieth-century innovations in the field of education have been egalitarian in nature, the great majority clearly have been, whether equality is thought of in terms of economics, sex, race, or ethnicity. The key educational developments of the present century have been far too numerous to discuss in detail, but a summary list would have to include at least the following: the vast expansion of federal aid to local schools; the increase in educational opportunities for racial and ethnic minorities; the growing democratization of school governance; the proliferation of vocational schools; the rise of high-quality white suburban schools and the concomitant deterioration of inner city schools; the universalization of secondary education; the elimination of sexual and racial quotas from most, if not all professional schools; the decreased emphasis on competition and grades and greater stress on psychological counseling; the spread of child-centered experimental movements, sparked by the thought of such reformers as John Dewey and Francis W. Parker; the popularization of the Montessori method of pedagogy; the permeation of educational theory by the concepts of Freudianism; the advent of open admissions to public colleges and universities; the rising importance of technological training; the expansion of state-supported two-year community colleges; the rapid inflation in educational costs at all levels; the democratization and modernization of curricular offerings;[18] the application of television and other media to the solution of educational problems; the precipitate decline of foreign languages, philosophy, and the humanities; the transformation of universities from selective to mass institutions; and, most important of all from the perspective of this study, the nearly universal acceptance of the notion that equality of educational opportunity is an idea whose time has come.[19]

In the early 1900s, the young people who were most deprived of equal educational opportunity were those with mental or physical handicaps: the deaf, the blind, the dumb, the crippled, and the mentally defective. That, fortunately, is no longer true for teaching the handicapped is now an integral and expanding part of the U.S. school system. As two examples of this, the federal government today subsidizes the publication of Braille books for state schools, and most local governments have for a long time supported programs to teach the handicapped. In 1958, Congress made a major contribution by appropriating one million dollars to train teachers of mentally retarded children; and since that beginning, federal aid to the handicapped has steadily increased. So, it might be added, has aid to the gifted child.

Since World War I, the issue of educational equality has become both more politicized and more subject to judicial litigation. In the first quarter of this century the main focus of the issue was not sexual or racial bias but alleged religious discrimination in the schools. In 1919, for example, Nebraska passed a law forbidding the teaching of any subject in any language but English. By the terms of the law, foreign languages might be taught, but only to students who had successfully passed the eighth grade. This caused a problem for a certain Mr. Meyer, who taught in a parochial school and used a German Bible history as a reading and religious text. He was indicted for violating the 1919 law; and after being tried and convicted, he appealed his conviction to the U.S. Supreme Court.

In 1923 the Supreme Court confronted the question: Was the Nebraska statute a violation of the liberty protected by the Fourteenth Amendment? In a seven-two opinion, the Court answered yes.[20] Mere use of the German language, the Court held, could hardly be harmful to students; and in any case, Meyer's right to teach, and the parents' right to hire him were within the liberty guaranteed by the Fourteenth Amendment. The Court further held that a state might take many kinds of action to improve the quality of its schools, so long as it did not violate the constitutional rights of students, be they native-born or foreign-born. As Justice McReynolds, speaking for the majority, put it, "a desirable end cannot be promoted by prohibited means."[21]

Two years later the Supreme Court had to grapple with an even more fundamental question that raised in an acute form the issue of religious equality in education. The question was: Can a state require children to attend public rather than parochial schools and thus force them to violate their religious principles? The Court's answer was a unanimous no.

The case originated in the fall of 1922 in strongly Protestant Oregon when the state legislature passed a Compulsory Education Act directing every child between the ages of eight and 16 to attend public school. Parents or guardians who prevented a child from attending public school would be guilty of a misdemeanor. The plaintiffs in the case were the Society of Sisters of the Holy Names of Jesus and Mary, whose members operated a number of private schools in Oregon in accord with the tenets of the Roman Catholic Church. After passage of the law, the society challenged it in court, arguing that its provisions violated the right of parents to choose schools where their children would get appropriate moral and religious training.

Again the Court held in effect that private school patrons have rights equal to those of public school patrons, and it reiterated the point that no constitutional rights may be abridged by state legislative action having no reasonable relation to some purpose within the competency of the state. Arguing for both diversity and equality, the Court held that the state has no right to compel the standardization of children by forcing them to attend public school institutions only. Speaking again for the Court, Justice McReynolds concluded that "the Act of 1922 unreasonably interferes with the liberty of parents and guardians to direct the upbringing and education of children under their control."[22] Protestant as well Catholic egalitarians agreed with that conclusion.

Almost half a century later, another educational equality case, turning on the rights of private school pupils, was decided by the Supreme Court. The case was brought by Wisconsin authorities against members of the Amish Church in an effort to force Amish families to obey the state's compulsory school attendance law that obligated all children to attend public or private school until the age of 16. The Amish parents refused to send their children to school beyond the eighth grade. Their refusal stemmed from a deep conviction that the values generally inculcated by secondary schooling are in opposition to the religious values and general way of life of the Amish people. The Amish have traditionally educated their children through private elementary school for the limited purposes of teaching them to read the Bible, be good farmers, and develop into good Christian citizens.

Chief Justice Burger, writing for the Court, upheld the right of Amish parents to keep their children out of public high school on the ground that the Wisconsin compulsory school attendance law infringed both the First and Fourteenth Amendments. The Court conceded that states have a valid interest in universal education so long as they do not abridge other legitimate interests, but held that in the case of the Amish, a profound religious belief was being unconstitutionally abridged. In the words of the majority opinion, "A way of life that is odd or even erratic but interferes with no rights or interests of others is not to be condemned because it is different."[23] The Amish, of course, constitute but a small Protestant sect in the United States, yet their victory in this case, though it annoyed some secular majoritarians, gave a boost to the equality claims of all U.S. minorities. It was also inegalitarian in the sense that it guaranteed the Amish the right to get *less* education than other people get.

Parochial school students, backed by their determined parents, had earlier won an important equality victory in Congress when that body, often unfriendly to minority demands, passed the School Lunch Act of 1946 and included parochial schools in its grant-in-aid program to the states. The issue in this instance involved not merely the educational equality claims of religious minorities but also the more basic question of church-state relations in a democratic society. Catholic spokesmen and some Protestant leaders have always insisted that parochial schools are just as entitled to the new forms of state aid as public schools, and they consider a state's refusal to grant such aid to their schools as a denial of educational equality. Mainstream Protestants, on the other hand, have generally opposed aid to parochial schools on the grounds that laws authorizing it violate the First Amendment and abridge the basic freedoms of taxpayers who send their children to the public schools. In a complex series of post-World War II church-state cases, the Supreme Court has held that there can be cooperation between church and state in the matter of schools *so long as state aid goes to parochial school students and not directly to the schools themselves.* These cases have badly split the Court, and the results have not entirely satisfied either Catholic egalitarians or First-Amendment Protestant and other libertarians.

In the first postwar church-state school case, the Supreme Court voted five to four to uphold a New Jersey law authorizing the reimbursement of parents of both public and parochial school students who used public transportation to get to school. Rejecting a taxpayer's claim that the law violated the First Amendment's ban on establishment of religion, the Court held that the transportation of children to their schools, whether public or private, was functionally similar to the provision of police protection at school crossings, the availability of fire protection, and the communal sharing of sewer facilities and sidewalks. Justice Black, speaking for the majority, conceded that the law approached the limits of the state's discretionary power but was nontheless constitutional. In a bitter dissent, Justice Jackson wrote that the majority opinion reminded him of Byron's heroine Julie, who "whispering 'I will ne'er consent'—consented."[24]

In the following year the Court disappointed religious conservatives by holding unconstitutional an elaborately organized system of religious instruction *in* the public schools of Champaign, Illinois, which was implemented by a private organization, the Champaign Council on Religious Education. The opinion was nearly unanimous (only Justice Reed dissented), and its central holding was that the Champaign system "falls squarely under the ban of the First Amendment."[25]

Then, four years later, the Court shocked liberals by validating a New York City *released-time* program, which operated during school hours but not on school property and without the use of school personnel. Justice Douglas, writing for a six-three majority, noted that "we are a religious people whose institutions presuppose a Supreme Being." Thus it is "obtuse reasoning," he continued, to use the First Amendment to support a "philosophy of hostility to religion." Again sharply dissenting, Justice Jackson observed that "the wall of separation between church and state has become even more warped and twisted than I anticipated."[26]

In the 1960s, the Warren Court re-opened and intensified the religion-in-the-schools controversy and, more often than not, sided with the secularists, even to the point of forbidding prayers and Bible readings in the public schools.[27] That, of course, infuriated Catholic conservatives, along with Protestant fundamentalists, who together precipitated a bitter public debate on the whole question, a debate which is still going on. Both secularists and religious conservatives maintain that they suffer a diminution of freedom as well as equality when the Supreme Court rules against them. And like all litigants, they demand absolute justice. In any event, the ideals of both freedom and equality are intimately involved in the controversy.

Of all the post-World War II school cases, the most controversial and historic was certainly the 1954 *Brown* case that overturned *Plessy.* As shocking as *Brown* was to southern white supremacists, its general outlines could have been predicted by a careful study of a sequence of cases going back to the 1930s. In 1938, for example, the Court held that Missouri's refusal to admit a black applicant to its state law school violated the equal protection clause of the Fourteenth Amendment.[28] Ten years later, in another law school case, the Court held that as long as Oklahoma furnished white persons with legal education, qualified black applicants were "entitled to secure legal education afforded by a state institution."[29]

Then, moving closer to *Brown,* the Court held in 1950 that an improvised Texas law school for one black student did not furnish blacks with true legal education equality;[30] nor did Oklahoma's in-school segregation of a black law student meet the demands of the Fourteenth Amendment.[31] Having won the right to law school desegregation, the NAACP promptly initiated the *Brown* litigation and began a full-scale assault on elementary and secondary school segregation.

The central holding of *Brown* I was stated in a single paragraph:[32]

> We conclude that in the field of public education the doctrine of "Separate but equal" has no place. Separate educational facilities are inherently unequal. Therefore, we hold that the plaintiffs and others similarly situated for whom the actions have been brought are, by reason of the segregation complained of, deprived of the equal protection of the laws guaranteed by the Fourteenth Amendment.

Along with invalidating southern and midwestern Jim Crow schools, the Court, in a related case, outlawed public school segregation in the District of Columbia.[33] Here the legal problem was different, as there is no equal protection clause in the Bill of Rights restricting federal authority. As a result, the Court was forced to invalidate school segregation in the nation's capital on the basis of the due process clause of the Fifth Amendment.

On May 31, 1955, after additional arguments had been heard concerning the formulation of decrees to provide appropriate relief to black students, the Court announced its enforcement ruling in *Brown* II. Rejecting the NAACP's request for immediate relief, the justices ordered the lower courts "to take such proceedings and enter such orders and decrees consistent with this opinion as are necessary and proper to admit to public schools on a racially nondiscriminatory basis *with all deliberate speed* the parties to these cases."[34] [Emphasis added by author.]

Brown I destroyed the *separate but equal* doctrine, and *Brown* II launched the new *with all deliberate speed* formula on its erratic carrer. But perhaps more important was the fact that in the two *Brown* decisions, the Warren Court was in effect constitutionalizing the grand assertion of the Declaration of Independence that all men are created equal—before the schoolhouse as well as before the law. In the process the Court was finally recognizing that education in the modern world is indeed a kind of socio-psychic credit card, without which one is wholly unequal to those who possess it.

The first reactions of the South's segregationists to *Brown* were strangely muted and fatalistic, although from the first the extreme racists anathematized the decision with verbal fire and brimstone. Then, beginning about 1956, the segregationists in charge of the South's state and local governments decided to launch a full-scale counterrevolution against court-ordered integration. After Virginia's Senator Harry Byrd used the phrase *massive resistance* in a Senate debate on the South's reaction to *Brown*, the entire movement was soon bearing that label. As an organized movement, Massive Resistance endured for about ten years, during which time it was responsible for an enormous amount of bigotry, vigilantism, and calculated murder. It took the concerted efforts of the president, the FBI, the military, Congress, and the courts to contain and eventually roll back the white South's extraordinary venture into counterrevolutionary defiance of federal authority.[35]

Speaking as states'-rightist libertarians, the South's white supremacists denounced *Brown* for a variety of reasons. It violated *stare decisis*. It curtailed their liberty of association. It denied their children freedom of choice in school matters. It put the neighborhood school in jeopardy. It was the first step toward destruction of de facto separation of the races. It ignored divine and natural law. It subverted the Jeffersonian principle of states' rights. It was a shamelessly loose construction of the Fourteenth Amendment. It put the rights of black people above the liberties of whites. And it converted the Supreme Court into a national school board.

The white South's case against *Brown* was formally set forth in the so-called Southern Manifesto or Declaration of Constitutional Principles that was introduced into Congress on March 12, 1956. Despite the fact that the manifesto had no legal standing and required no congressional action. it bore the signatures of 19 senators and 77 representatives from 11 southern states and was thus a powerful propaganda weapon in the Massive Resistance movement. The fact that the manifesto was a mixture of distorted history, fallacious political theory, and thinly-disguised racism did not in the least bother the average southerner.[36]

Southerners have always made more history than they can consume locally; and, not surprisingly, the problems and traumas spawned by the *Brown* decision inevitably affected every part of the nation. The Massive Resistance counterrevolution may have made few actual converts north of the Mason-Dixon Line, yet a strong undercurrent of sympathy for the southern myth of states' rights, cleverly manipulated by southern power elites, became apparent in many states outside the South. That undercurrent helped to bring Nixon to the White House in 1968, as, four years later, the cumulative resentment of *Brown* enabled him to carry every single state of the old Confederacy and to convert Mississippi into one of the most Republican states of the Union in terms of presidential politics.

In the end, however, Massive Resistance was able to do little more than delay the inevitable advent of school desegregation. For after Congress passed a series of tough civil rights laws, and after HEW began vigorously to enforce them, the South's dual school system rapidly disintegrated and survives today only in the private segregationist academies that dot the southern landscape. The *coup de grâce* came in 1969 when the Supreme Court directed that school districts must "operate now and hereafter only unitary schools."[37] There is now, ironically, more school segregation in the North than in the South, largely because of racial housing patterns.

As school integration brought a measure of greater educational equality throughout the South, and as the echoes of Massive Resistance faded away, there was for a time relative tranquility on the public school scene. But that tranquility was rudely shattered when George Wallace "discovered" busing as a campaign issue in the 1972 Florida presidential primary, a discovery promptly taken up by President Nixon and countless other opportunistic politicians. Indeed, in an amazingly brief time, antibusing rhetoric and demonstrations had become the new incarnation of Massive Resistance. Perhaps no other issue save Vietnam has posed such a grave challenge to U.S. democracy in the past decade as the issue of "forced busing," and "No issue has offered so few opportunities for conflict resolution and creative statesmanship."[38]

Blacks appeared generally to favor busing if their children actually were sent to superior schools, while the unreconstructed Massive Resisters vehemently opposed it when used to promote racial balance in segregated schools. They did so, they argued, not for racist reasons but for reasons of health and safety. Their egalitarian opponents rejected such reasoning as mere rationalizations for what they considered a new manifestation of virulent white supremacy racism.

The right of school boards or judges to order busing to remedy school violations of the equal protection guarantee was confirmed by a 1971 Supreme Court decision that originated in North Carolina's Charlotte-Mecklenburg school system. In a unanimous opinion, the Court held that school authorities have an obligation to take affirmative action to effect integration; and when that is not done, district judges have broad equitable power to fashion remedies, including busing, that will promote unitary school systems. The burden of proof remains on school authorities to satisfy the courts that their racial make-up is not the result of present or past discriminatory practices.[39]

In the summer of 1974, the Supreme Court delighted anti-egalitarians by invalidating a Detroit integration plan that required busing between Detroit and white suburban school districts. Writing for a five-four majority, Chief Justice Burger held that since the suburban districts *had not themselves discriminated*, Detroit would have to solve its school problems within its own borders.[40] The four dissenters in this case bitterly attacked the majority's reasoning, and black leaders everywhere were dismayed by what they viewed as a serious retreat from the lofty egalitarian principles of *Brown* and a tacit legitimation of northern de facto school segregation.

Conservatives clearly have used "forced busing" as a code-phrase for the putative deprivation of white liberties, if not subversion, while blacks have generally seen it as a way of vindicating the constitutional right of equal protection. Whatever one's personal views, there can be little doubt that the anti-busing rhetoric of conservatives and their manipulation of the counter-myth of freedom of choice represent[41]

> a delayed attempt by southern segregationists to "get" *Brown* and to achieve by indirection what the Massive Resistance counterrevolution was unable to achieve by direct action. It is [also] quite clearly an attempt by white southerners to keep blacks in their central-city ghetto schools and forever away from the lily-white, suburban "neighborhood schools." Doubtless there are many good reasons for wanting to minimize the busing of small children, but . . . it is hard to believe that the current anti-busing campaign is not, at least in part, racially motivated.

That judgment, of course, applies to the North as well as to the South. And it may well be, as blacks are increasingly saying: *The real issue is not the bus—it's us.*

Less intractable than busing but still divisive is the question of what to do about an estimated million students in the nation's school systems who speak little or no English. The issue rarely arose until the mid-1960s, when the melting pot myth was being debunked as racial and ethnic pride was soaring, along with efforts by minorities to revive their diverse cultural heritages. Ethnic pride and bilingualism seemed to go together in the new order.

In 1974, the issue was carried all the way to the U.S. Supreme Court, which held that San Francisco school authorities must either provide special instruction in Chinese for its eighteen hundred students of Chinese nationality or give them special remedial help in English. Concerning options, Justice Douglas, writing for the Court, observed that "Teaching English to the students of Chinese ancestry is one choice. Giving instruction to this group in Chinese is another. There may be others."[42]

Although the Court's opinion was a boon to non-English minorities, school boards around the nation were slow to act on the options suggested by Justice Douglas. That was largely because the opinion did not require school boards to initiate bilingual programs at once, and because HEW did little or nothing to push for such programs. As HEW goes, so go the school boards.

All that began to change around 1976, and today "bilingual projects are proliferating at an extraordinary rate."[43] That is quite a remarkable change, for before the 1970s "not a single state required bilingual teaching—and twenty-two forbade it by law."[44] Conservatives complain about the cost of such teaching, and many feel it is little more than a political ploy by minority groups, but there can be no doubt that well-conceived bilingual education, such as is now becoming common, is a vast expansion of educational equality for those children of many races and ethnic backgrounds who are virtually illiterate in English. It will doubtless not be a panacea, but it should increase their interest in school while reducing their astronomical dropout rates, especially in the big cities.

Yet another source of educational inequality in the United States has been the traditional system of decentralized school financing. That equality issue went to the Supreme Court one year before the San Francisco Chinese case was decided, and it resulted in a five-four victory for tradition. The four Nixon appointees and Justice Stewart made up the majority.

The case arose in San Antonio, Texas, where Chicano parents attacked the Texas system of school financing on the ground that the growing disparities between districts in population and taxable property were largely responsible for the differences in local expenditure for education. They asked that the Court require Texas to provide the same number of dollars per child in every school district throught the state, so that poor students might enjoy greater educational opportunity.

The Court majority disagreed with the Chicano litigants and upheld the San Antonio school financing system. They did so on several grounds. First, they argued that the class of students allegedly being disadvantaged was not susceptible to identification in traditional terms. Second, they stated that the equal protection clause of the Fourteenth Amendment does not require absolute equality or precisely equal advantages where wealth is at issue. Third, they noted that "Education . . . is not among the rights afforded explicit protection under our Federal Constitution. Nor do we find any basis for saying it is implicitly so protected." Fourth, they did not think that the financing system, despite reported disparities, was either irrational or intentionally prejudicial. Fifth, and last, they agreed that there was probably a need for reform in school tax systems, but they insisted that ultimate solutions must come from state lawmakers and the democratic process.[45]

Since the *San Antonio* decision was handed down, only a few states have made attempts to update their antiquated school financing laws. And unless the Supreme Court changes its mind and forces them to act, most are unlikely to do so. Of course, more tax money would not automatically result in better schools for the disadvantaged, but it would be a first step. Egalitarians, if they had a choice, would probably opt for the system adopted by Hawaii, where the state government is allowed to finance all public schools. Should all other states follow Hawaii's example, there would then no doubt be a demand to equalize all schools on a federal scale, a demand that would surely produce a bitter and explosive debate on the whole subject of educational equality. Such a debate might in fact be good.[46]

What is creating the most tension between libertarians and egalitarians today is not segregation, bilingual education, or school financing, but the issue of affirmative action programs and racial quotas, which are being vigorously pushed in various forms by both minority spokesmen and the bureaucracy of HEW. The phrase *reverse discrimination* is often used to denote both affirmative action and quotas, and it is fast becoming the most divisive issue in the whole field of civil rights. It is what busing used to be.

The critics of racial quotas and similar compensatory programs believe they are in step with Tocqueville and John Stuart Mill who, more than a century ago, warned of the *tyranny of the majority* in egalitarian democracies. They are also convinced that the pressures of minorities on school administrators to initiate affirmative action policies will ultimately result in a compulsive consensus that will diminish freedom far faster than it advances equality. On one point they and the militant egalitarians seem to be in accord, and that is that it is impossible to develop a powerful state for whatever purpose without creating implications in other spheres of activity, such as freedom patterns, which have profound effects on both society and government. The equality proponents, as always, are willing to take almost any risk to advance their cause. Libertarians would prefer to leave risk-taking to the private sector.

The issue of compensatory equality has become especially acute in the field of higher education, as evidenced by the much discussed *DeFunis* case. At issue in this case was "the whole concept of affirmative-action programs—programs that give preference to minority groups in such areas as school admissions and employment in order to compensate for past discrimination."[47] It was also a first test case.

The litigation was started by a Jewish Phi Beta Kappa student, Marco DeFunis, Jr., who was refused admission in 1971 to the University of Washington Law School. According to the record, "DeFunis's college grades and Law School Aptitude Test scores were higher than those of 36 minority students—blacks, Chicanos, Indians—who were accepted by the law school."[48] The University of Washington conceded that it used different criteria for processing minority-group law school applicants, but maintained that it had a compelling need to do so in order to overcome the scarcity of minority-group lawyers. DeFunis, who charged that he had been discriminated against, won his case at the trial level, where the judge ordered him to be admitted to the law school. Though the order was subsequently carried out, the judge's decision was appealed, and the case eventually reached the Supreme Court.

Rarely has the Supreme Court been faced with such a painful choice between freedom and equality, and the justices' disposition of the case was eagerly awaited by egalitarians and libertarians alike. Indeed, the litigation became so famous that more *amicus curiae* (friend of the court) briefs were filed in the case than in any other case ever argued before the U.S. Supreme Court. When the decision finally came, it was a disappointment to just about everybody for the Court dismissed the case, by a five-to-four vote, on the grounds that it had been rendered *moot* by DeFunis's impending graduation from law school. The dissenting justices, speaking through Justice Brennan, argued that avoidance of the constitutional issue disserved "the public interest."[49]

Fundamentally, the issue in the *DeFunis* case came down to an argument over the nature and scope of educational opportunity required by democratic principles. The argument might be posed in this fashion: *Should equality in the nation's schools and colleges mean merely traditional equality of basic opportunity, or should it mean equality of results?* The former view, favored by libertarians, mandates little more than state-supported schools, college scholarships for worthy students, and the absence of irrational discrimination in admissions or hiring. The latter, pushed by minority-group egalitarians, requires far more: affirmative action, preferential hiring, benign racial-ethnic quotas, and various other forms of compensatory justice.

Neither the majority nor the minority in *DeFunis* spoke the last word on the controversy, for the Supreme Court has already agreed to hear in its 1977-78 term a similar case from California. In that case the Supreme Court of California upheld a white student's claim that his refusal of admission to the medical school of the University of California at Davis was reverse discrimination, a decision which the university appealed. Many egalitarians opposed the university's decision to appeal, feeling that the litigation at issue is a particularly weak test for affirmative action and preferring to confine the damage to California. The U.C. Davis plan actually involves a quota system, and the disappointed white applicant, unlike DeFunis, was not admitted to the university's medical school. However the U.S. Supreme Court ultimately rules, it will shape the nation's employment and university-admissions policies for years to come. It will also be deciding how much reverse discrimination, if any, can be squared with the U.S. Constitution.

The enormous practical problems posed by the affirmative action issue are well illustrated by the following comments from a recent scholarly book:[50]

> A primary problem is the lack of knowledge; at this time no one knows how to improve significantly the performance of low achievers even if huge resources were made available ... The dilemmas of redistribution are severe because we insist upon promising equal results, which we do not know how to achieve ... Another dilemma is that redistribution policies that aim toward equality invariably create inequality... A "Karl Marx" bureaucracy might be worse than an "Adam Smith" one.

From the perspective of the disadvantaged, compensatory equality is not a freedom-slayer but a system of public-policy handicapping designed to counteract the injustice of nature and institutionalized racism. They insist that as less-skilled golfers are given a handicap in order that they may compete with more skilled ones, minorities are quite properly given compensatory assistance in higher education to better prepare them for competition with privileged majorities. What, they ask, could be fairer than that?

Furthermore, as egalitarians are quick to point out, affirmative action preferential treatment is not at all a new concept in the United States. Indeed, "Every law, every government decision awards benefits or imposes liabilities—that is, shows preference. Tax preference for agriculture and oil are obvious examples. But every variety of policy will benefit some and cost others—veterans benefits, highway and school construction, health care, alignment of election districts, labor laws, fluoridation of water."[51] Finally, egalitarians maintain that "While quotas are no panacea for curing our racial ills, they offer one constitutionally acceptable, sometimes constitutionally required, method for eliminating the adverse effects of past discrimination."[52] They are, in short, a means of implementing, not abridging, the equal protection guarantee of the Fourteenth Amendment.

Conservatives and moderate libertarians, especially those involved in education, remain unmoved by the egalitarians' rationale for compensatory equality. They almost always oppose the concept whether it is called affirmative action, sponsored mobility, contract compliance, minimum standards, enlightened personnel programs, or whatever. They remind their opponents that equality and justice used to mean *No Discrimination*, whereas now they have come to mean *Fair Shares—for the most demanding minority groups*. They insist, moreover, that all forms of educational quotas are paternalistic and demeaning, since they treat people not on an individual basis but as representatives of some racial or ethnic category. Even worse, they say, is the fact that the standard affirmative action program excludes as many people as it includes, and is thus totally alien to the U.S. tradition. For that and other reasons they condemn compensatory education programs as an undemocratic means to a democratic end and as inherently unfair in a representative, majoritarian polity.

Even when they agree that disadvantaged groups deserve special interim treatment, libertarians maintain that there is nothing magical about affirmative action programs, and that most of them turn out to be a "cure" that is worse than the disease. Permeating all their strictures on the new equality, three basic arguments stand out: that affirmative action remedies are unfair to white males and violative of the Civil Rights Act of 1964; that they produce counterproductive effects by dividing work staffs; and that they are excessively expensive and difficult to administer. Those libertarians who are not racists, and most are not, insist that there are reasonable alternatives to quotas and reverse discrimination that would be better adapted to achieving the desired ends.[53] What is needed, they suggest, is more patience and administrative imagination.

Egalitarians in the mid-1970s were particularly distressed by the number of old liberals who took up the right-wing cry that affirmative action is nothing more than affirmative discrimination. Such highly regarded writers as Martin Mayer, Edward Banfield, Daniel P. Moynihan, and Nathan Glazer, along with such liberal journals as *Harper's* and *Commentary*, have increasingly swung over to the view that recent egalitarian experiments in education have become costly failures administered by meddling bureaucrats.[54] Affirmative action, these liberal critics argue, has simply failed to help the mass of poor minorities because from the start it has been characterized more by anomalies and absurdities than by reason and common sense. Furthermore, while failing to improve the education of the disadvantaged, it has increased ethnic awareness in politics to a degree that is probably unhealthy.

Attorney General Edward Levi in the Ford Administration once solemnly warned that "a law against discrimination turns toward a law in favor of quotas."[55] And throughout his public career, Jimmy Carter until recently declined to endorse the concept of affirmation action programs. His Secretary of HEW, Joseph A. Califano, has often said that numerical goals, not arbitrary quotas, will be his approach to implementing affirmative action; but it appears that few Americans see any difference between goals and quotas. The important thing, of course, is whether the Supreme Court will perceive a difference—something that will perhaps be known in the near future. If recent decisions are any guide, the Burger Court may well declare discrimination constitutional if carried out in nondiscriminatory fashion. But that remains to be seen.

One of the most extraordinary educational developments of the 1970s was the widespread questioning of the value of higher education. Television documentary shows, such as *60 Minutes*, have examined this questioning, and scores of articles and books have been devoted to the subject. Until the late 1960s, it seemed that everybody in the United States wished to attend college, since higher education was widely viewed as a democratic panacea. But not any more. Disillusionment is now abroad in the land, and increasingly critics charge that "the so-called liberal arts education doesn't seem to prepare students for anything but teaching more liberal arts."[56] And as the cost of higher education has gone up, the payoff, it is charged, has gone down—"too many union cards in the marketplace."[57] Such allegations and many more have been made over the past few years by such distinguished educational critics as Paul Goodman, Everett Reimer, and Ivan Illich, who argued in his most controverial book that the contemporary school is rather like the medieval church in occupying a nearly unquestioned power over society.[58] In sum, what the critics are now demanding, and to some extent getting, is the demystification of the school, something that even professional educators admit is not entirely bad. The egalitarian implications of such a process are not entirely clear.

More disturbing to egalitarians was the publication in 1972 of a new study of inequality by Christopher Jencks, associate professor at the Harvard Graduate School of Education and lecturer in sociology. Professor Jencks raised anew the old question: Does education guarantee a decent life? What Jencks concluded, after a vast amount of computerized research, was that school does *not* really serve as a major vehicle of upward mobility or success in U.S. culture. Instead "schools serve primarily as selection and certification agencies, whose job is to measure and label people, and only secondarily as socialization agencies, whose job is to change people. This implies that schools serve primarily to legitimize inequality, not to create it."[59] He also suggested that the differential impact of the best schools as contrasted with the worst schools was minor, as blacks who attend desegregated schools achieve only a few points higher than those attending de facto segregated schools.

Although the press interpreted Jencks' findings to mean that schools make no difference in improving life chances, that was not accurate, since Jencks conceded that schools may produce happiness, bring about the reduction of racial antagonisms, and effect other desirable things. What was more to the point was his emphasis on schools as conserving mechanisms, reinforcing the existing distribution of resources and values. As for success in life, Jencks concluded that this comes primarily from luck, family status, and personality. As he had written several years earlier,

"Teachers are probably right in feeling that what their children need first and foremost is not academic skill but such 'middle-class' virtues as self-discipline and self-respect."[60]

Jencks' book generally received favorable reviews, but both conservatives and egalitarians attacked it. Conservatives attacked it for the revolutionary case it made for restructuring not education but society, while egalitarians criticized it for suggesting that busing and forced integration do little to advance minorities' equal educational opportunity. If Jencks is right, schools and colleges can no longer be viewed as prime lightning rods of the nation's hopes and frustrations: they must instead be viewed as peripheral institutions, perhaps even as irrelevant luxuries. The Jencks book, of course, is but one chapter in the continuing struggle between educational libertarians and egalitarians, yet it brought to the fore a number of important issues that require serious debate.

Despite all the controversy now swirling around U.S. schools and colleges, improvements continue to be made and the indomitable national quest for ever greater educational equality goes on as before. What is evolving in the nation's educational institutions, in typical U.S. fashion, is a kind of patchwork accommodation to mythic ideals, achieved by ad hoc responses to a succession of crises and problems. This type of policy incrementalism is, by its very nature, satisfactory neither to reformers nor to traditionalists. The former invariably call for more radical innovations; the latter, for fewer changes. For their part, militant egalitarians will doubtless keep harping on the fact that libertarianism, in the schools as elsewhere, simply institutionalizes and thus legitimates white racism. All of which makes one wonder if the values and ideas of the past are still viable today, or if democratic education has reached the end of the range of adaptability of its basic values and operative myths.

It is now clear that at a certain level of acquisition, educational equality metastasizes: *It both assumes a life of its own and takes control of its proponents to such a degree that its promotion becomes an obsession with them.* It is, indeed, as though equality, especially in education but also in other areas, has become a devouring metabolic disorder in the body politic, eroding social harmony and raising new problems of democratic governance as soon as old issues are resolved or muted. In this connection one is reminded of the Nietzschean term *ressentiment*, meaning envy, anger, and hatred toward those at the top. One is also reminded of Max Scheler's perceptive observation that[61]

> *Ressentiment* must . . . be strongest in a society like ours, where approximately equal rights (political and otherwise) or formal social equality, publicly recognized, go hand in hand with wide factual

differences in power, property and education . . . Quite independently of the characters and experiences of individuals, a potent charge of *ressentiment* is here accumulated by the very structure of society.

Whatever else the future may hold, it will unquestionably bring a mounting emphasis on equality of results by egalitarian activists who still regard education as a kind of panacea for their problems. They will insist with all the clout they can muster that the disadvantaged runners in the educational game must be compensated for their shackles, particularly for the exterior circumstances of birth and training which prevent their forging ahead. This, of course, is to say that they will not be trying so much to even out the race as to change its stakes and rules.[62]

In addition, one can safely predict that egalitarians, in the coming years, will be pushing for affirmative action in the field of higher education even more vigorously than in the recent past. Among other things, they will demand that colleges and universities undertake new and more strenuous efforts to seek out minority students who possess the talent and desire to profit from collegiate training. They will insist that imaginative programs of compensatory training be instituted for deprived students who have potential but are hobbled by poor preparation. And they will continue to advocate new institutional programs of financial aid and other help to minority graduate students. That, naturally, includes low-status females as well as racial and ethnic minorities. Above all, egalitarians will argue that diversity must be the future leitmotif of U.S. education. And as a corollary to that argument, they will insist that true democratic diversity can be realized as a national goal *only if race and sex, along with the history of past discrimination, are given due consideration.*

Middle-class white conservative males, for whom reverse discrimination has become an obsessive concern, show every indication of remaining as intransigent as their egalitarian opponents. They refuse to believe that preferential treatment for minority groups, however well intended, is worth the risks such a policy poses to personal freedom. They adamantly reject the view that the sins of the past can be atoned by discriminating against whites and males for that, they say, simply compounds the inequity. And they maintain that affirmative action really says to the luckless victim of an educational quota that he unfortunately belongs to a group whose arbitrary preferment is not in fashion this year or in this decade. What they are obviously demanding is that the courts once and for all declare that the Fourteenth Amendment is absolutely color-blind, and that *no* form of educational discrimination, however ingeniously contrived, is legitimate.

In sum, then, conservative libertarians remain firm in their belief that democracy merely requires an equal start in the race and not equality of performance, outcomes, or power. They also decry the linkage of the revolution of rising expectations with the quest for equality and, like Jefferson and Adams, they still talk unblushingly of a natural aristocracy of virtue and talents.[63] As is typically the case where equality and freedom clash, both sides are right up to a point. That, however, only states the dilemma: it offers no clues to solving the problem. Remedial clues, if they exist, have so far eluded our most creative policymakers.

NOTES

1. *Encyclopaedia Britannica: Macropaedia,* 15th ed., s.v. "Education, History of."
2. Ibid.
3. Ibid.
4. Ibid. Like gypsies, Spartan youths were trained to practice dissimulation, lying, and theft when dealing with outsiders.
5. *The Oxford Classical Dictionary,* 2nd ed., s.v. "Education."
6. An especially useful study of medieval universities is C.H. Haskins, *The Rise of Universities* (New York: Peter Smith, 1940). The book is actually a series of delightful short essays.
7. One of the best cultural studies of the seventeenth century is Carl Joachim Friedrich, *The Age of the Baroque, 1610-1660* (New York: Harper and Brothers, 1952). This is one of the volumes in the highly regarded *Rise of Modern Europe* series.
8. Seldes, p. 304. Earlier Erasmus had written that "A prince who is about to assume control of the state must be advised at once that the main hope of a state lies in the proper education of its youth." Ibid., p. 305.
9. See John Locke, *An Essay Concerning Human Understanding,* ed. Alexander C. Fraser, 2 vols (New York: Dover, 1959). As one should expect, Locke's ideas of education followed quite logically from his psychology, and they were generally more practical than the pedagogical doctrines of most of his contemporaries. The *tabula rasa* metaphor that underlay Locke's precepts for education apparently originated with Leibnitz, who constantly used it in criticizing him. Locke preferred the image of white paper as a symbol for the human mind at birth. The connection between Locke's general philosophy and his political and other thought is stressed in Walter M. Simon, "John Locke: Philosophy and Political Theory," *American Political Science Review* 45 (1951): 386-99.
10. For a modern edition of this work, see Jean-Jacques Rousseau, *Emile* (New York: Dutton, 1963).
11. Quoted in *International Encyclopedia of the Social Sciences,* s.v. "Rousseau, Jean Jacques."
12. Ibid.
13. The quotations by Webster, Lincoln, and Garfield are from Seldes, pp. 305, 307, 309.
14. *Encyclopaedia Britannica: Micropaedia,* 15th ed., s.v. "Pestalozzianism."
15. The Morrill Act, named for Republican Congressman Justin S. Morrill of Vermont, provided grants of land to state colleges in which the leading object

would be to teach subjects related to agriculture and the mechanic arts, without excluding general liberal arts courses. It likewise authorized training in military science. Under the act's provisions, roughly 11 million acres of land were granted by the federal government to the states for the support of the new land-grant or agricultural colleges. Later the land-grant colleges became the centers of experimental stations for agriculture and rural educational extension services. The basic precedent for national educational aid was the Northwest Ordinance of 1787, which provided that in the public domain (then mainly the Ohio Valley area) a plot of land would be reserved in every prospective township for the support of education.

16. Quoted in Seldes, p. 307.
17. See Dye, p. 67.
18. One might say that curricular modernization, at least on the collegiate level, began in the late nineteenth century when Harvard President Charles William Eliot replaced required with elective courses and elevated the sciences to a central position in the new Harvard program of liberal education. Eliot was also partly responsible for getting foreign languages and mathematics into the curriculum of U.S. junior high schools. His innovations, which were both elitist and egalitarian, were strongly resisted by old-fashioned authoritarian educators such as Noah Porter, president of Yale. Indeed, the Eliot-Porter conflict, though carried on at a fairly high level of abstraction, in many ways prefigured the twentieth-century struggle between pedagogical conservatives and progressives.
19. Since World War II, a large number of general histories of education have been published. Most of these deal with Western education, and are regularly reviewed in such professional journals as the *History of Education Quarterly*.
20. *Meyer* v. *Nebraska*, 262 U.S. 390 (1923).
21. Ibid.
22. *Pierce* v. *Society of Sisters of the Holy Names of Jesus and Mary*, 268 U.S. 510 (1925). The Court also held that the schools themselves had property for which they had a claim to protection under the Fourteenth Amendment.
23. *Wisconsin* v. *Yoder*, 406 U.S. 205 (1972).
24. *Everson* v. *Board of Education of Ewing Township*, 330 U.S. 1 (1947).
25. *McCollum* v. *Board of Education*, 333 U.S. 203 (1948).
26. *Zorach* v. *Clauson*, 343 U.S. 306 (1952).
27. See *Engel* v. *Vitale*, 370 U.S. 421 (1962); and *Abington School District* v. *Schempp*, 374 U.S. 203 (1963).
28. *Missouri ex rel. Gaines* v. *Canada*, 305 U.S. 337 (1938).
29. *Sipuel* v. *Board of Regents of University of Oklahoma*, 332 U.S. 631 (1948).
30. *Sweatt* v. *Painter*, 339 U.S. 629 (1950).
31. *McLaurin* v. *Oklahoma State Regents*, 339 U.S. 637 (1950).
32. *Brown* v. *Board of Education of Topeka*, 347 U.S. 483 (1954).
33. *Bolling* v. *Sharpe*, 347 U.S. 497 (1954).
34. *Brown* v. *Board of Education of Topeka*, 349 U.S. 294 (1955).
35. See Wilhoit, pp. 135-230.
36. See Ibid., pp. 285-87, for a complete copy of the Manifesto.
37. *Alexander* v. *Holmes County Board of Education*, 396 U.S. 19 (1969). Three other Supreme Court decisions were especially helpful in legitimating the black revolution in the field of educational equality. In *Cooper* v. *Aaron*, 358 U.S. 1 (1958), the Court warned that the rights of black children "can neither

be nullified openly and directly by state legislators or state executive officials nor nullified indirectly by them by evasive schemes for segregation." Six years later the Court ruled in *Griffin* v. *County Board of Prince Edward County,* 377 U.S. 218 (1964), that in closing the public schools while subsidizing private white schools, Prince Edward County authorities had "denied petitioners the equal protection of the laws." Then, one year before the *Alexander* decision, the Court held in *Green* v. *County Board of New Kent County,* 391 U.S. 430 (1968), that so-called freedom of choice school plans could be regarded as constitutionally acceptable only when they offered a "real promise of aiding a desegregation program" and where there were no alternative means to that objective "readily available." The most comprehensive study of the Supreme Court's original desegregation decision is Richard Kluger, *Simple Justice* (New York: Alfred A. Knopf, 1976). This is a dramatic account of an extraordinary chain of historical events.

38. Wilhoit, p. 276.
39. *Swann* v. *Charlotte-Mecklenburg Board of Education,* 402 U.S. 1 (1971).
40. *Milliken* v. *Bradley,* 418 U.S. 717 (1974).
41. Wilhoit, pp. 277-78.
42. *Lau* v. *Nichols,* 414 U.S. 563 (1974).
43. *Newsweek,* 7 February 1977, p. 64.
44. Ibid.
45. *San Antonio Independent School District* v. *Rodriguez,* 411 U.S. 1 (1973).
46. In a case initiated by John Serrano in 1968, the California Supreme Court, one of the most liberal courts in the nation, held in 1971 that the state's existing school funding programs discriminated against children in poor school districts and thus violated their constitutional right of equal protection. Although the legislature subsequently made efforts to reduce the school financing inequities, the Court held in late 1976 that the revised system still violated the state constitution's equal protection clause. These rulings were apparently the first in the nation to declare unconstitutional the traditional way of financing public schools mainly with property taxes. And despite the adverse ruling of the U.S. Supreme Court in the *San Antonio* case, the California opinion has apparently had a certain fall-out effect on other state legislatures and courts, most notably in New Jersey and Montana. In California, the state was given four years in which to implement a system that equalizes per-pupil expenditures throughout the state. Numerous other school financing cases are now in various stages of litigation in state courts.
47. Nina Totenberg, "Discriminating to end Discrimination," *The New York Times Magazine,* 14 April 1974, p. 9.
48. Ibid.
49. *DeFunis* v. *Odegaard,* 416 U.S. 312 (1974).
50. Frank S. Levy, Arnold J. Meltsner, and Aaron Wildavsky, *Urban Outcomes: Schools, Streets, and Libraries* (Berkely: University of California Press, 1974), pp. 248, 257, 259, 260. See also John D. Owen, *School Inequality and the Welfare State* (Baltimore: The Johns Hopkins University Press, 1974). Professor Owen links school inequality to the decentralized system of school finance which has characterized the development of U.S. educational institutions. He also shows how the traditional U.S. system of college scholarships, loans, and subsidized tuition rates has tended to support the educational advantages of the middle class.

51. Leonard A. Cole, *Blacks in Power: A Comparative Study of Black and White Elected Officials* (Princeton: Princeton University Press, 1976), p. 230.

52. Steven Nisenbaum, "Race Quotas," *Harvard Civil Rights-Civil Liberties Law Review* 8 (1973): 180.

53. Ibid., pp. 166-73.

54. See, for example, Nathan Glazer, *Affirmative Discrimination: Ethnic Inequality and Public Policy* (New York: Basic Books, 1976); and Martin Mayer, *Today and Tomorrow in America* (New York: Harper & Row, 1976).

55. *Des Moines Tribune,* 18 June 1977, p. 5.

56. Melvin Maddocks, "College as means to $ucce$$," *Des Moines Tribune,* 12 March 1976, p. 12.

57. Ibid.

58. See Ivan Illich, *Deschooling Society* (New York: Harper & Row, 1971).

59. Christopher Jencks, *Inequality: A Reassessment of the Effect of Family and Schooling in America* (New York: Harper & Row, 1972), p. 135.

60. Christopher Jencks, "A Reappraisal of the Most Controversial Education Document of Our Time," *New York Times Magazine,* 10 August 1969, p. 44. On this general subject, see also James S. Coleman, *Equality of Educational Opportunity* (Washington, D.C.: U.S. Government Printing Office, 1966); and Frederick Mosteller and Daniel P. Moynihan, eds., *On Equality of Educational Opportunity* (New York: Random House, 1972).

61. Quoted in Daniel Bell, "On Meritocracy and Equality," *The Public Interest,* Fall 1972, p. 51.

62. See Samuel Bowles, "Schooling and Inequality from Generation to Generation," *Journal of Political Economy* 80 (1972): S219-S251; and Herbert Gintis, "Education and the Characteristics of Worker Productivity," *American Economic Review* 61 (1971): 266-79. As socialist egalitarians, Bowles and Gintis argue that until the United States takes the radical step of democratizing its economic institutions, its schools cannot become appreciably less hierarchical or repressive.

63. See John R. Silber, "The Need for Elite Education," *Harper's,* June 1977, pp. 22-24. See also George F. Will, "Common Sense on Race," *Newsweek,* 24 January 1977, p. 80.

9

THE FUTURE IN PERSPECTIVE

This study has analyzed the ideas of freedom, equality, and social justice in a context of evolving policy issues and democratic ideology as well as in the light of experience as to the behavior of public policymakers. These dimensions of analysis are intricately related and obviously can never be fully separated in real life. But if there is one thing that stands out above all others in the book's analysis it is the fact that *notwithstanding the historic tension between freedom and equality in the United States, the nation's liberal democratic institutions have evidenced remarkable longevity and flexibility.* If the *have-nots* have, on occasion, succumbed to extremism, they have, for the most part, accepted the rules of the game and eschewed extra-legal violence in their quest for a fairer share of the nation's resources. Indeed, only during the Civil War and, to a lesser degree, during the 1960s did the freedom-equality dilemma degenerate into widespread violence that put in peril the stability of the Republic.

There are several reasons why U.S. democracy, so far at least, has been able to keep the equality struggle within manageable bounds and why the system has shown a resiliency rarely seen in other countries.

First of all there is the fact that almost all U.S. citizens accept the liberal values on which the country was established, with the result that a smothering consensus has developed concerning what can and cannot be achieved within the national polity.

Second, there has been a tendency in the past "to mute conflict by converting demands into economic form, where they could be satisfied by merely increasing the size of the total economic product, thus not taking anything away from the 'haves' while delivering tangible rewards to the 'have-nots.' "[1]

Third, there has been at work the stabilizing principle of cross-cutting cleavages, according to which class-based divisions are countered by other cleavages and by constantly shifting political coalitions.

Fourth, the deeply-ingrained centrist ideology of the nation has enabled the ruling elites to countervail far-out demands "by appearing to support the middle way every time—never too far in one direction or the other."[2]

Fifth, the U.S. political tradition of focusing on procedural regularity and legalism to the exclusion of substantive issues has made it easy for those in power to confuse their aspiring critics and maintain a high level of consensus for the status quo.

Sixth, the clever manipulation of such totemic symbols as law and order in times of crisis has been an especially useful ploy for containing the *have-nots* and engineering additional support for the supposedly neutral establishment.

Seventh, and last, sociopolitical integration in the United States has been strengthened by the ability of the political process to meet a substantial part of the expectations of most organized groups. No group, of course, realizes all its demands. But up to now at least, most groups have stopped short of seeking basic changes in the allocation of political and economic power. It can, therefore, be said that the recent triumphs of disadvantaged groups have had little to do with revolutionary politics but are rather a tribute to their combination of physical and moral vigor, their inflammable sense of the justness of their cause, their terrific tenacity, and their strenuous assertion of will at every point of access in the political process.

One cannot, of course, assume that the factors making for political integration will operate in the future as they have in the past. As this study has amply demonstrated, a number of stresses and strains have emerged since World War II that have led to a weakening of consensus and a growing polarization of libertarians and egalitarians. Moreover, these stress factors are not limited to the United States: they are present in nearly every democracy in the world and in many authoritarian states as well.

Today, for example, there appears to be a definite diminution in the scope of the liberal democratic consensus that up to this point has been so pervasive. Women, blacks, Chicanos, and young people, among others, are increasingly questioning established beliefs in every sphere of national life; and the more militant among these groups are now suggesting that they have been played for suckers. The traditional commitments to democratic assumptions are still the rule, but exceptions are proliferating, as are suspicions that *The System* and *The Establishment* now denote oppression, not equality in freedom.

There is also a possibility—indeed, a probability—that the ruling elites of the future will have more and more difficulty managing minority demands simply by converting them into economic terms. The orientation of U.S. citizens is, in many respects, far less materialistic than previously. Because of this, the channeling of freedom-equality issues into an economic equation will at the very least require more manipulative skills than were necessary heretofore. Decreasing materialism also means that the *have-nots* of the future are going to demand a higher quality of life as well as a larger share of the national income. They are beginning to learn what the established middle classes only recently learned: that man does not live by bread alone.

Regarding the stabilizing influence of cross-cutting cleavages, that phenomenon will doubtless continue to operate in U.S. pluralism, although polarization along class and racial lines may well become more important that it has so far been. Furthermore, if this occurs, it is not likely to be the *positive polarization* that Vice President Agnew promoted, but rather an ugly, divisive, and probably violent spectacle of confrontation politics which neither libertarians nor egalitarians can hope to win.

Despite the efforts of militant egalitarians on the Left and conservative libertarians on the Right to radicalize U.S. politics, centrism will almost surely remain the core ideology of mainstream Americans. Still, though few egalitarians are likely to become communists, as few conservatives will convert to fascism, the danger of a massive revitalization of the extreme Right and extreme Left persists and cannot be ignored by policymakers. Whether the pressures toward radicalism will lead to the kind of insurrectionary violence that was spawned by the confrontation between the black revolution and the Massive Resistance movement of the 1950s, no one can say. One can only emphasize that the roots of violence are just below the surface, and there is no shortage of freedom-equality issues to bring them to fruition.

As egalitarian demands escalate, the establishment will counterattack by trying to focus on procedural regularity and legalism, since these are principles about which relatively high levels of agreement may be anticipated. There can be no denying that such a focusing has been a useful stabilizing factor in the past; it may not, however, be quite so effective in the future. Minorities are getting wise to the establishment's tactic of casting fundamental issues into terms of procedural questions, and it is therefore unlikely that in future showdowns they will be so easily diverted from their goals by this ploy. At the very least, the greater awareness of minorities on this score will entail increased heat and bitterness in any future debate on freedom-equality issues.

Likewise, it is safe to predict that tomorrow's egalitarians will be less diverted by law and order cries than those of the past were. Egalitarians, like libertarians, want a stable-law-abiding society, but not at the expense of repealing the First and Fourteenth Amendments. Moreover, when it becomes apparent to all or most egalitarians that law and order is a code phrase of the *haves*, and that the establishment is not really neutral on most public issues, the disadvantaged are going to become far more difficult to deal with than formerly was the case. Their leaders know already that law is an instrument of social control favoring the status quo, and that the dice of politics are invariably loaded against outsiders. Increasingly the men and women in the ranks are becoming aware of these realities.

In respect to satisfaction of group wants, there will inevitably be new problems arising in this area for the simple reason that there are more organized pressure groups demanding more things than ever before. What is more important, this proliferation of group demands is occurring at the very time that national resources are being depleted and taxpayers' revolts spreading. Consequently, it may well be that the United States is "moving toward a politics resembling a zero-sum game, where everything one party wins comes out of the treasured possessions of the other side, making the latter a loser to the exact extent that the former becomes a winner."[3] It need hardly be added that if this turns out to be the case, all future efforts to maximize liberty and equality at the same time will be doubly difficult if not impossible.

As in the past, it seems certain that egalitarians will keep differing among themselves as to the most appropriate strategies and tactics to be used in pushing their demands for more equality. Over the past century or so, leaders of minority groups have devised a formidable array of strategies, many of them quite effective, and there is no reason to doubt that new and better ones will be created in the years ahead. Moderates are likely to continue accepting most of the premises of U.S. society while practicing strategies of incrementalim. That primarily means working for integration in all areas of life and vigorously pursuing the politics of access. Integration, of course, requires considerable self-denial on the part of proud minorities. Yet given the nation's pluralistic heritage, most groups seem to feel that rational compromise is worth the candle and promises the least tension between minority and dominant groups. As for the politics of access, it demands infinite patience and shrewd bargaining; but it has the advantage of being a comprehensive set of maneuvers, all highly respectable, that can be used to implement any number of tactical approaches.

Militant egalitarians, on the other hand, will obviously pursue more radical strategies in the belief "that the power structure cannot be dealt with except from a position of great internal strength, and that, basically, only self-interest and naked power shape political relationships."[4] Strategies of the militants will include compensatory equality, temporary withdrawal from coalition politics in order to build a political resource base, community control of as many fields of public policy as possible, and, on occasion, *creative violence* for the purpose of deriving maximal gains from confrontation politics. Extreme egalitarians, such as the communists, will also advocate a long-range strategy of revolution in accord with the classic Jacobin-Bolshevik archetype, which seeks to hasten the advent of a final showdown by exposing the *internal contradictions* in the existing system. In the final analysis, all militant egalitarian strategies rest on three premises:[5]

    1.   The "standard" view of the American political system is incorrect from the minority perspective.

    2.   The political system is morally wrong.

    3.   The political system must be changed.

In regard to future minority tactics, these will likely be even more varied and controversial than minority strategies, since they are the actual, everyday means by which strategies are implemented. Of course, all egalitarian tactics aim at destabilizing the system, but some are definitely more radical and conflict-inducing than others.

If the past can be relied upon to supply a key to the future, we can predict that tomorrow's minority tactics will include such things as coalition politics, bloc voting, strikes, demonstrations, boycotts, multi-form protests, myth-manipulation, ideological propaganda, icon-waving, symbol-spotlighting, nonnegotiable demands, and disruption. Old-fashioned libertarians will no doubt respond to these shock tactics as they have responded in the past—by denouncing them as immoral, illegal, and counterproductive. But tomorrow's activists are not likely to be deterred by self-righteous denunciations by their critics. Demonstrations, riots, rebellion, and system-destabilization have had a long history in the quest for equality in freedom. There is no sign that today's militants have any intention whatever of giving up this part of the democratic tradition.[6]

Conservative power elites, who have generally controlled public policy in the United States, will probably remain in control for some time to come. But in order to blunt the mounting assaults of militant egalitarians while securing their traditional liberties and privileges, they will need to become increasingly imaginative and innovative. Within the context of constitutional democracy, they can counter egalitarian demands with a number of responses that have not yet lost their efficacy. These include incremental change, muting of protest by symbolic (but not substantive) therapies, organizing establishmentarian coalitions such as the Nixon-Agnew Southern and Middle American strategies, coopting as many minority group leaders as possible, embracing parts of the egalitarian ideology, drawing a line and standing firmly on it, suppressing the more outrageous forms of dissent, harassing militants, and invalidating minority leadership in the way that J. Edgar Hoover and the FBI sought, unsuccessfully, to invalidate Dr. King's leadership. Some of these counter-responses are ugly and illegal; but they have all been tried in the recent past, and despite the post-Watergate morality, they may well be tried again. Obviously if carried too far, they would transform the nation into a police state where both freedom and equality would suffer.[7]

If they are smart, minority spokesmen in the future will increasingly stress the fact that in working for their own claims to equality, they are helping to secure the rights of all Americans. In this regard, they will be echoing the words of the great nineteenth-century black egalitarian, Frederick Douglass, who once declared that[8]

> No man can put a chain about the ankle of his fellow man, without at last finding the other end of it fastened about his own neck. The lesson of all the ages on this point is that a wrong done to one man is a wrong done to all men. It may not be felt at the moment, and the evil day may be long delayed, but so sure as there is a moral government of the universe, so sure will the harvest of evil come.

In the future, as in the past, the tone for U.S. political discourse is going to be set by the tension between liberty and equality. In fact, throughout U.S. history there has been a continual testing, probing, and realigning of these basic principles, with first freedom holding center stage and then equality. Thus, in the eighteenth and nineteenth centuries the principle of freedom predominated, while equality rose to the fore in the early twentieth century with the Progressive movement. Then, in pendulum-like succession came the economic libertarianism of the 1920s, Roosevelt's New Deal egalitarianism of the 1930s, Eisenhower's business-oriented conservatism, the New Frontier-Great Society war on poverty and racism, and, finally, the Nixon-Ford revival of Social Darwinism. The contours of Carter's Good Society are as yet but dimly discerned.

A particularly difficult problem for future policymakers will be that of coming to terms with the *future shock* resulting from the rapid transformation in the conceptualization of freedom and equality. Today new notions of both these principles are being vigorously pursued on every hand, as existing formulations undergo constant re-examination. And it is well to bear in mind that the outcomes from the public-policy process are both cause and effect of this ongoing conceptual evolution. This ideological development will not suddenly come to a halt. Rather it will go on and on, enormously complicating and exacerbating the already difficult tasks of public administrators.

Until a new consensual synthesis about the precise ralation of equality to freedom and justice can be devised, U.S. politics, one can state with assurance, will be more cacophonous than tranquil, more centrifugal than centripetal. The heart of the politics of the future will be the crucial confrontations, as inevitable as they are bound to be divisive, between the egalitarians' *therapeutic reform ethic* and the libertairans' *Protestant work ethic*. In such confrontations, egalitarians will continue to emphasize environmental determinism and judicial resolution of social problems, while libertarians will continue to stress individual autonomy and less dependence on judicial activism. The truth in this matter may not be equidistant between the two positions, but it stands somewhere between the ideals of total determinism and total free will. The task of tomorrow's statesmen will be to pinpoint the exact locus, while finding ways to harmonize the legitimate equality demands of minorities with the traditional libertarian commitments of the majority. In that task both the political arms of government and the judicial process will have vital, indeed indispensable, roles to play.

Egalitarians will only be fooling themselves if they expect conservatives to suddenly relax their visceral prejudice against radical conceptions of equality or give up the old Burkean notion that men have equal rights but not to equal things. Conservatives are fiercely committed to the old libertarian conceptions of justice which they believe have stood the test of time and therefore have established in their favor a presumption of legitimacy. Though right-wingers may be quick to embrace new-fangled technologies, especially when their profit potential is apparent, they are not about to succumb to the ideas of equality and justice implicit in the New Politics.

Conservatives today are particularly impatient with the increasing tendency of minorities to insist that every major social ill in the country can find its cure in some constitutional principle, and that the judiciary should boldly intervene to promote egalitarian reform. They prefer to leave the solution of social problems to the political branches of government, partly, it would appear, because those branches move more deliberately and tend to favor middle-class freedoms over lower-class equality. As Justice Harlan, a staunch conservative, remarked in a controversial re-apportionment case, "The Constitution is not a panacea for every blot upon the public welfare, nor should this Court, ordained as a judicial body, be thought of as a general haven for reform movements."[9] No conservative would dissent from that judgment.

It now appears certain that tomorrow's conservative libertarians will bear more than a passing resemblance to their nineteenth-century Social Darwinist forebears, especially in their conviction that since liberty permits men to accumulate capital, the fuel of progress, the advance of humanity is inexorably linked to the principle of personal freedom. Indeed, some are even now maintaining that the U.S. egalitarian tradition simply cannot survive when the relative merits of freedom and equality are judged solely on the basis of empirical facts. In this opinion they are reflecting the views of William Graham Sumner, who once wrote that[10]

> The assertion that all men are equal is perhaps the purest of falsehoods in dogmas that was ever put into human language; five minutes' observation of facts will show that men are unequal through a very wide range of variation. . . . If there is liberty, there will be inequality.

It was also Sumner, echoing Herbert Spencer, who wrote that "The history of the human race is one long story of attempts by certain persons and classes to obtain control of the power of the State, so as to win earthly gratifications at the expense of others."[11] and because of that history, he warned, libertarians must ever be vigilant.

Conservatives in the years ahead will not only revive Burke and Sumner and Spencer, as they are already doing, to support their arguments, they will also quite likely rehabilitate Calhoun, without, of course, his pro-slavery philosophy. They will certainly applaud Calhoun's remarks that[12]

> There is another error, not less great and dangerous. . . . I refer to the opinion, that liberty and equality are so intimately united, that liberty cannot be perfect without perfect equality. That they are united to a certain extent. . . is conceded. But to go further, and make equality of *condition* essential to liberty, would be to destroy both liberty and progress. The reason is, that inequality of condition, while it is a necessary consequence of liberty is, at the same time, indispensable to progress.

Libertarians, when all is said and done, are basically people who give liberty a preferred position in their scale of values. At least in that respect they are preeminently Calhounians, for it was Calhoun who always insisted that "Liberty leaves each free to pursue the course he may deem best to promote his interest and happiness, as far as it may be compatible with the primary end for which government is ordained."[13] Few libertarians are likely to become outright reactionaries and repudiate the idea of equality of opportunity. What is more probable is that they will keep supporting traditional political and legal conceptions of equality, which exclude the concept of equality of results, as the only legitimate meanings of the ideal.

Many, perhaps most, economic libertarians would like to see the world return to something like the Benthamite liberalism that characterized governmental policy throughout much of the nineteenth century. Today's descendants of the Philosophical Radicals—Rand, Helms, Buckley, Goldwater, Reagan, and Friedman—will no doubt continue to yearn for the days when personal liberty was valued far more than equality; but all the yearning in the world is not likely to revive those far-off days. For the simple truth of the matter is that the masses of the West would never tolerate a return to the long discredited *ill-fare state*.

Conservatives, understandably, are incensed at demagogic left-wing politicians who, they maintain, have made the common people more equality-conscious than they might otherwise have been, and who have been largely responsible for the recent downplaying of individual initiative. Here they are Hamiltonian to the core. For it was Hamilton, writing in *Federalist* No. 1, who tartly observed that "of those men who have overturned the liberties of republics, the greatest number have begun their career by paying an obsequious court to the [equality-obsessed] people; commencing demagogues, and ending tyrants."[14] No friend of democracy can ignore the danger that Hamilton warned against, whether the demagogue rants in the rhetoric of radicalism or of conservatism. The patriot James Otis showed good sense when he took as his personal motto the phrase, *Ubi libertas ibi patria* (where liberty dwells, there is my country). Enlightened democrats, whether conservative or egalitarian, will be hard put to find a better guide to justice, even if they disagree about the meaning of liberty.

It will be surprising if tomorrow's libertarians, after rahabilitating the Social Darwinists, do not go back even further and resurrect an equally persuasive conservative thinker, John Adams. Indeed, few people of any age have written as lucidly and meaningfully of the relation between freedom and equality as the nation's second president. Yet, sad to say, only a handful of scholars are now conversant with Adams' seminal thoughts on this vital subject. The following brief selections from the works of Adams will show why conservative libertarians ought to find him most congenial:[15]

> [Certain kinds of inequality] are common to every people and can never be altered by any because they are founded in the constitution

of nature. . . . [Moreover,] it must be remembered that the rich are *people* as well as the poor; that they have rights as well as others; that they have as clear and *sacred* right to their large property as others have to theirs which is smaller; that oppression to them is as possible and as wicked as to others; that stealing, robbing, cheating are the same crimes and sins, whether committed against them or others. The rich, therefore, ought to have an effectual barrier in the constitution against being robbed, plundered, and murdered, as well as the poor; and this can never be without an independent senate.

It is, of course, possible that only the most literate among libertarians will embrace the aristocratic conservatism of Adams, since for most people on the Right, classical liberalism is likely to prove more congenial. If that indeed turns out to be the case, the libertarians' favorite guru of the future will quite probably be Professor Milton Friedman of the University of Chicago. While he would certainly deny that he is against equality, Friedman's writings provide such a limited role for government that the effect of adopting his ideas as public policy would probably be a reduction in public support for the goals of egalitarians. In any event, libertarians of whatever stripe will take heart from Friedman's conclusion that governments should be judged best which have effectively[16]

maintained law and order, defined property rights, served as a means whereby we could modify property rights and other rules of the economic game, adjudicated disputes about the interpretation of the rules, enforced contracts, promoted competition, provided a monetary framework, engaged in activities to counter technical monopolies . . . , and . . . supplemented private charity and the private family in protecting the irresponsible, whether madman or child.

To the extent that they adopt the classical liberal philosophy of Friedman, tomorrow's libertarians can be counted on to oppose not only such activist egalitarian programs as welfare, affirmative action, quotas, and open admissions, but also such moderate policies as public housing, integration of suburbs by government pressure, retroactive seniority in employment, rent control, consumer-protection legislation, environmental clean-up programs, and social security expansion. True, libertarians have not been united in the past and they will not be united in the future. Yet the majority of them, including all who are on the right wing of the political spectrum, clearly have a nostalgic hankering for laissez-faire and for Adam Smith's *invisible hand*. Few, however, are as consistent as Friedman is, or as Smith was.

To a somewhat surprising degree, egalitarians are increasingly being placed on the defensive as they find it ever more difficult to engineer a broad national consensus for their major reform proposals, whether they relate to politics, criminal justice, the economy, or education. This is partly a legacy of the Nixon-Agnew years of *benign neglect*, but it is also related to the economic recession—*stagflation* the economists call it—that the country has been in since the early 1970s. Whatever the reasons, the damage has been done. And egalitarians now find it necessary to crusade vigorously against the New Minimalism in government, which seems to be soaring in popularity, and to point out constantly that the neo-Spencerian ideas of today's libertarians are nothing less than an ill-concealed blueprint for permanent inequality. Bitterly denying conservative charges that they are more interested in redistributing the world's wealth than in expanding it, egalitarians gravely predict that if conservative ideas become hardened into public policy, millions of workers will lose their jobs, cities will rot beyond repair; and with less government all along the line, blacks and other minorities will again find themselves at the mercy of racists, bigots, and reactionary states'-rightists.

Although many liberals and moderate egalitarians remain under the spell of the old Jeffersonian dream, the more aggressive proponents of equality are convinced that future victories over inequality will never come from reducing the size of government and returning to a self-winding economy. Only through vigorous, positive government, they argue, can anything approaching full equality in freedom ever be approximated. They believe, in other words, in the socialization of democracy via the benevolent state, for they agree with Arthur M. Schlesinger, Jr., that "Our democratic tradition has been at its best an activist tradition. It has found its fulfillment, not in complaint or in escapism, but in responsibility and decision."[17]

As long as conservative libertarians continue to oppose the activism of the Left, egalitarians must remain alert to the possibility of a revival of laissez-faire, at least in a modified form. For the moment, the so-called New Minimalism is the main focus of their anxieties, but of course they are concerned with anything that suggests a decline in the government's determination to fight inequality. These concerns were well expressed by Vernon E. Jordan, Jr., Executive Director of the National Urban League, when he wrote that[18]

> The siren song of less government is actually a strident march designed to keep black people and the poor in their place, penniless and powerless. . . .
> It's a curious phenomenon—the President and candidates for his office all running against the government they want to lead. . . .

The new minimalism only promises racial friction and continued depression. It tells us that less is more and that we should think small instead of embracing larger aspirations. It's better fitted to Cal Coolidge's simpler times than to today's complex society.

The conservative idea that the public sector in U.S. society ought to be reduced, which Jordan and others have long attacked, is in a sense an invitation to class politics; and if that idea continues to gain currency, it is probable that class politics of some sort will expand as the freedom-equality conflict intensifies. Of course, a free society without tensions and conflicts is unthinkable. For as long as inequalities remain that are not clearly based on personal merit, democratic politics will of necessity focus on the quest for equality—and sometimes quite stridently so. That quest, if it is to remain democratic, must be kept within legal bounds, or neither freedom nor equality will survive. Keeping it in such bounds will be easier for all concerned if conservatives will quit identifying a given status quo with the essence of civilization, and if militant egalitarians will remember that their passionate protests are as much an expression of self-interest as they are of some infallible dogma about society.

Quite clearly, any future equality movement that purports to shape a real world must first of all accept the limitations and possibilities of that world. Similarly, any right-wing libertarian movement that hopes to remain just and viable must demonstrate that it is more than an outlet for private grievances, plutocratic frustrations, and middle-class vested interests. All of this is but to suggest that the freedom-equality dilemma is **not merely a conflict** in national politics, it is likewise a conflict within each **and every** individual.

The class politics of the future will likely resemble the politics of the past **in at least** one important respect: libertarians are going to remain *trickle-down* democrats, while their egalitarian opponents will remain what they have always been—*trickle-up* democrats. The crucial distinction between these traditional schools of politics was spotlighted by William Jennings Bryan in his famous Cross of Gold speech before the 1896 Democratic Presidential Nominating Convention. He declared then that[19]

There are two ideas of government. There are those who believe that, if you will only legislate to make the well-to-do prosperous, their prosperity will leak through to those below. The Democratic idea, however, has been that if you legislate to make the masses prosperous, their prosperity will find its way up through every class which rests upon them.

Since at least the Constitutional Convention of 1787, the more astute U.S. politicians, such as Bryan, have been aware of the inherent tension between liberty and equality in the national heritage. Indeed, that tension formed the basis of our first real party struggle: that between the Federalists, who favored liberty and the new Federal Constitution, and the states'-rightist Antifederalists, who feared that the constitutional architects in Philadelphia had sacrificed equality for the privileged liberty of the upper classes. Given such a record of longevity, the tension between freedom and equality will undoubtedly survive in all areas of U.S. life, for generations to come. Most Americans, it can likewise be predicted, will go on avoiding the issue by claiming that they are committed to both principles. And they will be right—up to the point where their interests become directly involved. When that occurs, they will unhesitatingly prefer one over the other, which is precisely why freedom and equality have for so many years served as the structuring poles of U.S. political debate.

Whatever its problematic side-effects may be, and they exist, the quest for equality in freedom has always been a humanistic enterprise, a redemptive process that exemplifies what being human is all about. Today, moreover, the quest has acquired something resembling the mystique of religion and fairy tales. Certainly nobody has so far been able—though many have tried— to put the equality genie back into the bottle, and it seems unlikely that anybody ever will. It is simply a matter of democratic arithmetic that *where there is no equality, there is no freedom; and where there is no freedom, there is no justice.*

Well-intentioned pessimists have sometimes argued that mass egalitarian democracy, with its ubiquitous freedom-equality paradox, may be an experiment doomed to fail, though it is perhaps the only political experiment worth trying. There is no question about its experimental nature, but there is also no question about its enduring merits. For in the final analysis, the democratic quest for equality is anchored in human nature itself, a fact that imbues the quest with both a philosophy of life and a faith to live by. Who, then, can deny that the love and pursuit of equality constitute a fundamental expression of the moral nature and destiny of man?

Nobody can accurately predict the attitude of future generations toward freedom and equality, but it is certain that they will have to confront a question that remains both elementary and ultimate. The question is this: Given the nation's limited, dwindling resources, can full equality in freedom ever be practically realized; if so, will it be achieved through evolution or revolution? New conservatives and some old liberals keep raising the point that the growing emphasis on equality since the eighteenth century has led to centralized, bureaucratized government and destroyed diversity, autonomy, and cultural creativity—the very values we ought to be maximizing. Equality, they also suggest, has in effect become a *new despotism,* working hand in hand with coercive government under the symbolic accoutrements of constitutional democracy.[20] Of course, the postulation of egalitarianism as the chief foe of liberty is neither new nor free of ideological bias. Yet there can be no blinking the fact that liberty and equality, in the real world, do increasingly seem antipodal rather than complementary.

Nevertheless, the dream persists, and the politics it inspires is neither illusion nor aimless rhetoric. To the oppressed of every age, it must seem that equality is forever on the scaffold, inequality forever on the throne—a view easily justified by a look at the facts. There is, however, nothing wrong with the democratic dream of equality, which seeks to balance the real on the ideal. The problem is the majority's response to the minority dreamers. It has well been said that "We may kill our dreamers, but not their dreams."[21] And for all the vaunted virtues of realism, the dream of equality is still necessary if we as a nation are to transform what we are now *into what we may become.* Ever relevant are the eloquent words of Dr. Martin Luther King, Jr., delivered from the steps of the Lincoln Memorial:[22]

> I still have a dream. It is a dream deeply rooted in the American dream. I have a dream that one day this nation will rise up and live out the true meaning of its creed: "We hold these truths to be self-evident that all men are created equal."

Perhaps, as the future unfolds, it will develop that the libertarian drive and egalitarian quest are not really so different after all but are the same democratic force at its negative and positive poles, out of which comes a current that fuses the materials of justice as no single political myth could do. It is generally agreed that liberty and equality were the two principal visions that inspired the foundation of the United States, yet even a cursory glance at the nation's history reveals that these visions have never been effectively merged. The democratic agenda of the future will contain no more urgent business than the accomplishment of that merger.

Democracy's freedom-equality paradox, serious though it is, is not so critical a problem as to require an Isaiah coming down from the mountain in goatskins to prophesy our doom. There is every reason to believe that freedom, equality, and constitutional democracy *will* survive, *provided* we face up to the issues inherent in the paradox and refuse to be panicked into either reactionary or utopian solutions. The democratic urge for equality, as Tocqueville so aptly stressed, is indeed insatiable. But that simple fact, far from dividing us, should be viewed by democrats everywhere as humanity's greatest challenge and opportunity.

NOTES

1. Dolbeare, *Directions,* p. 345.
2. Ibid., p. 346.
3. Ibid., p. 356.
4. Makielski, p. 175.
5. Ibid., pp. 181-82. Three fine general works dealing with militant strategies are John R. Howard, ed., *Awakening Minorities* (New Brunswick, N.J.: Transaction Books, 1970); Kenneth Kenniston, *Young Radicals* (New York: Harcourt, Brace and World, 1965); and Edgar Litt, *Ethnic Politics in America* (Glenview, Ill.: Scott Foresman, 1970). The Litt work is particularly interesting, since it appraises several minority strategies, with special reference to how they relate to specific goals.
6. The best studies of minority tactics are Saul Alinsky, *Rules for Radicals: A Pragmatic Primer for Realistic Radicals* (New York: Random House, 1971); August Meier, ed., *The Transformation of Activism* (Chicago: Aldine, 1970); and Chuck Stone, *Black Political Power in America* (Indianapolis: Bobbs-Merrill, 1968).
7. Concerning the issue of response and counterresponse, see Morris Janowitz, *The Social Control of Escalated Riots* (Chicago: University of Chicago Press, 1968); Fred Powledge, *Black Power White Resistance* (Cleveland: World, 1967); and Jerome H. Skolnick, *The Politics of Protest* (New York: Ballantine, 1969).
8. Quoted in Larry I. Peterman and Louis F. Weschler, eds., *American Political Thought: Readings* (New York: Appleton-Century-Crofts, 1972), p. 246.
9. *Reynolds* v. *Sims,* 377 U.S. 533 (1964).
10. A.G. Keller and M. Davie, eds., *Essays of William Graham Sumner* (New Haven: Yale University Press, 1934), Vol. 2, p. 96.
11. Quoted in Dolbeare, *Directions,* p. 236.
12. Quoted in Peterman and Weschler, p. 155.
13. Richard Crallé, ed., *The Works of John C. Calhoun* (New York: D. Appleton and Co., 1854), Vol. 1, p. 52.
14. Clinton Rossiter, ed., *The Federalist Papers: Hamilton, Madison, Jay* (New York: The New American Library, 1961), p. 35.
15. Quoted in Dolbeare, *Directions,* pp. 134, 138.
16. Friedman, p. 34.
17. Quoted in Dolbeare, *Directions,* pp. 405-06.
18. Vernon E. Jordan, Jr., "My Turn: The New Minimalism," *Newsweek,* 23 February 1976, p. 9.
19. William Jennings Bryan, *The First Battle* (Chicago: W.B. Conky Co., 1896), p. 205.
20. See in this regard Robert Nisbet, *Twilight of Authority* (New York: Oxford University Press, 1976). Nisbet's book is the latest in a long series of pessimistic works bemoaning the decline of the West. His main criticism of

egalitarianism seems to be that it is a leveling, anti-quality phenomenon. Though sometimes insightful, the criticism is basically a mixture of polemics and prophecy.

21.   Charles V. Willie, "The American dream: illusion or reality?", *Harvard Magazine,* July-August 1977, p. 38.
22.   Quoted in Dye, p. 324.

BIBLIOGRAPHY

Articles in Books, Journals, and Periodicals

Alker, Hayward, and Russet, Bruce. "On Measuring Inequality."
  Behavioral Science 9 (July 1964): 207-18.
Armor, David. "The Evidence on Busing." *The Public Interest,* Summer
  1972, pp. 90-126.
Bell, Daniel. "On Meritocracy and Equality." *The Public Interest,*
  Fall 1972, pp. 29-68.
Bowles, Samuel. "Schooling and Inequality from Generation to
  Generation." *Journal of Political Economy* 80 (May/June 1972):
  S219-S251.
Chase, Clinton, and Pugh, Richard C. "Social Class and Performance on
  an Intelligence Test." *Journal of Educational Measurement*
  8 (Fall 1971): 197-202.
Cohen, Wilbur J. "Toward the Elimination of Poverty." *Current History,*
  June 1973, pp. 268-72.
Coleman, James S. "Equality of Educational Opportunity: Reply to
  Bowles and Levin." *Journal of Human Resources* 3 (Spring 1968):
  237-46.
Duncan, Otis Dudley. "Discrimination Against Negroes." *Annals of the
  American Academy of Political and Social Science* 371
  (May 1967): 85-103.
Garvey, George. "Inequality of Income: Causes and Measurement."
  Studies in Income and Wealth 15 (1952): 27-47.
Gintis, Herbert. "Education and the Characteristics of Worker
  Productivity." *American Economic Review* 61 (May 1971): 266-79.

Goldwater, Barry. "The Conscience of a Conservative." In *American Government: The Clash of Issues,* edited by James A. Burkhart, Samuel Krislov, and Raymond L. Lee, pp. 188-89. 3rd ed. Englewood Cliffs, N.J.: Prentice-Hall, 1968.

King, Martin Luther, Jr. "Letter from Birmingham Jail." In *American Political Thought: Readings,* edited by Larry I. Peterman and Louis Weschler, pp. 312-20. New York: Appleton-Century-Crofts, 1972.

Marmor, Theodore. "On Comparing Income Maintenance Alternatives." *American Political Science Review* 65 (March 1971): 83-96.

Metzger, L. Paul. "American Sociology and Black Assimilation: Conflicting Perspectives." *American Journal of Sociology* 76 (January 1971): 627-47.

Nisenbaum, Steven. "Race Quotas." *Harvard Civil Rights-Civil Liberties Law Review* 8 (January 1973): 128-80.

Rackman, Emanuel. "Judaism and Equality." In *Nomos IX: Equality,* edited by J. Roland Pennock and John W. Chapman, pp. 154-76. New York: Atherton Press, 1967.

Schatz, Andrew. "Comments: Gagging the Press in Criminal Trials." *Harvard Civil Rights-Civil Liberties Law Review* 10 (Summer 1975): 608-52.

Sigmund, Paul E. "Hierarchy, Equality, and Consent in Medieval Christian Thought." In *Nomos IX: Equality,* edited by J. Roland Pennock and John W. Chapman, pp. 134-53. New York: Atherton Press, 1967.

Silber, John R. "The Need for elite Education." *Harper's,* June 1977, pp. 22-24.

Stanley, John. "Poverty on the Land." *The Commonweal,* 18 November 1955, pp. 161-63.

Sumner, William Graham. "From What Social Classes Owe to Each Other." In *Directions in American Political Thought,* edited by Kenneth M. Dolbeare, pp. 230-43. New York: John Wiley & Sons, 1969.

Tuddenham, Read D. "Soldier Intelligence in World Wars I and II." *American Psychologist* 3 (February 1948): 54-56.

Wilson, Woodrow. "The Nature of Democracy in the United States." In *The Political Thought of American Statesmen: Selected Writings and Speeches,* edited by Morton J. Frisch and Richard G. Stevens, pp. 270-85. Itasca, Ill.: F.E. Peacock Publishers, 1973.

BOOKS

Alinsky, Saul. *Rules for Radicals: A Pragmatic Primer for Realistic Radicals.* New York: Random House, 1971.

Allen, Francis A. *The Borderland of Criminal Justice.* Chicago: University of Chicago Press, 1964.

Amundsen, Kirsten. *The Silenced Majority: Women and American Democracy.* Englewood Cliffs, N.J.: Prentice-Hall, 1971.

Andrews, William G. *Coordinate Magistrates: Constitutional Law by Congress and President.* New York: Van Nostrand, Reinhold, 1969.

Bagdikian, Ben H. *The Shame of the Prisons.* New York: Pocket Books, 1972.

Banfield, Edward C. *The Unheavenly City.* Boston: Little, Brown, 1970.

Barker, Ernest, ed. *The Politics of Aristotle.* London: Oxford University Press, 1948.

Bax, E. Belfort. *Rise and Fall of the Anabaptists.* London: S. Sonnenschein, 1903.

de Beauvoir, Simone. *The Second Sex.* New York: Bantam Books, 1961.

Becker, Carl. *The Heavenly City of the Eighteenth Century Philosophers.* New Haven: Yale University Press, 1932.

Beitzinger, A.J. *A History of American Political Thought.* New York: Dodd, Mead, 1972.

Bellamy, Edward. *Equality.* New York: D. Appleton, 1897.

Benedict, Ruth. *Race, Science and Politics.* New York: Viking Press, 1943.

Bequaert, Lucia H. *Single Women: Alone and Together.* Boston: Beacon Press, 1976.

Bigongiari, Dino, ed. *The Political Ideas of St. Thomas Aquinas: Representative Selections.* New York: The Hafner Library of Classics, 1963.

Bird, Caroline. *Born Female: The High Cost of Keeping Women Down.* New York: David McKay, 1968.

Boorstin, Daniel. *The Genius of American Politics.* Chicago: University of Chicago Press, 1953.

Brown, Ford K. *Life of William Godwin.* New York: E.P. Dutton, 1926.

Buckley, William F. *Up from Liberalism.* New York: Honor Books, 1959.

Butz, Otto. *Of Man and Politics, An Introduction to Political Science.* New York: Holt, Rinehart and Winston, 1963.

Carmichael, Stokely, and Hamilton, Charles V. *Black Power: The Politics of Liberation in America.* New York: Vintage, 1967.

Cassirer, Ernst. *The Philosophy of the Enlightenment.* Princeton: Princeton University Press, 1951.

Chafe, William H. *Women and Equality: Changing Patterns in American Culture.* New York: Oxford University Press, 1977.

Clark, Ramsey. *Crime in America.* New York: Simon and Schuster, 1970.

Cobb, Roger, and Elder, Charles. *Participation in American Politics: The Dynamics of Agenda-Building.* Boston: Allyn and Bacon, 1972.

Cobban, Alfred. *Rousseau and the Modern State.* London: George Allen and Unwin, 1934.

Cole, Leonard A. *Blacks in Power: A Comparative Study of Black and White Elected Officials.* Princeton: Princeton University Press, 1976.

Cole, Margaret. *Robert Owen of New Lanark.* New York: Oxford University Press, 1953.

Coleman, James S. *Equality of Educational Opportunity.* Washington, D.C.: U.S. Government Printing Office, 1966.

Collier, John. *The Indians of the Americas.* New York: W.W. Norton, 1947.

Cortner, Richard C. *The Apportionment Cases.* Knoxville: University of Tennessee Press, 1970

Cranston, Maurice. *John Locke; A Biography.* New York: Macmillan, 1957.

Czajkowski, C.J. *The Theory of Private Property in Locke's Political Philosophy.* Notre Dame, Ind.: University of Notre Dame Press, 1941.

Dahl, Robert A. *A Preface to Democratic Theory.* Chicago: University of Chicago Press, 1956.

_____.*Pluralist Democracy in the United States: Conflict and Consent.* Chicago: Rand McNally, 1967.

Davidson, Chandler. *Biracial Politics: Conflict and Coalition in the Metropolitan South.* Baton Rouge: Louisiana State University Press, 1972.

Deckard, Barbara Sinclair. *The Women's Movement: Political, Socioeconomic, and Psychological Issues.* New York: Harper & Row, 1975.

Deloria, Vine, Jr. *Behind the Trial of Broken Treaties.* New York: Delta, 1974.

_____.*Custer Died for Your Sins: An Indian Manifesto.* New York: Macmillan, 1970.

Dolbeare, Kenneth M., and Dolbeare, Patricia. *American Ideologies: The Competing Political Beliefs of the 1970s.* 3rd ed. Chicago: Rand McNally, 1978.

Downie, Leonard, Jr. *Justice Denied: The Case for Reform of the Courts.* Baltimore: Penguin Books, 1972.

DuBois, W.E.B. *The Souls of Black Folk.* Chicago: A.C. McClurg, 1903.

Dye, Thomas R. *Power and Society: an introduction to the social sciences.* North Scituate, Mass.: Duxbury Press, 1975.

Fainsod, Merle, Gordon, Lincoln, and Palamountain, Joseph C., Jr. *Government and the American Economy.* 3rd ed. New York: W.W. Norton, 1959.

Firestone, Shulamith. *The Dialectic of Sex: The Case for Feminist Revolution*. New York: Morrow, 1970.

Flexnor, Eleanor. *Century of Struggle: The Woman's Rights Movement*. Cambridge, Mass.: Harvard University Press, 1959.

Frankel, Charles. *The Democratic Prospect*. New York: Harper & Row, 1962.

Frazier, E. Franklin. *Race and Culture Contacts in the Modern World*. Boston: Beacon Press, 1965.

Friedan, Betty. *The Feminine Mystique*. New York: W.W. Norton, 1963.

Friedman, Milton. *Capitalism and Freedom*. Chicago: University of Chicago Press, 1962.

Galbraith, John Kenneth. *Economics and the Public Purpose*. Boston: Houghton Mifflin, 1973.

_____. *The Affluent Society*. Boston: Houghton Mifflin, 1958.

Glazer, Nathan. *Affirmative Discrimination: Ethnic Inequality and Public Policy*. New York: Basic Books, 1976.

Glock, Charles Y., and Stark, Rodney. *Christian Beliefs and Anti-Semitism*. New York: Harper & Row, 1966.

Godin, Jean. *Social Solutions*. Translated by Marie Howland. New York: Lovell, 1886.

Goldwater, Barry. *Where I Stand*. New York: McGraw-Hill, 1964.

Gooch, G.P. *English Democratic Ideas in the Seventeenth Century*. New York: Harper & Row, 1959.

Gosnell, Harold F. *Democracy: The Threshold of Freedom*. New York: Ronald Press, 1948.

Gough, John. *John Locke's Political Philosophy*. Oxford: Clarendon Press, 1950.

Gould, William B. *Black Workers in White Unions: Job Discrimination in the United States*. Ithaca, N.Y.: Cornell University Press, 1977.

Haas, Ernst B. *Beyond the Nation-state: Functionalism and International Organization*. Stanford, Calif.: Stanford University Press, 1964.

Harrington, Michael. *Socialism*. New York: Saturday Review Press, 1972.

_____. *The Other America: Poverty in the United States*. Baltimore: Penguin Books, 1962.

Hartz, Louis. *The Liberal Tradition in America*. New York: Harcourt Brace and World, 1955.

Hayek, Friedrich. *The Road to Serfdom*. Chicago: University of Chicago Press, 1944.

Hearnshaw, F.J.C., ed. *The Social and Political Ideas of Some Great French Thinkers of the Age of Reason*. London: Harrap, 1930.

Heilbroner, Robert L. *The Quest for Wealth: A Study of Acquisitive Man*. New York: Simon and Schuster, 1956.

Hellman, Ellen, ed. *Handbook on Race Relations in South Africa.* London: Oxford University Press, 1949.

Howard, John R., ed. *Awakening Minorities.* New York: Aldine, 1970.

Illich, Ivan. *Deschooling Society.* New York: Harper & Row, 1971.

Janowitz, Morris. *The Social Control of Escalated Riots.* Chicago: University of Chicago Press, 1968.

Jencks, Christopher. *Inequality: A Reassessment of the Effect of Family and Schooling in America.* New York: Harper & Row, 1972.

Kelsen, Hans. *Vom Wesen und Wert der Demokratie.* Tuebingen: Mohr, 1929.

Kenniston, Kenneth. *Young Radicals.* New York: Harcourt, Brace and World, 1965.

Kershaw, Joseph A. *Government Against Poverty.* Chicago: Markham, 1970.

Kittrie, Nicholas N. *The Right to be Different.* Baltimore: Penguin Books, 1971.

Klassen, Peter James. *The Economics of Anabaptism, 1525-1560.* The Hague: Mouton, 1964.

Kluger, Richard. *Simple Justice.* New York: Alfred A. Knopf, 1976.

Kolko, Gabriel. *Wealth and Power in America.* New York: Praeger, 1962.

Kornhauser, William. *The Politics of Mass Society.* Glencoe, Ill.: Free Press, 1959.

Kraditor, Aileen, *Up From the Pedestal.* Chicago: Quadrangle Books, 1968.

Krislov, Samuel. *The Supreme Court in the Political Process.* New York: Macmillan, 1965.

Lakoff, Sanford A. *Equality in Philosophy.* Cambridge: Harvard University Press, 1964.

Lampman, Robert J. *The Share of Top Wealth-holders in National Wealth.*

Princeton: Princeton University Press, 1962.

Lasswell, Harold D. *Politics: Who Gets What, When, How.* New York: McGraw-Hill, 1936.

Lee, Calvin B.T. *One Man, One Vote: WMCA and the Struggle for Equal Representation.* New York: Charles Scribner's Sons, 1967.

Lerner, Max. *America As A Civilization: Life and Thought in the United States Today.* New York: Simon and Schuster, 1957.

Levitan, Sar. *The Great Society's Poor Law.* Baltimore: The Johns Hopkins University Press, 1969.

Levy, Leonard W. *Against the Law: The Nixon Court and Criminal Justice.* New York: Harper & Row, 1974.

Lewis, Anthony. *Gideon's Trumpet.* New York: Random House, 1964.

Lindsay, A.D. *The Modern Democratic State.* New York: Oxford University Press, 1943.

Litt, Edgar. *Ethnic Politics in America.* Glenview, Ill.: Scott Foresman, 1970.

Lynd, Staughton, and Alperovitz, Gar. *Strategy and Program: Two Essays Toward a New American Socialism.* Boston: Beacon Press, 1973.

Madsden, William. *The Mexican-Americans of South Texas.* New York: Holt, Rinehart, and Winston, 1964.

Makielski, S.J., Jr. *Beleaguered Minorities: Cultural Politics in America.* San Francisco: W.H. Freeman, 1973.

Marcus, Jacob R. *The Jew in the Medieval World: A Source Book, 315-1791.* New York: Meridian, 1938.

Mayer, Martin. *Today and Tomorrow in America.* New York: Harper & Row, 1976.

Mayo, Henry B. *An Introduction to Democratic Theory.* New York: Oxford University Press, 1960.

McDonald, Lee Cameron. *Western Political Theory, From its Origins to the Present.* New York: Harcourt, Brace & World, 1968.

McWilliams, Wilson Carey. *The Idea of Fraternity in America.* Berkeley: University of California Press, 1973.

Meier, August, ed. *The Transformation of Activism.* Chicago: Aldine, 1970.

Meiklejohn, Alexander. *Political Freedom: The Constitutional Powers of the People.* New York: Harper & Row, 1960.

Miller, Jean Baker. *Toward a New Psychology of Women.* Boston: Beacon Press, 1976.

Millet, Kate. *Sexual Politics.* Garden City, N.Y.: Doubleday, 1970.

Mills, C. Wright. *The Power Elite.* New York: Oxford University Press, 1956.

Mitau, G. Theodore. *Decade of Decision: The Supreme Court and the Constitutional Revolution, 1954-1964.* New York: Charles Scribner's Sons, 1967.

Mitford, Jessica. *Kind and Usual Punishment.* New York: Alfred A. Knopf, 1973.

Morgan, Robin, ed. *Sisterhood is Powerful.* New York: Vintage, 1970.

Moynihan, Daniel P. *The Politics of a Guaranteed Income: The Nixon Administration and the Family Assistance Plan.* New York: Random House, 1973.

Nathan, Richard P. *Jobs and Civil Rights: The Role of the Federal Government in Promoting Equal Opportunity and Employment and Training.* Washington, D.C.: Brookings Institution, 1969.

Nisbet, Robert. *Twilight of Authority.* New York: Oxford University Press, 1976.

Nozick, Robert. *Anarchy, State and Utopia.* New York: Basic Books, 1974.

Okun, Arthur M. *Equality and Efficiency: The Big Tradeoff.* Washington, D.C.: Brookings Institution, 1975.

Owen, John D. *School Inequality and the Welfare State.* Baltimore: The Johns Hopkins University Press, 1974.

Peeks, Edward. *The Long Struggle for Black Power.* New York: Charles Scribner's Sons, 1971.

Pennock, J. Roland, and Chapman, John W., eds. *Nomos IX: Equality.* New York: Atherton Press, 1967.

Piven, Frances Fox, and Cloward, Richard A. *Regulating the Poor: The Functions of Public Welfare.* New York: Random House, 1971.

Powledge, Fred. *Black Power White Resistance.* Cleveland: World, 1967.

Rawls, John. *A Theory of Justice.* Cambridge: Harvard University Press, 1971.

Renjai, M. *Democracy, The Contemporary Theories.* New York: Atherton Press, 1967.

Rendon, Armando. *Chicano Manifesto.* New York: Macmillan, 1971.

Rothbard, Murray. *For A New Liberty.* New York: Macmillan, 1973.

Rowbotham, Sheila. *Woman's Consciousness, Man's World.* Baltimore: Penguin Books, 1973.

Schapiro, J. Salwyn. *Condorcet and the Rise of Liberalsim.* New York: Harcourt, Brace, 1934.

Shaw, George Bernard. *Essays in Fabian Socialism.* Edinburgh: Clark, 1932.

Sigmund, Paul E. *Nicholas of Cusa and Medieval Political Thought.* Cambridge: Harvard University Press, 1963.

Skolnick, Jerome H. *The Politics of Protest.* New York: Ballantine, 1969.

Sohner, Charles P. *American Government and Politics Today: A Concise Introduction.* Glenview, Ill.: Scott, Foresman, 1973.

Stone, Chuck. *Black Political Power in America.* Indianapolis: Bobbs-Merrill, 1968.

Tawney, R.H. *Equality.* London: George Allen and Unwin, 1964.

Tierney, Brian. *Foundations of the Conciliar Theory.* New York: Cambridge University Press, 1955.

Tocqueville, Alexis de. *Democracy in America.* Edited abridged by Richard D. Heffner. New York: The New American Library, 1961.

Thorson, Thomas Landon, ed. *Plato: Totalitarian or Democrat?* Englewood Cliffs, N.J.: Prentice-Hall, 1963.

Valentin, Hugo. *Anti-Semitism Historically and Critically Examined.* New York: Viking Press, 1936.

Verba, Sidney, and Nie, Norman H. *Participation in America: Political Democracy and Social Equality.* New York: Harper & Row, 1972.

Weber, Max. *Protestant Ethic and the Spirit of Capitalism.* Translated by
  Talcott Parsons. London: Allen & Unwin, 1930.
Wells, H.G. *The New Machiavelli.* New York: Duffield, 1927.
Wicker, Tom. *A Time To Die.* New York: Quadrangle Books, 1975.
Wilhoit, Francis M. *The Politics of Massive Resistance.* New York:George
  Braziller, 1973.
Williamson, Chilton. *American Suffrage from Property to Democracy,
  1760-1860.* Princeton: Princeton University Press, 1960.
Woodcock, George. *William Godwin.* London: Porcupine Press, 1946.
Yates, Gayle Graham. *What Women Want: The Ideas of the Movement.*
  Cambridge: Harvard University Press, 1975.

U.S. Supreme Court Cases

Abington School District v. *Schempp,* 374 U.S. 203 (1963)
Alexander v. *Holmes County Board of Education,* 396 U.S. 19 (1969)
Baker v. *Carr,* 369 U.S. 186 (1962)
Benton v. *Maryland,* 395 U.S. 784 (1969)
Bolling v. *Sharpe,* 347 U.S. 497 (1954)
Bridges v. *California,* 314 U.S. 252 (1941)
Brown v. *Board of Education of Topeka,* 347 U.S. 483 (1954)
Brown v. *Board of Education of Topeka,* 349 U.S. 294 (1955)
Calder v. *Bull,* 3 Dallas 386 (1798)
Carlson v. Landon, 342 U.S. 524 (1952)
Chimel v. *California,* 395 U.S. 752 (1969)
Cooper v. *Aaron,* 358 U.S. 1 (1958)
DeFunis v. *Odegaard,* 416 U.S. 312 (1974)
Doe v. *Bolton,* 410 U.S. 179 (1973)
Dred Scott v. *Sandford,* 19 Howard 393 (1857)
Engel v. *Vitale,* 370 U.S. 421 (1962)
Escobedo v. *Illinois,* 378 U.S. 478 (1964)
Everson v. *Board of Education of Ewing Township,* 330 U.S. 1 (1947)
Frontiero v. *Richardson,* 411 U.S. 677 (1973)
Furman v. *Georgia,* 408 U.S. 238 (1972)
Geduldig v. *Aiello,* 417 U.S. 484 (1974)
Gideon v. *Wainwright,* 372 U.S. 335 (1963)
Goldman v. *United States,* 316 U.S. 129 (1942)
Green v. *County Board of New Kent County,* 391 U.S. 430 (1968)
Griffin v. *County Board of Prince Edward County,* 377 U.S. 218 (1964)
Hurtado v. *California,* 110 U.S. 516 (1884)
Kahn v. *Shevin,* 416 U.S. 351 (1974)
Katz v. *U.S.,* 389 U.S. 347 (1967)

Weems v. *United States,* 217 U.S. 349 (1910)
Weinberger v. *Weisenfeld,* 420 U.S. 636 (1975)
Wesberry v. *Sanders,* 376 U.S. 1 (1964)
Wisconsin v. *Yoder,* 406 U.S. 205 (1972)
Wolf v. *Colorado,* 338 U.S. 25 (1949)
Zorach v. *Clauson, 343 U.S. 306 (1952)*

INDEX

Date Due